'Given the growing significance of internationalisation of education in both local public schools and private international schools across East and West and the Global South and North, this edited volume critically engages with core theoretical and empirical issues concerned with internationalising schools. The volume is empirically well grounded and theoretically incisive. It is a product carefully orchestrated by stellar researchers in the field.'

—**Professor Moosung Lee**, *Centenary Professor,*
University of Canberra, Australia

'This book is an important and very worthwhile addition to the recent literature on school internationalisation. Written by authors from a range of educational backgrounds and contexts, each chapter brings insightful theoretical and practical knowledge to bear on the key issues and possibilities facing the internationalisation of schools today. Whether readers are interested in global policy directions, theoretical approaches, or practical examples, this book has something to offer. The analysis contained within does not shy away from addressing core questions which remain about the international practices of schools, and the editors have executed the task of forging a cohesive and focused book with skill and acumen. I highly recommend it.'

—**Andrew Peterson**, *Professor of Character and*
Citizenship Education, Jubilee Centre for
Character and Virtues, University of
Birmingham, UK

'The spotlight of this edited volume of essays is on internationalisation in education. Finally, we have an important landmark reference that reveals the multiple ways in which internationalisation is practiced in diverse educational contexts, and where a repertoire of theories is used astutely to critically analyse how internationalisation is put into action. This book is necessary, and intriguing work for all who study internationalisation in education.'

—**Aaron Koh**, *Associate Professor, The Chinese*
University of Hong Kong, China

'Various processes of new class formation are now evident around the world, with schools playing a major role in creating transnational elites. This collection of original papers brings together scholars, both established and emerging, to consider the contentious and contradictory nature of these processes. The papers show in particular how the discourses of internationalisation are deployed to socially differentiate categories of students and schools.'

—**Fazal Rizvi**, *Professor in Global Studies in Education,*
The University of Melbourne, Australia

'This wide-ranging, cross-disciplinary anthology of essays could not have come at a more needed time as the topic of globalization and internationalization in schooling comes under the pressure of a wider policy environment in key Western states that now tends toward feral nationalism and localism and boundary maintenance as underscored by Brexit-Trump. Contributors to this volume are to be commended for grappling with internationalization and globalization in education by interrogating commonly accepted starting points and connecting richly layered empirical studies with thoroughgoing theoretical insights and with a strong commitment to policy reflection and intervention. A particularly compelling feature of this collaborative scholarly effort is the depth and breadth of subject matter considered and the evident commitment of contributors to work across the often presumptive and calcifying divides lodged in North/South geographies. This volume should be required reading for those interested in the economic, cultural and political transformations associated with globalization that are now fully articulated to schooling in even the most remote zones of the globe. The Machinery of School Internationalisation in Action: Beyond the Established Boundaries should be required reading for both scholars and practitioners interested in the impact of internationalization and globalization in schooling and the implications for change and transformation in the tumult of the contemporary era.'

—**Cameron McCarthy,** *University Scholar, Former Director of Global Studies Education, University of Illinois, USA*

The Machinery of School Internationalisation in Action

Drawing on scholarship from the field of internationalisation in higher education and other theoretical influences in education policy, comparative education and sociology of education, this edited collection offers a much-needed extension of discussion and research into the compulsory schooling context.

In this book, established and emerging scholars provide an authoritative set of conceptual tools for researchers in the field of internationalisation of compulsory schooling. It provides an overview of the current knowledge base and ways in which future research could engage with gaps in understandings. Through detailed case studies of the multiple forms of internationalisation present within schools and schooling systems, the volume considers why and how processes of internationalisation are shaping compulsory schooling today.

This book will offer scholars and educators a clearer, more coherent set of conceptual frameworks within which to position their work in sociology of education, global studies in education, and international and comparative education, helping to develop a more comprehensive understanding of the many ways that compulsory schooling is being internationalised, and with what consequences.

Laura C. Engel is Associate Professor of International Education and International Affairs at George Washington University, USA

Claire Maxwell is Professor of Sociology at the Department of Sociology, University Copenhagen, Denmark

Miri Yemini is Senior Academic Faculty and Comparative Education Scholar at Tel Aviv University, Israel

Education in Global Context
Series editor: Lois Weis

Education in Global Context takes seriously the transnational migration of commerce, capital and peoples, and the implications of such for education and social structure in global context. Globalization—in the world economy, in patterns of migration, and increasingly in education—affects all of us. The increasingly globalized and knowledge-based economy renders the linkages between education and social and economic outcomes and arrangements empirically "up for grabs" in a wide variety of nations while simultaneously more important than ever. This series underscores the consequences of the global both internationally and here at home while simultaneously stressing the importance of a paradigmatic shift in our understanding of schooling and social/economic arrangements.

The Machinery of School Internationalisation in Action
Beyond the Established Boundaries
Edited by Laura C. Engel, Claire Maxwell and Miri Yemini

Social Class and Education
Global Perspectives
Edited by Lois Weis and Nadine Dolby

Confucius and Crisis in American Universities
Amy Stambach

Globalizing Educational Accountabilities
Bob Lingard, Wayne Martino, Goli Rezai-Rashti and Sam Sellar

Elite Schools
Multiple Geographies of Privilege
Edited by Aaron Koh and Jane Kenway

Global Liberalism & Elite Schooling in Argentina
Howard Prosser

The Machinery of School Internationalisation in Action

Beyond the Established Boundaries

Edited by
Laura C. Engel, Claire Maxwell
and Miri Yemini

NEW YORK AND LONDON

First published 2020
by Routledge
52 Vanderbilt Avenue, New York, NY 10017

and by Routledge
2 Park Square, Milton Park, Abingdon, Oxon OX14 4RN

Routledge is an imprint of the Taylor & Francis Group, an informa business

© 2020 Taylor & Francis

The right of Laura C. Engel, Claire Maxwell and Miri Yemini
to be identified as the authors of the editorial material, and of
the authors for their individual chapters, has been asserted in
accordance with sections 77 and 78 of the Copyright, Designs
and Patents Act 1988.

Library of Congress Cataloging-in-Publication Data
A catalog record for this title has been requested

ISBN: 978-0-367-23587-1 (hbk)
ISBN: 978-0-429-28062-7 (ebk)

Typeset in Sabon
by Apex CoVantage, LLC

Printed and bound in Great Britain by
TJ International Ltd, Padstow, Cornwall

Contents

Introduction

Laura C. Engel, Claire Maxwell and Miri Yemini

Schooling around the world has changed significantly over the past several decades, in part due to the effects of globalisation—from the escalation of transnational flows of people, leading to increased diversification of student populations in classrooms; to the growing use of new technologies, which transform pedagogies in schools; to shifting labour markets, which put significant pressures on schools to prepare graduates for these changing workplaces. Whether positioned as a challenge or an opportunity, these changing dynamics have undoubtedly repositioned the aims and practices of schooling towards meeting the needs of a creative and innovative knowledge-based global economy, as well as simultaneously promoting a discourse of inclusive, participatory, sustainable and humanistic forms of education. Alongside and because of the pressures to globalise, schools must contend with increasingly neoliberalised modes of governance, which have stimulated the privatisation, marketisation and commercialisation of the traditionally public provision of education. Internationalisation, as a possible response of schools to a globalised world and more globally connected modes of governance, has raised the central question of whether these changes are increasing or potentially reducing inequalities at local, national and international levels.

New developments in education policies, programmes and practices that are responsive to globalisation and involve some sort of interaction with global, international, multilingual, inter- and multi-cultural dimensions are often placed under the umbrella term of internationalisation, a notably disparate and under-theorised concept, which originally was more common in higher education (Yemini, 2015). Taking the above as a fast evolving and problematic context in which education must develop and thrive, and concerned with the lack of theoretical clarity being drawn on to advance our understandings of the genesis, processes and outcomes of 'internationalisation', we have curated this edited collection. Through this book we seek to offer both established and emerging scholars in the field an authoritative reference point for this area of study, and shape its future development so that researchers might work in a more coherent and collective manner to address this critical arena of education policy and practice.

Unlike the field of internationalisation in higher education, which is more established and shares some common definitions and frameworks within its scholarship, research on internationalisation in compulsory (primary/secondary) schooling is composed of contributions which draw on a wide range of theories, references a relatively disparate number of key texts and defines the concept of internationalisation very broadly (Engel, 2014; Engel & Siczek, 2017; Fielding & Vidovich, 2017; Maxwell & Yemini, 2019). Concepts such as global citizenship, global competence, cosmopolitan citizenship, intercultural competence, among others, are frequently drawn on in discussions about internationalisation (Auld & Morris, 2019; Yemini, 2014). While organisations like the International Baccalaureate Organisation (IBO), the United Nations Educational, Scientific and Cultural Organization (UNESCO) and the Organisation for Economic Co-operation and Development (OECD) are each seen as key actors in mobilising the internationalisation of education, each of these institutions proposes and promotes it quite differently, and in fact, at times, offers opposing propositions of what internationalisation can and should mean in schooling settings.

This definitional 'slipperiness' is not aided by the fact that scholarship related to internationalisation of schooling tends to rely largely on Knight's (2004, 2008) now seminal definition of internationalisation in higher education. And yet, schooling settings are significantly different contexts from higher education, demanding new conceptual attention to what more precisely it means to internationalise schooling systems and, more importantly, how internationalisation might influence the teaching and learning processes in schools in various places. The most significant tension within schooling (not similarly experienced by higher education) is that compulsory education traditionally had the objective of socialising children and young people to take up local and national values, while simultaneously preparing young people to enter the 21st century knowledge economy, develop the awareness and the skills necessary to tackle global issues and form relationships across cultural divides. Given the prominence of the United Nations' Sustainable Development Goals (SDGs), which require that nation-states provide high quality schooling for everybody and, via the SDG global indicator 4.7.1, ensure that 'global citizenship education and education for sustainable development, including gender equality and human rights, are mainstreamed in national education policies, curricula, teacher education and student assessment', an inter-connectivity between people and the broader global community is now an expectation within education provision everywhere. How does the imperative to internationalise therefore shape these twin objectives of education today?

In order to engage with the conceptual 'messiness' within the field, and to begin a conversation about motivations, practices and outcomes around internationalisation at the local, national and international levels, we have brought together scholars (established and emerging) variously undertaking innovative research either in terms of the conceptual resources they are drawing on or in relation to the empirical focus of their studies. This book also integrates several chapters written by practitioners currently working in the field. By highlighting more grounded perspectives of practitioners and combining these with solid theoretical contributions, the book builds on the importance of integrating 'stories from the field', increasingly recognised as important in the field of international higher education (Streitwieser & Ogden, 2016). This book's inclusion of scholar-practitioners therefore provides yet another vital perspective on how and why internationalisation is being implemented in various schooling contexts.

Through detailed case studies examining multiple forms of internationalisation present in different schools and schooling systems, this edited collection offers readers (i) a clearer, more coherent set of conceptual frameworks within which to position their work; (ii) a perspective and understanding of the multiple ways compulsory schooling is being internationalised, including factors that both facilitate and/or constrain internationalisation in schools, and how its outcomes across schooling types, countries and by different social groups differ; and (iii) an overview of the current knowledge base, pointing to ways in which future research could engage with gaps in our understandings. A central thread throughout the collection is a question of whether and how forms of internationalisation can be understood as articulations of elitism and imperialism, or whether in fact internationalisation facilitates opportunities for re-negotiating relations of power in local, national and international settings.

State of the Art

Internationalisation is a well-documented phenomenon in higher education. A common starting place is Knight's (2008) definition of internationalisation as 'the process of integrating international, intercultural or global dimensions into purpose, functions and delivery of postsecondary education at the institutional and national levels' (p. xi). Constructed rather rapidly over the past several decades, this body of literature has established several important dimensions of internationalisation. First, literature points to the drivers and rationales of internationalisation (Qiang, 2003; van der Wende, 2001; Warner, 1992). For example, scholars emphasise that internationalisation is 'not an aim in itself, but a way to ensure that higher education responds to a growing need for openness and cooperation, continuously enhances its quality and responds to the increasingly global challenges' (Deca, Egron Polak, & Fit, 2015, p. 130). Second, scholarship on internationalisation of higher education underscores the broad components of internationalisation in different institutions and national settings, examining characteristics, gaps and outcomes of internationalisation practices. Here, literature frequently categorises institutional programmes, policies and activities of internationalisation either as 'abroad' or 'at home' (Knight, 2008), while also emphasising that the deepest approach to internationalisation is what scholars refer to as the process approach, which seeks to inculcate internationalised outlooks and practices throughout an institution's teaching and learning (de Wit, 2002). Third, research within the higher education space has focused on the distinctive processes and programmes of internationalisation in different institutions and systems (Hudzik, 2012; Knight, 2008). Increasingly there is an acknowledgment of the extent to which internationalisation either limits or facilitates broader educational aims of inclusion, equity and quality in different contexts (de Wit & Jones, 2018).

Although the body of literature on internationalisation is well-established in higher education, a conceptual framing of internationalisation in school settings is less clear. There are limited examples where internationalisation has been explored at the school level, and in very few cases, in early years settings (Cambridge & Thompson, 2004; Fielding & Vidovich, 2017; Hayden, 2011; Naumann, 2018; Oonk, Maslowski, & Van der Werf, 2011). In particular, questions of policy borrowing, influences of intergovernmental organisations and effects of neoliberalism have been a main focus of studies of internationalisation at the school level (Pak & Lee, 2018; Yemini, 2015). As such, research into internationalisation in education overall tends to be far more fragmented than in the higher education sector, lacking connections to a comprehensive, commonly engaged theoretical framework. It might be in part due to the fact that internationalisation in schools was traditionally linked to international schooling, which has been, at least in the past, a small, segregated and exclusive sector, aimed to serve the children of highly mobile and privileged families. Since internationalisation was not originally developed as integral to the core activities in state schools, its research emerged from various theoretical and methodological positions without a formal grounding or self-sustained tradition.

As a common thread, internationalisation both for higher education and schooling has emerged as a process or approach to mediate and address the challenges related to the various dynamics and conditions brought about by globalisation, making internationalisation (as an institutional response to globalisation) more universal. Altbach and Knight (2007) argued that the following would continue to both challenge and foster developments around internationalisation in education: the need to turn an economic profit; keep up provision while extending access; the use of English as a main language of instruction; internationalisation of the curriculum; promotion of e-learning; quality assurance and control that mirrors approaches used elsewhere; and regional and national policies (such as the Bologna Process) being followed. Risks of the growing presence of commercialisation in internationalisation initiatives, as well as increased global demands for English language use in education, are viewed by many as potentially diminishing the central values inherent in earlier definitions of internationalisation, particularly those connected to collaboration and cross-cultural dialogue (Brandenburg & de Wit, 2015; Francois, 2015).

Schools are particularly implicated in these dynamics as they are frequently caught between the nation-state's goals of local and national socialisation/citizen formation and broader demands to impart students with English language, technology skills and an overarching orientation to global economic competitiveness. The rise of a neoliberal form of globalisation has placed greater emphasis on the significance of 21st century skills, frequently referred to as global competencies. Moreover, mass migration has created conditions in education whereby many classrooms and schools are now serving more culturally and linguistically diverse populations. At the same time, shifting labour markets have encouraged the cross-border movement of highly mobile populations giving rise to a global middle class, which has increased demands for internationalised schooling and amplified existing gaps in economic and educational opportunities (Maxwell & Yemini, 2019; Weenink, 2008).

Different from the objectives of higher education in many systems, trends to internationalise through compulsory schooling are in some sense contradictory to the sector's underlying rationale around nation-state building and socialisation (Coulby & Zambeta, 2005). As mass schooling emerged with the aim of transmitting a dominant social, cultural and political system to young people so as to facilitate the creation of a cohesive nation-state (Bromley, 2011), schools were exploited for the construction of closed national communities whereby citizens in the same geographic territory were conceptualised as a homogenous group, with an ethno-culturally distinct polity. Compulsory schooling in many systems has leaned towards more subtractive policies, divesting societies of particular cultural and linguistic resources in the name of social cohesion and the formation of the 'ideal' national citizen. These models still exist, pushing mass schooling towards localism and nationalism, in contrast to the more recent global trends depicted earlier. Thus, schools are located at a challenging junction of contradicting pressures. On one hand, the state prioritises the 'nation' over other categories and legitimates education policies, curricula and reforms that are consistent with this logic. On the other hand, competing internal and external forces are pushing schools towards greater cosmopolitanism that prioritises the 'world' and legitimates discourses and practices that transcend the nation.

There are other contrasting aims of internationalisation, including a broader tension between collaboration and competition (Engel & Siczek, 2018; Tarc, 2009; Torres, 2015). Some scholars see these values or objectives as irreconcilable differences, whereby internationalisation is either understood as an individual, private good to enhance competitiveness *or* as a collective public good to enhance solidarity. These divergences have elicited questions about whether it is possible then to concurrently cultivate values of nationalism and globalism, solidarity and competition, empathy and protection from external threats (Engel & Siczek, 2018; Mitchell, 2003; Ortloff & Shonia, 2015; Tarc, 2009; Torres, 2015). Several of the leading international organisations seem to have taken positions: the IBO, for example, has promoted international solidarity over economic competitiveness (Tarc, 2009) while UNESCO (2014) positions both of these aims as compatible whereby competition is thought to breed the kinds of innovations needed in a collaborative global world.

Given these tensions and the lack of coherence in the field, there is a notable fragmentation in both the conceptual landscape related to internationalisation of schools, as well as its practices. Examples of the 'global turn' in compulsory schooling are increasingly prevalent, whether in a focus on shifts in education policy formation (see e.g. Ball, 2012; Engel, 2009; Lingard, Sellar, Hogan, & Thompson, 2017; Rizvi & Lingard, 2009; Verger, 2011), in the reorientation of schooling towards a global society (Pak & Lee, 2018; Torres, 2015; Yemini, Goren, & Maxwell, 2018), or the complex relationships of internationalisation with elite class structures in both urban and postcolonial settings (Kenway, Fahey, Epstein, Koh, McCarthy, & Rizvi, 2017; Maxwell, Deppe, Krüger, & Helsper, 2018; Maxwell & Yemini, 2019). Yet, to date, very little has intentionally and comprehensively focused on internationalisation of schooling. In particular, we believe there is a critical need to focus on the *machinery* of internationalisation: its distinctive parts, effects, outcomes, implications and the rationales that both help facilitate and/or impede its construction in systems around the world. In most of this book's contributions, authors tackle the why and how questions related to enactment of internationalisation, thus directly enriching the field theoretically and empirically.

Furthermore, the book seeks to directly tackle the tensions found in the field to date. The chapters therefore, as a collection, move us beyond a focus on one country or region (e.g. Israel or Europe), one kind of school (e.g. independent or fee-based 'international' schools), or how internationalisation affects understandings of particular articulations of education (e.g. elite forms of education). The book considers the how and why of internationalisation of schooling, potential conceptual tools that might bring the field together and the specific tensions understood as besetting the desires and imperatives to internationalise. Furthermore, the three of us as co-editors, along with the collaborators of this book, represent a cross-national team of established and emerging scholars tackling these critical questions, a nod to the need to internationalise who studies this issue, and the focus and scope of the enquiry.

Chapter Overviews

Chapter 1 by Euan Auld and Paul Morris—
The OECD's Assessment of Global Competence:
Measuring and Making Global Elites

Auld and Morris' chapter examines the historical development of the Programme for International Student Assessment (PISA) 2018 assessment of global competence, situated potentially as a leading measure of internationalisation in an evidence-based global landscape. As the OECD has positioned itself as the major assessor of the SDG 4.7.1 on global citizenship, this chapter considers the implications of such an assessment, including the extent to which it may narrowly serve global elitism. The chapter argues that the rationale and nature of the OECD's measurement has been superficially influenced by the organisation's attempt to position itself as the primary agency responsible for tracking progress on the UN's SDGs. Auld and Morris' analysis suggests that the OECD's measurement remains focused on its vision of fostering individuals that can compete in a global economy, a vision at odds with the UN's original conception of global citizenship. This is related in part to the organisation's core mission and the groups involved in constructing the measurement. With the potential to be utilised as a yardstick for internationalisation in schools and societies, the authors argue that the OECD's measurement may contribute to the process of making and legitimating global elites.

Chapter 2 by Johanna Waters and Rachel Brooks—
Geographies of Connection? The Chicken Project and Other
International Acts by State Secondary Schools in England

This chapter focuses on three state-funded secondary schools in England, supported by secondary web-based analysis of 50 schools, providing important views of non-fee-based schools' approaches to internationalisation. The chapter provides insights into the motivations of state-funded schools to pursue internationalisation, including the extent to which schools explicitly addressed terms like 'global citizen', 'global worker', and/or 'cosmopolitan capital'. Using data related to the 'chicken project' (an overseas service-learning 'charity' project), the chapter examines the ways that a school's international pursuits and approaches can on the one hand engage young people in humanistic pursuits at a global level, building broader global social consciousness, and on the other hand reinforce neo-colonialism through global charity.

Chapter 3 by Tristan Bunnell—The 'Internationalisation of
Public Schooling' in Practice: A 'Skeptical Reality' Approach

This chapter focuses on the diverse pathways of internationalisation by examining the growth of the International Baccalaureate (IB) programmes in public schools in the US (Chicago), Ecuador and Japan. Although scholars suggest that the IB provision is being massified, Bunnell argues that in practice, it only benefits a very small proportion of the world's middle/upper-middle class populations living in urban areas. Developing a framework based on the skeptical reality approach, the chapter argues that there are very few interactions between public schooling and the IB. The skeptical reality framework takes as its starting point an understanding that nation-states are actively harnessing international opportunities and changes to meet their own needs. Thus, rather than expecting globalisation to be taking away agency from nations, the analytical approach is to seek to examine how nations are meeting their own needs in a globalising context.

Chapter 4 by Laura C. Engel and Heidi Gibson— Equal Global Futures? Pathways of Internationalisation in US Schooling

The focus of this chapter is on internationalisation of public schooling systems in the United States, adding perspectives on the multiple pathways of internationalisation within a federalised or multi-level context, where local and state authorities have greater autonomy to innovate. The chapter focuses on several key examples within the US: North Carolina, Illinois and Washington, DC, which reflect different combinations of formal recognition of individual student achievements, school- and district-wide global designations and supports, teacher professional development, and mobility programmes. Although varied, the authors argue that internationalisation initiatives have been framed in a more pragmatic, skills-based orientation and in less ideological, values-based ways. As such, they have garnered policy support in US states and districts, allowing them to be sustained even in the 'America First' era. However, in framing internationalisation as largely about individual and national competitiveness, the authors argue that critical opportunities may be missed both to build understanding across divisions within the US and globally, and to address the possibility of increased inequities resulting from uneven application of global education initiatives.

Chapter 5 by Katerina Bodovski and Ruxandra Apostolescu—The Pull and Push Forces in the Internationalization of Education in Russia

This chapter provides a historical overview of internationalisation in pre-Soviet, Soviet and post-Soviet Russia, and in doing so, explores the contradictory processes whereby the Russian education system is gravitating towards, and pulling away, from internationally oriented trends in education. The authors examine the possible role internationalisation can play in a post-Soviet cultural environment where nationalistic and locally oriented pressures are interwoven with the desire to dominate the global education arena. As these processes within and across national systems are often ambiguous, Bodovski and Apostolescu develop a flexible theoretical model of three dimensions: Pragmatic, cultural and political. They argue that this model can be especially useful to the study of internationalisation in other post-socialist systems.

Chapter 6 by Jason Beech and Jennifer Guevara—
Multiple Internationalizations: The Idiosyncratic
Enactment of the International Baccalaureate in
State Schools in Costa Rica, Peru and Buenos Aires

The chapter by Beech and Guevara examines the internationalisation of schools in Latin America. Its specific focus is on the introduction of the International Baccalaureate Diploma Programme (IBDP) in state schools in Peru, Costa Rica and the city of Buenos Aires. It draws on qualitative interviews and focus groups at local school, national and global levels (including the International Baccalaureate Organization), as well as document analysis and class observations. The chapter makes two primary contributions to internationalisation: (1) It generates new knowledge about the International Baccalaureate Organization, one of the leading global organisations focused on internationalisation of schooling; (2) its cross-national and multi-levelled focus allows for a better understanding of *how* the IBDP is operationalised differently in local and national political contexts. In particular, the chapter illuminates the central rationales and the infrastructures within systems that underlie and facilitate the IBDP in public systems, thus illustrating an understanding of the mechanisms by which the global model of the IBDP is solidified in distinctive systems.

Chapter 7 by Vina Adriany—On Being Local and
International: Indonesian Teachers' Experiences
in an International Kindergarten

This chapter draws on a post-colonial lens to examine the dynamics of local Indonesian teacher experiences in an international kindergarten in Indonesia. The focus is on early childhood education, which has increasingly become an attractive space for families seeking an internationalised education for their young children. Yet, there is an uneven set of policies and practices for overseas (often Global North) and local Indonesian teachers, as demonstrated in salary levels and general regard for professional experience. Drawing on the narratives of three kindergarten teachers, this chapter sheds light on both the structural inequalities that persist in internationalised settings in the Global South, but also the agency of local Indonesian teachers, who develop collaborative relationships with international/ex-patriot teachers. As such, this chapter helps illuminate the micro-politics of inequalities related to insider-outsider and hybrid identities developed around and through internationalised schooling spaces.

Chapter 8 by Boris Prickarts—Inclusive Internationalisation in an International School in Amsterdam—Illusion or Reality?

This chapter focuses on a unique case of an international school in the Netherlands, which was established to make accessible a globally oriented education to less affluent families, and create a teaching space where immigrant families, middle-class Dutch children and ex-patriate professionals would seek to have their children educated. The chapter examines the history leading to this unique educational provision and suggests how the school is facilitating a pedagogical space oriented towards cross-cultural dialogue and learning. The focus on this school model illustrates the ways in which an internationalised school can remain dedicated to equal access to global opportunities at the same time as meeting the demands of globally mobile, middle class families.

Chapter 9 by Sherry Hattingh—Pedagogy for Internationalisation: An Australian Secondary School Case Study

Hattingh's chapter offers an overview of the literature on how schools can engage with internationalisation, focusing specifically on four dimensions: the organisation and management of the school; the school culture; how cultural knowledge is offered to the students; and the teaching and learning approach. After introducing the context in which Australia is seeking to recruit more international students to complete their compulsory school, Hattingh examines how one case study school has engaged with efforts to internationalise. She specifically develops the concept of 'pedagogy for internationalisation'—illustrating the ways the school models this and the challenges in implementing this well.

Chapter 10 by Tatiana Fumasoli—Learning From Internationalisation Scholarship in Higher Education: Commonalities, Divergences and Possible Research Directions for Internationalisation in Schools

This chapter approaches the field of internationalisation in schooling from the standpoint of a scholar immersed in research within the field of higher education. It outlines the instrumental and normative rationales, processes and outcomes of student and staff mobility, home and abroad internationalisation, as well as institutional building, such as creating international branch campuses. By highlighting the actors involved at global, national, institutional and classroom levels, it elaborates on the possible borrowing of internationalisation models from higher education to schooling. Finally, the author reflects on the empirical findings presented in several studies in this book, suggesting possible future research directions, challenges and opportunities in developing this type of research in school contexts.

Conclusion: Central Contributions

Through its ten chapters, the book makes several key contributions. First, this edited volume provides scholars in the field with a more solid and self-sustaining grounding by offering important theoretical resources and extending the empirical foci of the research to date on internationalisation. While in the past researchers have turned to work on internationalisation in higher education for inspiration, we would urge scholars to now borrow ideas gleaned from this emerging work within compulsory schooling (see Fumasoli, Chapter 10). This may also facilitate a greater discussion between sectors, as we suggest there is an increasing expectation that students have an internationally oriented education before entering university.

At a more conceptual level, the chapters in the book collectively point to the idea that the 'national' versus the 'global' is not a zero-sum game, as has been framed as a tension in the literature on internationalisation (see e.g. Tarc, 2009) and globalisation (see e.g. Engel, 2009), but rather can be facilitated together in highly complex ways, deserving of conceptual and empirical attention in future research. For example, our book provides insights into ways that internationalisation is facilitated through the work of influential global agents and stakeholders, including the OECD (see Chapter 1) and the role of the IBO in schooling (Chapters 3 and 6), and that while this scholarship could at the outset suggest convergence around the promotion of internationalisation at a global and national levels, many of the studies included in this book suggest the emergence of multiple 'forms' of internationalisation. Engel and Gibson (Chapter 4), Bodovski and Apostolescu (Chapter 5), and Beech and Guevara (Chapter 6), for example, each illustrate the ways in which internationalisation is in effect mediated at national and, in fact, local levels, while Adriany (Chapter 7), Prickarts (Chapter 8) and Hattingh (Chapter 9) bring in school-level dynamics. Further, the idea developed by Engel and Gibson in their chapter on internationalisation in three US states suggests that internationalisation as a process can be promoted even within an overarching trend toward nationalism. Thus, it could offer insights to those studying internationalisation of both schools and universities in systems experiencing nationalistic currents, as in the case of Israel, China and Cuba, for example (Bamberger, Morris, & Yemini, 2019).

As future research considers the recontextualisation of global forms of internationalisation in different local, sub-national and national settings, the book offers a few frameworks to help support understanding of how and under what circumstances internationalisation is leveraged and implemented. For example, multiple forms of internationalisation are affected by different combinations of agents and circumstances, including for example, the OECD (Chapter 1), the IBO (Chapter 6), nation-states and sub-national agendas (Chapter 2, 4, 5 and 6), but also individual stakeholders at the local level, including both head teachers and teachers (Chapters 7, 8 and 9). Here we find the focus on actor-network theory (Chapter 6) to be useful in framing and illuminating the combinations of actors and the relationships forming between the actors involved in internationalisation. Beyond actors, several chapters underscore the importance of historicization and the push/pull factors inherent in the ways in which internationalisation dynamics as a trajectory of policy gets framed and implemented in different settings and across time (Chapters 3, 4, 5, 6 and 8). The skeptical reality approach (Chapter 3) is one mechanism for ensuring that national interests are attended to in scholarship related to internationalisation. Whether the needs of 'the national' become more diffuse and the dominance of the local or regional increase needs to be examined further, and the skeptical reality approach may also be a useful analytical framework for such contexts too.

Many of the chapters point to the desirability of internationalisation across national settings, pointing to the ways in which internationalised schooling may well be a growing global trend implicated in global standardisation movements in education. In different ways, authors engage in the implications of such a global movement. Some of the chapters seem to question the role of internationalisation in fostering social inclusion and equality in local, sub-national, national and global settings, despite its promises, and see the increased demand and supply of internationalised public schools as intimately associated with elitism, ultimately fostering opportunities for the global middle and elite classes (Maxwell & Yemini, 2018; Maxwell & Yemini, 2019; Kenway et al., 2017; see also Bunnell this book, Chapter 3). This book helps illuminate these threads, examining the dynamics of internationalisation, elitism and neo-colonialism. At a more global level, for example, Auld and Morris (Chapter 1) argue that the assessment of global competences by OECD might act as a form of Western dominance given its focus on a ranking or yardstick for internationalisation. At a national level, Waters and Brooks (Chapter 2) focus on students' participation in international service projects showcases the tensions between building global social consciousness of students from the Global North at the same time as neo-colonialism is reinforced. At a local level, Adriany (Chapter 7) examines the micro-politics of inequality facing local Indonesian teachers within an international kindergarten in Indonesia, reproducing neo-colonial relationships. Collectively these chapters suggest that there are multiple forms of balance between neo-colonialism, elitism, and internationalisation, and not necessarily one or the other.

And yet, if globalisation can be assumed to be a proxy of diversity (due to increased global migration patterns whereby, for example, mass migration has increased from 173 million international migrants in 2000 to 258 million in 2017 (United Nations Department of Economic and Social Affairs, Population Division, 2017)), school spaces are tasked not only with addressing the outcomes of increased global mobility patterns, but also enacting the promise of internationalisation—that is, of cultivating common values of collaboration, mutual respect, and protecting cultural and linguistic diversity. In some systems, public or state schools serving populations of students of lower socio-economic status backgrounds may also tend to accommodate higher proportions of students of colour than schools serving students of higher socio-economic status backgrounds, as suggested by Prickarts (Chapter 8). Here, internationalisation of public or state schools bolstering more diverse populations may well act as a promising opportunity to reduce inequality, a point also underscored by Engel and Gibson (Chapter 4), Prickarts (Chapter 8) and Hattingh (Chapter 9), who each frame more inclusive forms and practices of internationalisation. Furthermore, the book also presents interesting ways that internationalisation may in fact serve opportunities to advance global social consciousness (Waters & Brooks, Chapter 2; Prickarts, Chapter 8) and offer avenues for the formation of collaborative relationships across national and cultural boundaries (Adriany, Chapter 7). Future directions in the field of internationalisation therefore mandate further research both on the challenges, as well as the opportunities, for schooling to meet the promise of internationalisation towards human capital development *and* the common public good.

Apart from contributing to scholarship, one of the book's main contributions is to facilitate the establishment of a global network of researchers and practitioners whose work offers opportunities to extend the field. We see great advantage to working interdisciplinarily and cross-nationally, and this book is another important step in serving those goals. Pulling together both emergent and established scholars, as well as theoretical and more practitioner-based analyses, we hope this book is but the start to many fruitful collaborations helping to develop further scholarly contributions on internationalisation of schooling.

References

Altbach, P. G., & Knight, J. (2007). The internationalization of higher education: Motivations and realities. *Journal of Studies in International Education*, 11(3–4), 290–305.

Auld, E., & Morris, P. (2019). Science by streetlight and the OECD's measure of global competence: A new yardstick for internationalisation? *Policy Futures in Education*, 1478210318819246.

Ball, S. (2012). *Global Education Inc.: New policy networks and the neo-liberal imaginary*. New York: Routledge.

Bamberger, A., Morris, P., & Yemini, M. (2019). Neoliberalism, internationalisation and higher education: Connections, contradictions and alternatives. *Discourse: Studies in the Cultural Politics of Education*, 40(2), 203–216.

Brandenburg, U., & De Wit, H. (2015). The end of internationalization. *International Higher Education*, (62). https://doi.org/10.6017/ihe.2011.62.8533

Bromley, P. (2011). Multiculturalism and human rights in civic education: The case of British Columbia, Canada. *Educational Research*, 53(2), 151–164.

Cambridge, J., & Thompson, J. (2004). Internationalism and globalization as contexts for international education. *Compare*, 34(2), 161–175.

Coulby, D., & Zambeta, E. (2005). *World yearbook of education 2005: Globalization and nationalism in education*. London: Routledge.

de Wit, H. (2002). *Internationalization of higher education in the United States of America and Europe. A historical, comparative, and conceptual analysis*. USA: Greenwood.

de Wit, H., & Jones, E., (2018). Inclusive internationalization: Improving equity and access. *International Higher Education*, 94, 16–18.

Deca, L., Egron-Polak, E., & Fit, C. R. (2015). Internationalisation of Higher Education in Romanian National and Institutional Contexts. In A. Curaj, L. Deca, E. Egron-Polak, & J. Salmi (eds.). *Higher education reforms in Romania: Between the Bologna process and national challenges* (pp. 127–148). London: Springer.

Engel, L. C. (2009). *New state formations in education policy: Reflections from Spain*. Rotterdam: Sense Publishers.

Engel, L. C. (2014). Global citizenship and national (re)formations: Analysis of citizenship education reform in Spain. *Education, Citizenship and Social Justice*, 9(3), 239–254.

Engel, L. C. & Siczek, M. (2017). A cross-national comparison of international strategies: National competitiveness or global citizenship? *Compare: A Journal of Comparative Education*, 48(5), 749–767.

Engel, L. C., & Siczek, M. (2018). Framing global education in the United States: Policy perspectives. In L. D. Hill & F. J. Levine (Eds.), *Global perspectives in education research* (pp. 26–47). London: Routledge. Fielding, M., & Vidovich, L. (2017). Internationalisation in practice in Australian independent secondary schools: A global-local nexus? *Compare: A Journal of Comparative and International Education*, 47(2), 148–162.

Francois, E. J. (2015). *Building global education with a local perspective: An introduction to global higher education*. New York: Palgrave Macmillan.

Hayden, M. (2011). Transnational spaces of education: The growth of the international school sector. *Globalisation, Societies and Education*, 9(2), 211–224.

Hudzik, J. (2011). *Comprehensive internationalization: From concept to action*. Report, Washington, DC: NAFSA.

Kenway, J., Fahey, J., Epstein, D., Koh, A., McCarthy, C., & Rizvi, F. (2017). *Class choreographies: Elite schools and globalization*. London: Palgrave Macmillan.

Knight, J. (2004). Internationalization remodeled: Definition, approaches, and rationales. *Journal of Studies in International Education*, 8(1), 5–31.

Knight, J. (2008). *Higher education in turmoil: The changing world of internationalisation*. Rotterdam: Sense Publishers.

Lingard, B., Sellar, S., Hogan, A., & Thompson, G. (2017). *Commercialisation in public schooling (CIPS)*. Sydney: New South Wales Teachers Federation.

Maxwell, C., & Yemini, M. (2018). Discourses of global citizenship education: The influence of the global middle-classes. In A. Peterson, G. Stahl, & H. Soong (Eds.), *The Palgrave handbook of citizenship and education*. Basingstoke: Palgrave Macmillan.

Maxwell, C., & Yemini, M. (2019). Modalities of cosmopolitanism and mobility: Parental education strategies of global, immigrant and local middle-class Israelis. *Discourse: Studies in the Cultural Politics of Education*, 1–17.

Maxwell, C., Deppe, U., Krüger, H. H., & Helsper, W. (Eds). (2018). *Elite education and internationalisation: From the early years into higher education*. Basingstoke: Palgrave Macmillan.

Mitchell, K. (2003). Educating the national citizen in neoliberal times: From the multicultural self to the strategic cosmopolitan. *Transactions of the Institute of British Geographers*, 28(4), 387–403.

Naumann, I. K. (2018). Internationalising early childhood education, or embedding international children into local contexts? In C. Maxwell, U. Deppe, H. H. Krüger, & W. Helsper (Eds.), *Elite education and internationalisation: From the early years into higher education* (pp. 181–188). Basingstoke: Palgrave Macmillan.

Oonk, H., Maslowski, R., & Van der Werf, G. (2011). *Internationalisation in secondary education in Europe: A European and international orientation in schools policies, theories and research*. Groningen: IAP.

Ortloff, D. H., & Shonia, O. N. (2015). Teacher conceptualizations of global citizenship: Global immersion experiences and implications for the empathy/threat dialectic. In B. Maguth & J. Hilburn (Eds.), *The state of global education: Learning with the world and its people* (pp. 78–91). London: Routledge.

Pak, S. Y., & Lee, M. (2018). 'Hit the ground running': Delineating the problems and potentials in State-led Global Citizenship Education (GCE) through teacher practices in South Korea. *British Journal of Educational Studies*, 66(4), 515–535.

Qiang, Z. (2003). Internationalisation of higher education: Towards a conceptual framework. *Policy Futures in Education*, 1(2), 250.

Rizvi, F., & Lingard, B. (2009). *Globalizing education policy*. New York: Routledge.

Streitwieser, B., & Ogden, A. (2016). International higher education's scholar-practitioners: Bridging research and practice. Oxford: Symposium Books.

Tarc, P. (2009). *Global dreams, enduring tensions: International baccalaureate in a changing world*. New York: Peter Lang.

Torres, C. A. (2015). Solidarity and competitiveness in a global context: Comparable concepts in global citizenship education? *The International Education Journal: Comparative Perspectives*, 14(2), 22–29.

United Nations Department of Economic and Social Affairs, Population Division (2017). *International migration report 2017: Highlights (ST/ESA/SER.A/404)*. New York: United Nations.

UNESCO (2014). *Global citizenship education: Preparing learners for the challenges of the 21st century.* Paris: UNESCO.

van der Wende, M. C. (2001). Internationalisation policies: About new trends and contrasting paradigms. *Higher Education Policy, 14*(3), 249–259.

Verger, A. (2011). Framing and selling global education policy: The promotion of public-private partnerships for education in low-income countries. *Journal of Education Policy, 27*(1), 109–130.

Warner, G. (1992). Internationalization models and the role of the university. *International Education Magazine, 8*(1), 21.

Weenink, D. (2008). Cosmopolitanism as a form of capital: Parents preparing their children for a globalizing world. *Sociology, 42,* 1089–1106.

Yemini, M., Goren, H., & Maxwell, C. (2018). Global citizenship education in the era of mobility conflict and globalisation. *British Journal of Educational Studies, 66*(4), 1–10.

Yemini, M. (2014). Internationalization of secondary education—Lessons from Israeli Palestinian-Arab schools in Tel Aviv-Jaffa. *Urban Education, 49*(5), 471–498.

Yemini, M. (2015). Internationalisation discourse hits the tipping point: A new definition is needed. *Perspectives: Policy and Practice in Higher Education, 19*(1), 19–22.

1   The OECD's Assessment of Global Competence

Measuring and Making Global Elites

Euan Auld and Paul Morris

Chapter 1 is adapted from an article by Auld and Morris (2019), published in *Policy Futures in Education*, titled 'Science by Streetlight and the OECD's measure of global competence: a new yardstick for internationalisation?'

Introduction

The Organisation for Economic Development (OECD) compares triannually the academic performance of 15-year-olds globally through its Programme for International Student Assessment (PISA), describing the assessment as 'the world's premier yardstick for evaluating the quality, equity and efficiency of school systems' (OECD, 2012, p. 11). With this yardstick, it pursues its core mission of promoting 'Better Policies for Better Lives'. Its testing empire has been extended to cover, adults, 4–5-year-olds, teachers and university students, and in the 2018 PISA cycle 'global competence' was included as a domain in PISA for the first time. Through its comparative assessments, the OECD has asserted itself as an influential player in the global governance of education, exerting a significant but uneven influence on national education systems (Kallo, 2009; Martens, 2007; Sellar & Lingard, 2014).

The OECD's assessments have served in some nations to redefine the aims of schooling by encouraging the narrowing of curricula to raise performance on its key domains, and the organisation explicitly advocates for the integration of its test components in local curricula (e.g. OECD, 2012; Schleicher, 2018). Through these processes, the OECD's assessments have emerged as a powerful tool for 'internationalisation' that has the capacity, via comparative measurements, to affect entire education systems from kindergartens to higher education. When extended to measuring the global competence of 15-year-olds, PISA has the potential to be used as the measure of the effectiveness of internationalisation and global education policies and practices in schools, and the basis for identifying and advocating the 'best practices' for its achievement.

Although the pursuit of 'Global Citizenship' has long been a central goal of internationalisation efforts in schools, especially 'International Schools' and curricular initiatives such as the Model United Nations (UN), and has been explicitly promoted by UNESCO (e.g. 2012), its inclusion in the UN's Sustainable Development Goals (SDG's) (target 4.7), has significant ramifications. When translated into the language of assessment, 'global citizenship' (UNESCO, 2014) becomes global *competence/competencies* or *skills* (OECD, 2018a). This chapter builds upon an earlier article by the authors (Auld & Morris, 2019), and focusses on the OECD's measurement of global competence through an analysis of (i) key documents and presentations produced by the OECD; (ii) related documents, in particular those relating to the SDGs; and (iii) academic commentaries and critiques. Documents were analysed with regard to their rhetorical goals, recognising that these transcend specific texts to encompass the broader organisational agenda.

The structure of this chapter addresses sequentially the critical questions concerning the OECD's measurement of global competence: why was it undertaken; how was it defined; who defined it; and how are the challenges inherent in its measurement overcome? The domains measured regularly by PISA (science, maths and literacy) are far more established than global citizenship, which largely operates as a floating signifier and conveys a diverse range of meanings. Oxley and Morris (2013) identify eight different conceptions of Global Citizenship, and there is also evidence that the concept is understood and represented in school curricula differently across nations (Goren & Yemini, 2017). A similar absence of uniformity is evident in how Global Citizenship is defined by different international agencies, and by the OECD over time. This definitional variety and lack of clarity is emblematic of the desires to 'internationalise' schooling, we argue, and therefore the attempt to 'measure' it globally is highly problematic for a process that is usually contextual and can potentially extend relations of inequality within and across countries.

We demonstrate that the OECD's conception of global competence is an ahistorical and depoliticised entity, focusing on the cognitive domain through the measurement of pupils' understanding. This focus on what is easiest to measure is fundamentally in tension with the organisation's quest to measure the non-cognitive and to promote the 'appreciation of cultural diversity', as the model 'global citizen' ultimately sounds like a model OECD intern (see OECD, 2018c) or member of the global middle class (Maxwell & Yemini, 2018). Consequently the role of such schools which cater for the global middle class as models of 'best practice' will be legitimated and strengthened, making and legitimating global elites (Maxwell, 2018).

We suggest the measure of global competencies has in its final form been influenced by the OECD's attempt to secure its own role in measuring and tracking progress on the UN's SDGs. In pursuing this goal, the organisation has belatedly aligned its definition of global competencies with the SDGs and will use the data to identify and promote the causes of high-performance on PISA within its Learning 2030 Framework. Although few countries elected to participate in the PISA 2018 assessment of global competence, the OECD has previously launched its new assessments in a small number of pilot nations, using this to demonstrate the viability of its measurement before extending their reach in subsequent cycles.

Surveying the OECD's Measure of Global Competence

Rationales

From 2013, a multitude of reasons for assessing global competencies were presented by the OECD, but the overall narrative which runs through the documents involves the OECD portraying itself as responding to two exogenous forces. First, it is depicted as an inevitable response to the irresistible impact of globalisation and technological change. Second, it claims it is undertaking the task in response to the demand of policy makers and educational leaders who are seeking to address those impacts. Though the PISA Governing Board's interest in global competence as a new assessment domain has unclear origins and was arguably influenced by the US international education strategy for 2012–2016 (see Engel & Siczek, 2018), here we focus on the rationales that were explicitly provided in key OECD reports (Reimers, 2013; OECD, 2014, 2016a, 2018a).

The first explicit statement that the OECD was considering assessing Global Competencies appeared in a strategy paper authored by Professor Fernando Reimers[1] (2013). Reimers' rationale closely followed that defined by UNESCO (2013), positioning global education as 'the new civics of the 21st century' and observing that 'citizenship is embedded in a mesh of relationships that are global as well as local' (p. 1). Reimers argued that comparative research was particularly useful for supporting this task, with the final inference: 'building on the successful record of the PISA studies, [the OECD] is well positioned to assume a leadership role in advancing the development and implementation of cross-national assessments of global competencies of students' (p. 2).

The following year, the PISA governing board (2014) met to discuss the PISA 2018 Framework Plans, with global competence on the agenda. The interest in Global Competencies takes the same starting point as Reimers and UNESCO, highlighting the necessity of developing attitudes, knowledge and skills that will enable students to contribute positively to the global community. The rationale then shifts in line with the organisation's economic mission, emphasising that

> education needs to adapt its program and take account of what students will need in their future lives . . . [as] the requirements of the global knowledge required in the 21st century society go far beyond the traditional literacies.
>
> (p. 6)

A further departure emerges in the assertion that the inclusion of additional domains such as global competence will be used to 'enable interpretation of PISA outcome data and increase the likelihood of revealing causality' (OECD, 2014, p. 7), specifically regarding the education policies and practices associated with high performance on PISA.

The report presents its assessment model for PISA 2018 and states 'the purely cognitive and essentially non-cognitive form a continuum, from skills to behaviours and attitudes, from tools for working to living in the world' (p. 7). Whereas the OECD generally tends to highlight a 'web of correlations' that could 'conceivably affect [students'] performance' (e.g. OECD, 2012, p. 23), the rationale here emerges that by assessing more domains the organisation will get closer to identifying causally significant features of education systems that produce the right kind of knowledge workers for the global economy. Global Competencies thus becomes an additional variable within the overarching schema of 21st century requirements and skills. This ties into the OECD's mission to identify and advocate the education policies and practices associated with higher education performance as measured by its assessments.

Two years later, Gabriela Ramos, OECD Chief of Staff, opens the report *Global Competency for an Inclusive World* by stating that 'citizens need not only the skills to be competitive and ready for a new world of work, but more importantly they also need to develop the capacity to analyse and understand global intercultural issues' (OECD, 2016a). Andreas Schleicher, OECD Director of Education and Skills, follows with a more familiar economic framing:

> The more interdependent the world becomes, the more we rely on collaborators and orchestrators who are able to join others in work and life. Schools need to prepare students for a world in which people need to work with others of diverse cultural origins, and appreciate different ideas, perspectives and values.
>
> (OECD, 2016a)

In a BBC Press Release, Schleicher (2016) stated that 'there is such a need for *new rankings* to show young people's competence in a world where globalisation is a powerful economic, political and cultural force'.

Moreover, it is noted that education leaders around the world are increasingly talking about the need to teach 'global competences'. This is identified as an undervalued part of the school curriculum on the grounds that its inclusion will help reduce sources of conflict in societies and produce a multitude of worthwhile benefits. The specific role of the OECD in developing measurements is then reframed as responding to policymakers needs, by providing a system for measuring and comparing performance.

At this stage, and despite global citizenship's inclusion in SDG 4.7, there is still no explicit mention of the SDGs amidst the rationales. The assessment framework was, however, updated and integrated into the OECD's emerging *Education 2030 Framework* (OECD, 2016a, p. 2). The document emphasises 'the need to find a new concept of growth', one that 'may not be a quantifiable concept, based solely on maximising economic gains, but a multidimensional concept that includes care for the environment and social harmony, as well as acceptable levels of security, health, and education' and which covers 'quantitative and qualitative indicators, including subjective well-being and quality jobs', ensuring 'the benefits of growth are fairly shared across society' (OECD, 2016a, p. 1).

Although there is no mention of the SDGs, global competencies/citizenship or sustainability in the 2016 framework, the OECD would later state that its *Learning Framework 2030* (OECD, 2018a) 'contributes to the UN 2030 Global Goals for Sustainable Development (SDGs), aiming to ensure the sustainability of people, profit, planet and peace, through partnership' (p. 3). That is, the basic framework originally conceptualised under the OECD's new paradigm for development was retrofitted to incorporate specific aspects of the SDGs and thereby to align more closely with the UN's post-2015 agenda.

In 2018, the organisation found its final positioning. The foreword by Ramos reiterates the two main rationales:

> Reinforcing global competence is vital for individuals to thrive in a rapidly changing world and for societies to progress without leaving anyone behind. . . . Citizens need not only the skills to be competitive and ready for a new world of work, but more importantly they also need to develop the capacity to analyse and understand global and intercultural issues. . . . Together, we can foster global competence for more inclusive societies.
>
> (OECD, 2018a, p. 2)

Schleicher, however, presents an altogether different rationale to his OECD 2016a opening:

> In 2015, 193 countries committed to achieving the UN's 17 Sustainable Development Goals (SDGs), a shared vision of humanity that

provides the missing piece of the globalisation puzzle. The extent to which that vision becomes a reality will depend on today's classrooms. . . . This has inspired the OECD's PISA, the global yardstick for educational success, to include global competence in its metrics for quality, equity and effectiveness in education. PISA will assess global competence for the first time ever in 2018. In that regard, this framework provides its conceptual underpinning.

(OECD, 2018a, p. 2)

The claim that the UN's SDGs *inspired* the OECD to include Global Competencies in its metrics looks like an exercise in *post hoc* rationalisation given that the decision to assess Global Competencies was considered five years earlier and then explicitly linked to the SDGs in 2018. The main text nuances Schleicher's rationale, and a section titled 'why do we need global competence?' answers: (i) to live harmoniously in multicultural communities; (ii) to thrive in a changing labour market; (iii) to use media platforms effectively and responsibly; and (iv) to support the SDG's. Of these, the second most clearly fits the OECD's initial framework, which focused squarely on cognitive skills in education and their implications within a competitive global knowledge economy. The subsection elaborates:

Educating for global competence can boost employability. Employers increasingly seek to attract learners who easily adapt and are able to apply and transfer their skills and knowledge to new contexts. Work readiness in an interconnected world requires young people to understand the complex dynamics of globalisation, be open to people from different cultural backgrounds, build trust in diverse teams and demonstrate respect for others.

(p. 5)

This statement represents continuity with the initial rationale presented in 2014, and reiterated in 2016, which indicated that global competency would form part of the broader continuum of cognitive and non-cognitive skills necessary to function as a global knowledge worker, and the inclusion of which would enhance the organisation's capacity to make causal judgements on education performance and future economic competitiveness. The other rationales are secondary to the organisation's central mission, while the section 'To support the Sustainable Development Goals' states: 'educating for global competence can help form new generations who care about global issues and *engage in tackling* social, political, economic and environmental challenges' (p. 5).

Having established the importance of global competence under the SDGs, the OECD poses the question: 'Should we assess global competence?' (p. 6). It duly answers in the affirmative, stating that high demands can only be met 'if education systems define new learning objectives based on a solid framework, and use different types of assessment to reflect on the effectiveness of their initiatives and teaching practices' (p. 5). The assessment is identified as laying the foundations for pursuing the OECD's motto of identifying Better Policies for Better Lives:

> A fundamental goal of this work . . . [is] to support evidence-based decisions on how to improve curricula, teaching, assessments and schools' responses to cultural diversity in order to prepare young people to become global citizens.
>
> (OECD, 2018a, p. 6)

The OECD's traditional emphasis on global knowledge workers is thus substituted for globally competent citizens, with the latter encompassing and nuancing the former to accommodate the SDGs but not replacing it. This preserves and strengthens the OECD's broader ambitions in education governance, with PISA incorporated into the OECD Learning Framework 2030 and positioned as a benchmark of progress on the UN's SDGs. PISA is already being used by the UNESCO Institute for Statistics to identify basic minimum standards of education quality and to track progress on SDG 4.1 (see UIS, 2018) and the Learning Framework 2030 is intended as a barometer for all nations. In this respect, the post hoc rationalisation and discursive alignment with the SDGs has implications for how internationalisation will be conceived, developed and delivered as it filters down and is translated into 'evidence-based decisions' for national education systems.

This shift in rationales is mirrored in the way Global Competencies was redefined, which we explore later.

(Re)defining Global Competence

The definitions of global competence have varied over time. Here we survey the definitions that appeared in key publications before turning to look more closely at the individuals involved in developing them. In 2013, Reimers presented the rationale for assessing global competence with regard to its status as 'the new civics' for the 21st century, distinguishing two approaches that focused on *knowledge* and *dispositions*:

> the skills and mind habits to understand global interdependence, and to live with meaning and direction in contexts where global interactions increase exponentially.
>
> (Reimers, 2013, p. 2)

During these early phases the OECD canvassed a range of ideas and definitions and this continued in the 2014 document, in which the intent to include Global Competency in the 2018 PISA cycle was confirmed. Noting the need to encompass both knowledge and behaviours in any definition and drawing 'heavily on Pearsons' existing expertise and knowledge of what works in PISA' (OECD, 2014, p. 8), the OECD presented the following definition:

> the capacity of an individual to understand that we learn, work and live in an international, interconnected and interdependent society and the capability to use that knowledge to inform one's dispositions, behaviours and actions when navigating, interacting, communicating and participating in a variety of roles and international contexts as a reflective individual.
>
> (OECD, 2014, p. 9)

The OECD (2014) stressed that its definition might change as the Global Competence Expert Group considered 'the knowledge, skills, attitudes, and behaviours that comprise global competence' (p. 10). In 2016, and despite framing the rationale largely in terms of the need to develop 'globally minded' workers in the foreword, Schleicher (OECD, 2016a) enunciated a more elaborate definition of global competence, which moves it towards a focus on global issues and intercultural sensitivity:

> the capacity to analyse global and intercultural issues critically and from multiple perspectives, to understand how differences affect perceptions judgements, and ideas of self and others, and to engage in open, appropriate and effective interactions with others from different backgrounds on the basis of a shared respect for human dignity.
>
> (OECD, 2016a, p. 4)

The final definition (OECD, 2018a) contains two significant changes from the (2016a) definition. First, the expectation that pupils are critical and reflect on their own perceptions of others was removed. Second, the quest for 'human dignity' was replaced by 'to act for collective well-being and sustainable development', as follows:

> the capacity to examine local, global and intercultural issues, to understand and appreciate the perspectives and world views of others, to engage in open, appropriate and effective interactions with people from different cultures, and to act for collective well-being and sustainable development.
>
> (OECD, 2018a, p. 7)

The reasons for these changes are not specified but the focus on 'understanding' aligns it with what is more readily measurable than critical reflection (or engagement). Similarly, the removal of reference to 'respect for human dignity' allows a focus on cognitive aspects (knowledge, skills and attitudes), and it allows the exercise to avoid assessing 'values'. The direct references to sustainability and well-being introduced in 2018 follows the amended rationale and strengthens the OECD's quest to assess the SDGs through its Learning Framework 2030 (OECD, 2018b). This extends beyond the cognitive-economic focus into the non-cognitive aspects of education to align with the UN's post-2015 agenda, effectively developing a yardstick for 'internationalisation' defined in terms of students' 'global competence' and underpinned by the OECD's economic vision.

Once the assessment has been established, OECD publications actively encourage the integration of test components across school curricula to improve results against its global standard, leveraging peer pressure and the strategic use of media channels to overcome resistance to reform (see OECD, 2012; Schleicher, 2018).

The Nature of the Global Citizen

The OECD (2018a) divides Global Competency into four dimensions (knowledge, values, attitudes and skills), and targets four primary rationales: to live harmoniously in multicultural communities; to thrive in a changing labour market; to use media platforms effectively and responsibly; and to support the SDGs. In terms of Oxley and Morris's (2013) analysis of the conceptions of global citizenship, the focus is on a cultural/social/sustainable conception rather than a critical or political one that requires active engagement. The OECD portrays the 'global' as an ahistorical, depoliticised and fixed entity to be accepted as it is. Schools are expected to teach pupils about globalisation and provide them with the skills to adapt to it. Any consideration that the world has been shaped through conquest, racism, nationalism and religious mission, inter alia, and that the barriers to human dignity operate both within and across nations and cultures is absent.

Similarly, with specific regard to the 2016a OECD document, Ledger, Their, Bailey and Pitts (2019) comment:

> [It] presumes that young people need to change to meet the world of the future, rather than suggesting that we should work systemically to construct alternative futures to meet the needs of the young.
>
> (21)

A further insight is provided by analysing the nature of the globally competent 15-year-old citizen which the OECD envisages, and his/her inverse, 'the globally incompetent citizen'. The former, who will score highly on the test, is one who has experienced other cultures, is bi-lingual and has access to social media and a liberal, internationally oriented education, i.e. a member of the global elite. In contrast, the 'anti-global' student is monolingual, probably socio-economically disadvantaged and has limited exposure to other cultures, social media and internationalised education. Ledger et al.'s (2019) detailed analysis of the sample assessment items provided describes the model student:

> A globally competent person feels confident and happy about travelling to other countries, implying that if one hails from a background where this is not a norm, and feels apprehensive about such new experiences, one is not globally competent (p. 24). . . . The ideal globally competent student has money to donate to charity, has a home in which they can host exchange students, has met people from many countries, and goes to a school which is able to offer exchange programmes. These variables essentially describe the habitus of a global elite, making it hard to see how a child from a lower socio-economic background and/or an attendee of a poorly funded local school could possibly score well on this scale.
>
> (p. 25)

This outcome is predictable, given that the OECD has grafted goals and ideas associated with the SDGs upon its economic mission. That is, of the four rationales presented (to live harmoniously in multicultural communities; to thrive in a changing labour market; to use media platforms effectively and responsibly; and to support the SDGs) the OECD remains oriented towards the way in which global competence will enable students to flourish as a knowledge worker in a changing global labour market.

Further insights into the problems which the test faces are provided by the sample Questionnaire items; many of these require pupils to express their extent of agreement/disagreement with statements such as:

- Immigrants who live in a country for several years should have the opportunity to vote in elections.
- Immigrants should have the opportunity to continue their own customs and lifestyle.
- I want to learn how people live in different countries
- I am interested in how people from various cultures see the world.
- I am interested in finding out about the traditions of other cultures.

These underline the focus on measuring intercultural awareness and the extent of tolerance within a nation towards foreigners. In the absence of any publicly available analysis of how the validity of these items has been established it is unclear how contextual variations will be addressed: for pupils who live in multicultural urban societies currently seeking to integrate large influxes of immigrants and refugees (e.g. Italy and Germany) their responses will be influenced by their lived experiences, including the coverage of that topic in the domestic media and by local politicians. For other pupils, who live in relatively homogeneous societies (e.g. Japan) or where the media is centrally controlled (e.g. China), their answers will be essentially hypothetical and rooted in a very different set of experiences.

The OECD's conception of a global citizen is best understood with attention to those involved in its construction. The OECD (2018a) claims that their framework is:

> the product of a collaborative effort between the countries partici-
> pating in PISA and the OECD Secretariat.
>
> (p. 1)

In practise, the framework was developed by OECD staff and various experts they commissioned, and the core group was termed the Global Competence Expert Group (CEG). Grotlüschen (2017) provides a detailed analysis of the personnel involved from 2013 and concludes:

> Overall, the group never was very global; it never included countries which are less familiar with the English language than the former Commonwealth and Asian countries. There is no contribution from Latin America and Africa.

Similarly, Ledger et al. (2019) conclude:

> Despite OECD nominally espousing a version of global compe-
> tency based on multiple perspectives and understanding cultural differences, (our) findings show evidence of an OECD conversation impoverished by a limited degree of diversity of scholars, publication types, backgrounds, and viewpoints (p. 33) . . . a mistake that runs afoul of the very purpose of educating for global competency.
>
> (p. 38)

Ledger et al. (2019) notes the glaring paradox, namely that the OECD relied on a small group of experts, primarily drawn from the USA and UK, to develop the global competence framework. Ultimately, these nations have not only withdrawn from the test of global competence but are in many respects responsible for shaping the nature of 'the global' and its ongoing problems. Recent reports (BBC, 2018) suggest that more than half of the countries involved in PISA (including England, the United States, Germany, France, Denmark, the Netherlands, Finland and Ireland) decided not to take the global competency test, and only about 28 countries have agreed to do so. In essence, richer nations have promoted and developed a test that is to be administered to lower income nations.

Dealing With the Challenges: Science by Streetlight

The ambition of constructing a meaningful 'yardstick of education quality' and promoting the transfer of 'better policies' from high-performing systems requires a series of problematic assumptions (see Auld & Morris, 2014; 2016). The OECD must demonstrate that (i) the aims and outcomes of education systems are directly commensurable and are accurately captured by their assessments (in this instance, a universal conception of global competence). To be meaningful, the OECD traditionally claims that (ii) systems' performance on their tests can be directly related to future competitiveness in the global knowledge economy. This is now supplemented by claims that improvement on the assessment domains is central to achieving the UN's SDGs, with collective well-being at the apex of its Learning Framework 2030. To identify policy lessons, the OECD must assume that (iii) the causes of high-performance exert an independent, constant and predictable effect, are absolute and universal and therefore are readily transferrable. To support the transfer of these 'better policies', (iv) causality must be located within school systems' practices and structures.

The foundations for bypassing these issues are laid in the construction of the measurement itself. The OECD gains legitimacy from government endorsements and references from policymakers (Rautalin & Alasuutari, 2009), and it relies heavily on the media to popularise its assessments (Grey & Morris, 2018). In 2016, Global Competencies were promoted because it would help 'to counter the discriminatory behaviours *picked up at school and in the family*' (2016a, p. 2). It is illustrative of the OECD's depoliticised perspective that the school and the family are identified as the sole sources of what it terms 'discriminatory behaviour' (which is not clearly defined), whilst no reference is made to national governments, the media or politicians. Two years on, the OECD (2018a) stated, 'PISA will provide a comprehensive overview of education systems' efforts to create learning environments that invite young people to understand the world beyond their immediate environment' (p. 5). The challenge of commensurability in assessing global competence is identified:

> The most salient challenge for the PISA assessment is that—through a single international instrument—it needs to account for the large variety of geographic and cultural contexts represented in participating countries.
>
> (OECD, 2018a, p. 21)

Two strategies are employed to anticipate this challenge before it is explicitly stated. First, it is addressed tangentially through a boxed insert titled 'Defining Culture', which is not discussed in the main text and states inter alia:

> 'Culture' is difficult to define because cultural groups are always internally heterogeneous and contain individuals who adhere to a range of diverse beliefs and practices. Furthermore, the core cultural beliefs and practices that are most typically associated with any given group are also constantly changing and evolving over time.
>
> (OECD, 2018a, p. 8)

Culture is thus portrayed as fragmented, atomistic and fluid, and consequently, individuals can be members of a host of different but shifting cultures but all fall under the inescapable influence of globalization, and hence partake in global citizenship. The second strategy also involves the use of a boxed insert titled 'Perspectives on Global Competence From Different Cultures', which recognises the Western perspective adopted by the OECD and explains:

> However, related concepts exist in many countries and cultures around the world. One interesting perspective on global competence comes from South Africa and involves the concept of Ubuntu. . . . There are other similar concepts to Ubuntu found in different cultures around the world including in indigenous cultures in the Andes and in Malaysia. Collective identity, relationships and context (as impacted by historical, social, economic and political realities) all become major emphases in other cultural discourses on global competence.
>
> (OECD, 2018a, p. 19)

Cultures are now portrayed as coherent, homogeneous, stable and rooted in different societies, and while they may be slightly different from Western conceptions, they nonetheless share common features. The message, reiterated in the main text, is that the OECD are measuring the essence of both Western and non-Western views of global competence. The challenge of culture and Western hegemony is neatly identified, marginalised and resolved, and the focus shifted on to how it is learnt within schools.

The OECD's conception of a competent global citizen is constructed on Western cultural foundations which focus on the individual. Just as the rationale and definitions had shifted over time to follow *what should be measured*, the aspects measured (i.e. the *de facto* definition) again simply follow *what can be measured*. The actual assessment does not measure the qualities stated under the official definition, and social skills and attitudes are limited to background information (values or engagement are not assessed at all—*see list of domains below*). Three domains of global competence are identified, and the methods of assessment are:

1. Knowledge . . . Cognitive test and questionnaire
2. Cognitive skills . . . Cognitive test and questionnaire
3. Social skills and attitudes . . . Questionnaire only

(OECD, 2018a, p. 22)

Values are included as a fourth domain in the framework but described as 'beyond the scope of the PISA 2018 assessment'. As noted previously, however, the official definition of Global Competency is not actually being *assessed* as the organisation focuses on what is more easily measured. In so doing, the OECD provides an illustration of a classic methodological problem; namely the 'streetlight effect', which involves a tendency to search for an object where the lighting is best, not where it is located (Freedman, 2010). In this case the lighting is best if they focus on assessing and comparing the cognitive domain.

A challenge of a more technical nature arises from the nature of the assessment items described previously. Most 15-year-olds will be able to discern the most virtuous answer from the questions, and the tests may provide a good indication of national differences in their willingness to provide the virtuous answer. A variant of that problem is recognised when it is explained that:

People from some cultural backgrounds tend to exaggerate their responses to typical questionnaire items based on a Likert-type scale . . . whereas others tend to take a middle ground.

(OECD, 2018a, p. 22)

The problem is however solved because:

The responses to the questionnaire items will thus not be used to position countries and students on a scale. Instead, they will be used only to illustrate general patterns and differences within countries in the development of the skills and attitudes that contribute to global competence among 15-year-old students, as well as to analyse the relationship between those skills and attitudes and students' results on the cognitive test.

(OECD, 2018a, p. 22)

In essence, by presenting the questionnaire data in a way which shows 'general patterns and differences' rather than as a league table, the problems are overcome. The eventual league table will continue to focus on where the light shines brightest; that is, the cognitive tests and their economic implications. Although the questionnaire items (social skills and attitudes) will not actually be used to determine rankings, they will be used in combination with other components to nuance the interpretation of PISA data and as a basis for promoting specific reforms. For example, nations in which students score well on the cognitive tests and demonstrate high levels of global competence will be clustered to present 'meaningful configurations' and then used as a basis for identifying the underlying policies and practices associated with these (and presumably other) desirable outcomes. These will include policies and practices associated with high levels of 'global competence' and degrees of 'internationalisation' within school systems, and potentially individual schools (see PISA for Schools).[2]

Conclusion

Our analysis challenges many of the basic claims made by the OECD. The claim that they were inspired by the SDGs emerged long after the decision to proceed and the development work had begun. The claim that the exercise was 'a collaborative effort between the countries participating in PISA' is partly true, as the individuals responsible for developing the measurement were drawn from the USA and UK. However, those nations then elected not to participate in the optional assessment of global competence. The OECD's claim that it successfully devised a universal and accurate measure capturing the essence of both Western and non-Western views of global competence is not supported. On the contrary, the OECD's measure of a globally competent student is one who is rooted in an elite, Western liberal tradition, an act of 'elite-making' that further privileges well resourced groups (Maxwell, 2018). By measuring others on that metric, we legitimize our values and require others to embrace and deliver them in schools.

The OECD's definition of global competence shifted markedly, and the final version was notable for its inclusion of 'sustainable development' and 'collective wellbeing'. We interpret this as a late attempt by the OECD to position itself as the primary agency responsible for measuring and monitoring progress on the SDGs in education, extending its new paradigm for development through the OECD Learning Framework 2030. As a one-off exercise, we argue its key role is to legitimise the 'conceptual underpinnings' of its Learning Framework 2030 by demonstrating its capacity to measure global competence. Aligning its agenda and assessments with the UN's SDGs provides a moral legitimacy the OECD has not enjoyed with the traditional PISA initiative and its narrow economic focus. Crucially, a key feature of the initiative is the integration of the OECD assessment technologies into national assessment infrastructures under the imperative of 'capacity building', with the goal of aligning, or replacing, national assessments with a global standard and giving nations access to a community of international experts that will help improve performance on the key indicators.

Global competence will now be one of the domains covered by these indicators. If, as with its other assessments, this influences curriculum and schooling, it has the further potential to influence expectations of 'being international' in these nations, which may in turn affect 'the formation of student subjectivities and imaginaries' (Maxwell, 2018, p. 349).

Dill (2013) identifies two competing features in global citizenship education: (1) a global consciousness that includes an awareness of other perspectives, a vision of oneself as part of a global community, and a moral conscience to act for the good of the world; and (2), global competencies that include skills and knowledge for economic success in global capitalism. We suggest the OECD has adopted the language of the former in pursuit of the latter as it seeks to expand the domain and power of its assessment. While the former is broadly in line with the outlook and policies being pursued by nations that were influential in developing the measure, such as the United States (see Engel & Siczek, 2018), Engel and Siczek (2017) point out that internationalisation strategies that are competitive in orientation actually limit possibilities of advancing central tenets of global citizenship. In short, the OECD has failed its own assessment.

Caution should be exercised when the results of the assessment are released and the OECD proceeds to identify policies and practices associated with 'global competence'. Precedents suggest that (Auld & Morris, 2019): (i) the OECD will present its assessment of global competence as the 'world's premier yardstick' of internationalisation/ global education in school systems, recommending schools copy the policies of high performing nations and integrate PISA components into curricula to enhance students' global competence; (ii) where stakes are high, the yardstick will encourage gaming the system to improve scores; and, (iii) it will allow policy makers to ignore those aspects of schooling (e.g. the promotion of instrumental and nationalistic values) that undermine the promotion of a global consciousness and what goes on beyond the school gates (UNESCO/MGIEP (2017).

If the new assessment does gain traction it has the potential to frame debates regarding internationalisation for the various stakeholders trying to develop policy initiatives and approaches to 'internationalising' schools across the globe. Therein lies another conundrum, are global competencies such as tolerance, cooperation and interdependence enhanced by encouraging nations to compete with and outdo each other on a questionable metric?

Notes

1. Fernando Reimers is a professor at the Harvard Graduate School of Education and directs the Global Education Innovation Initiative.

2. The OECD's PISA for Schools is intended as a 'tool for school leaders across the world to understand their 15-year old students' abilities to think critically and apply their knowledge creatively in novel contexts'. Available online at: www.oecd.org/PISA/pisa-for-schools/. In the future this would also include information on students' 'global competence' and internationalisation.

References

Auld, E., & Morris, P. (2014). Comparative education, the 'New Paradigm' and policy borrowing: Constructing knowledge for educational reform. *Comparative Education, 50*(2), 129–155.

Auld, E., & Morris, P. (2016). PISA, policy and persuasion: Translating complex conditions into education 'best practice'. *Comparative Education, 52*(2), 202–229.

Auld, E., & Morris, P. (2019). Science by streetlight and the OECD's measure of global competence. *Policy Futures in Education.* doi:10.1177/1478210318819246

BBC. (2018, January 24). *England and US will not take PISA test in Tolerance.* www.bbc.com/news/business-42781376

Dill, J. S. (2013). *The longings and limits of global citizenship education: The moral pedagogy of schooling in a cosmopolitan age.* New York: Routledge.

Engel, L. C., & Siczek, M. M. (2017). 'A cross-national comparison of international strategies: Global citizenship and the advancement of national competitiveness'. *Compare: A Journal of Comparative and International Education,* online 28 July.

Engel, L. C., & Siczek, M. M. (2018). Framing global education in the united states: Policy perspectives. In L. D. Hill & F. J. Levine (Eds.), *Global perspectives on education research.* New York: Routledge.

Freedman, D. H. (2010). *Wrong: Why experts keep failing us.* Little: Brown and Company.

Goren, H., & Yemini, M. (2017). Global citizenship education redefined—A systematic review off empirical studies on global citizenship education. *International Journal of Educational Research,* (82), 170–183.

Grey, S., & Morris, P. (2018). PISA: Multiple 'truths' and mediatised global governance. *Comparative Education, 54*(2), 109–131.

Grotlüschen, A. (2017). Global competence—Does the new OECD competence domain ignore the global South? *Studies in the Education of Adults.* doi:10.10 80/02660830.2018.1523100

Kallo, J. (2009). *OECD education policy: A comparative and historical study focusing on the thematic reviews of tertiary education.* Jyvaskyla: Finnish Research Association.

Ledger, S., Their, M., Bailey, L., & Pitts, C. (2019). OECD's approach to measuring global competency: Powerful voices shaping education. *Teachers College Record, 121*(8).

Martens, K. (2007). How to become an influential actor—the 'comparative turn' in OECD education policy. In A. Rusconi & K. Lutz (Eds.), *Transformations of the state and global governance.* London: Routledge, pp. 40–56.

Maxwell, C. (2018). Changing spaces—The re-shaping of (elite) education through internationalization. In C. Maxwell, U. Deppe, H. H. Kruger, & W. Helsper (Eds.), *Elite education and internationalisation: From the early years into higher education.* Basingstoke: Palgrave Macmillan.

Maxwell, C., & Yemini, M. (2018). Discourses of global citizenship education: The influence of the global middle-classes. In A. Peterson, G. Stahl, & H. Soong (Eds.), *The Palgrave handbook of citizenship and education*. Basingstoke: Palgrave Macmillan.

OECD. (2012). Lessons from PISA for Japan, strong performers and successful reformers in education. Paris: OECD.

OECD. (2014). *PISA 2018 framework plans: 38th meeting of the PISA governing board*. EDU/PISA/GB (2014)16 24-Nov-2014. Dublin. Retrieved from OECD: www.uvm.dk/-/media/UVM/Filer/Om-os/PDF16/160315-Bilag-16,-d-,-PISA-2018-Framework-Plans.ashx?la=da.

OECD. (2016a) *Global competency for an inclusive world: Programme for the international student assessment*. Paris: OECD. Retrieved from www.oecd.org/pisa/aboutpisa/Global-competency-for-an-inclusive-world.pdf.

OECD. (2018a). *Preparing our youth for an inclusive and sustainable world: The OECD PISA global competence framework*. Paris. Retrieved from OECD: www.oecd.org/pisa/Handbook-PISA-2018-Global-Competence.pdf.

OECD. (2018b). *The future of education and skills: Education 2030*. Paris: OECD.

OECD. (2018c). *The OECD internship programme*. Retrieved from www.oecd.org/careers/internshipprogramme.htm

Oxley, L., & Morris, P. (2013). Global citizenship: A typology for distinguishing its multiple conceptions. *British Journal of Educational Studies*, 61(3), 301–325. doi:10.1080/00071005.2013.798393

Rautalin, M., & Alasuutari, P. (2009). The uses of the national PISA results by Finnish officials. *Journal of Education Policy*, 24(5), 539–556.

Reimers, F. (2013). Assessing global education: An opportunity for the OECD. Retrieved from www.oecd.org/pisa/pisaproducts/Global-Competency.pdf

Schleicher, A. (2016, May 27). PISA tests to include 'global skills' and cultural awareness, *BBC*. Retrieved from www.bbc.com/news/business-36343602

Schleicher, A. (2018). *World class: How to build a 21st-century school system*. Paris: OECD.

Sellar, S., & Lingard, B. (2014). The OECD and the expansion of PISA: New global modes of governance in education. *British Educational Research Journal*, 40(6), 917–936.

UNESCO. (2012). Global education first initiative: An initiative of the United Nations secretary-general. Paris: UNESCO. Retrieved from https://issuu.com/globaleducationfirst/docs/gefi_brochure_eng

UNESCO. (2013). Global citizenship education: An emerging perspective, *Outcome document of the technical consultation on global citizenship education*. Paris: UNESCO. Retrieved from http://unesdoc.unesco.org/images/0022/002241/224115E.pdf

UNESCO. (2014). *Global citizenship education: Preparing learners for the challenges of the 21st century*. Paris: UNESCO.

UNESCO. (2016). *Education 2030: Incheon declaration and a framework for action for the implementation of sustainable goal 4*. Retrieved from http://uis.unesco.org/sites/default/files/documents/education-2030-incheon-framework-for-action-implementation-of-sdg4-2016-en_2.pdf

UNESCO Institute for Statistics (2018). *Quick guide to education indicators for SDG4*. Montreal, Canada: UNESCO Institute for Statistics. Retrieved from http://uis.unesco.org/sites/default/files/documents/quick-guide-education-indicators-sdg4-2018-en.pdf

UNESCO/MGIEP. (2017). *Rethinking schooling for the 21st century*. New Delhi, India: Mahatma Gandhi Institute for Peace and Sustainable Development.

2 Geographies of Connection? The Chicken Project and Other International Acts by State Secondary Schools in England

Johanna Waters and Rachel Brooks

Introduction

> Expensive school trips to far-flung corners of the globe are fast becoming the norm, not just in elite, private schools, but in ordinary state secondary schools up and down the country.
>
> (Weale, 2018, n.p.)

> What we've got to try and manage, I think, is that when we go, we don't just sort of turn up looking like we're, you know, the good guys from Europe with lots of money.
>
> (Art teacher, School #3)

This chapter considers the question of how and why some state secondary schools (and not others) in England are engaging, in various ways, with what could be called international projects. It is well known that the independent school sector, particularly private and high-fee schools in England,[1] incorporate various international ventures into their learning experiences (including, perhaps most obviously, multifarious school trips and expeditions overseas), even when these are less openly celebrated than are schools' 'local' engagements (Brooks & Waters, 2015; Waters & Brooks, 2015). Less clear is the extent to which 'ordinary', publicly funded state schools are also embracing a form of internationalism in their activities, in the face of funding cuts and enduring pressures on resources. Simply put, international activities are expensive—both in terms of actual financial burdens on schools and staff time—but (we have been told) go largely unrecognised and unrewarded by the 'system' (such as Ofsted).[2] As part of the project described in this chapter, we carried out research within three state secondary schools in England (in the counties of Oxfordshire, Warwickshire and Surrey) and conducted a web analysis of 50 additional schools, in order to establish what, if any, 'international' activities and projects they were engaging in, how and why. We spoke to staff (including head teachers) and pupils, attended lessons and were shown various depictions (such as art work and video clips) of the international activities that schools were undertaking. The research was conducted during 2016, in the period in which campaigning for 'Brexit' versus 'Remain' (relating to European Union membership) was underway. Interestingly, related ideas entered the discussions to a greater or lesser extent, indicating the role that political discourse at different levels (national/supranational) can play in attitudes towards internationalisation.

In this project, we seek to understand the nature of state-schools' international engagements in light of the wider literature on 'international education', which largely posits the valuable nature of internationalisation and international credentials (often discussed in terms of the acquisition, by students, of embodied cultural capital—see Waters, 2006; Yang, 2018). The chapter begins with a discussion of the internationalisation of education, and how the scope and remit of the debate has broadened in recent years (from a narrow early focus on higher education student mobility) to include the concept of 'internationalisation at home' at the level of 'ordinary' schools. Arguably, the internationalisation of higher education is qualitatively different from that at school: 'Schools are . . . more naturally indrawn and internally organised than higher education institutions, due to tight local and governmental regulations and resource dependence on formal governmental funding sources (Hayden, 2011)' (Yemini, 2014, p. 474). And yet, as Yemini (2014) interestingly observes:

> the increasing efforts of globalization and demanding efforts of universities and colleges to internationalize in every sphere of life suggest that internationalization does not suddenly emerge in tertiary education but rather continues from the bottom levels in secondary schools and even earlier.
>
> (p. 474)

The intriguing implication of this quotation is that internationalisation somehow *begins* at school level. Schools could be seen to initiate the process of internationalisation within and among young people, albeit with a potentially different purpose (tied to ideas of global citizenship and 'expanding of horizons') compared to higher education (which tends to be far more pecuniary in motivation). Our findings explore some of these motivations and purposes of schools' internationalisation.

The chapter moves on to consider the promotion of the idea of 'global citizenship' by the United Nations and how this may or may not 'filter down' into schools wedded to particular curricula. We are cognisant of international variation in these issues, and consider the significance of geographical context. We then discuss the importance of politics and ethics in internationalisation and the ongoing tensions between a humanistic desire for social justice and, at the same time and in opposition, the drive within schools to produce neoliberal global workers (what Mitchell [2003] has called 'strategic cosmopolitans'—see also Cheng, 2015a, 2015b). We look at a particular initiative called 'The Chicken Project'— held up by one school as a perfect showcasing of internationalisation in action. We consider this project in terms of the broader questions we are posing around the 'kinds' of internationalisation on display. Finally, the chapter attempts to frame the outcomes or consequences of these schools' activities in terms of the literature around 'geographies of [international] connection' (Featherstone, 2008): 'the forms of political identity and agency they have shaped can animate contemporary political imaginaries' (p. 2). Featherstone's argument concerns the theorisation of 'counter-global' networks and the forms of alliances and solidarities generated by them. Claiming that schools' engagements with international education represent a type of 'subaltern politics' might be a step too far; overstating the significance of what they are achieving. It is, however, nevertheless productive to think through schools' international activities in ways that counter or rub against a potentially neoliberal and glib perspective of internationalisation as the creation of 'global citizens'. Thus, we are searching, in this chapter, for more creative (less hackneyed, more nuanced) perspectives on international education and schooling.

Review of the Literature

Internationalisation in Education

Internationalisation within the education system can clearly take many forms. While in this chapter we focus on specific initiatives within and out with the curricula, the broader literature attests to the wide variety of ways in which schooling and higher education have been 'internationalised'. Historically, internationalisation has been closely allied to student mobility—with students crossing national borders to pursue degree-level study and, increasingly, compulsory education (Brooks & Waters, 2011; Ong, 1999). Over recent years, however, internationalisation has been pursued by various other means. Indeed, we have seen significant growth of the number of transnational education providers—offering an ostensibly international 'educational experience' to students within their home nation (e.g. Geddie, 2012; Waters & Leung, 2012). Again, this has been most common at the level of higher education (through the establishment of branch campuses), but there has been recent growth in the number of 'franchise schools', particularly in Southeast Asia and the Middle East, owned by 'parent schools' in the Global North (Brooks & Waters, 2015), while 'international schools', set up initially to serve expatriate communities, have become increasingly popular among local populations (Hayden, 2011). 'Internationalisation at home' has also been given increasing attention—through, for example the development of curricula with a more explicitly global focus; programmes to develop 'global citizens'; bi-lingual and multi-lingual education; and greater recognition of the potential diversity of pupils within individual classrooms (Brown & Jones, 2007; Harrison, 2015; Maxwell, 2018). Borrowing from Knight (2008), Engel et al. (2016) adapted these ideas to distinguish between internationalisation 'at home' and 'abroad'. They understand 'at home' to involve school-level strategies with a focus on curricula or extra-curricula activities, standards development, pedagogy and teacher training. Conversely, 'abroad' entails the international mobility of both students and staff, study abroad opportunities and the diversifying of the staff and student body.

Changes 'at home' vis-à-vis internationalisation have been driven by a multitude of influences including the emergence of more competitive global markets in education; international education coming to be viewed as a mechanism for social reproduction and/or social mobility; the impact of large-scale migration; and the affordances of new technologies and cheap transport (Yemini, 2014). International organisations have also exerted influence. Indeed, the United Nations Educational, Scientific and Cultural Organisation (UNESCO) has promoted global citizenship education as a key part of its United Education Programme, and it was one of three priorities on the United Nation's Secretary-General's 'Global Education First Initiative', launched in 2012 (Pais & Costa, 2017). Underpinning such initiatives is a belief that, as a result of shifts in the relationship between individuals, governments and political institutions, 'citizens' rights, identities, and sites of civic engagement can be derived from global, national and local spaces, rather than exclusively from nation-state institutions' (Hammond & Keating, 2017, p. 3).

Geographies and Local Variation

Although processes of internationalisation have been identified in most parts of the world, there are significant spatial disparities in how these unfold. Student mobility tends, for example, to be seen as a movement from the Global South to the Global North, while transnational education is typically provided by institutions located within more affluent, Anglophone nations (Brooks & Waters, 2011). Research has also demonstrated how the way in which internationalisation is played out within schools can depend, quite significantly, on a variety of contextual factors. Previous research that we have conducted, analysing the websites and other publicity material of elite English schools, has shown that the *national* context can affect the extent to which internationalisation is foregrounded (Brooks & Waters, 2015). In contrast to studies conducted elsewhere in the world, which have argued that highlighting international activities is often used as an important marketing tool, to attract middle class families in particular (see, for example, Aguiar and Nogueira's

[2012] study of Brazilian schools and Yemini [2014] for Israel), our research indicated that while the schools in our sample tended to demonstrate a high level of internationalisation (such as many international pupils and significant numbers of students progressing to overseas universities), this was typically downplayed in the marketing materials. This, we argue, was because of the way in which an 'English' identity was central to their appeal:

> 'Englishness' is likely to be strongly desired by those international pupils who cross national borders for their education, by virtue of its association with prestigious and traditional forms of education, access to elite social networks, the value of British educational credentials in the global marketplace, and the opportunity to become fluent in a dominant world language.
>
> (Brooks & Waters, 2015, p. 225)

In addition, however, given the spatial disparities in the global field of education and the persistence of neo-colonial influences, we suggested that 'Englishness' was likely to be valued equally highly by British families seeking an elite schooling for their children—and deemed more desirable than 'international' alternatives.

Differences can also be observed at the *school level* within particular nation-states. Yemini and Fulop (2015), for example, have shown how, in Israel, schools demonstrate diverse patterns of internationalisation that are associated with their pupil population and status. This diversity is also related to the broader political context and the ideological and political orientation of teachers. For example, focussing specifically on Israeli Palestinian-Arab schools, Yemini (2014) shows how, in one school in her research, 'international' activities were defined as those that brought the Palestinian-Arab pupils into contact with Jewish students (in Israel). This, she argues, is explained by the 'history of discrimination by the state government [which] creates a situation where Israeli Palestinian-Arabs relate to "regular Israelis" or Israeli Jews as others or foreigners' (p. 491).

Politics and Ethics of Internationalisation of Education

A key theme in the literature on international education and global citizenship is the tension between, on the one hand, the commitment to social justice and humanist values that often underpin such initiatives, at least in their initiation and intention, and the values that become embodied in practice. Indeed, a significant body of work has shown how many international education policies and programmes become orientated around the production of 'global workers' rather than 'global citizens', and are framed within neoliberal perspectives (Mitchell, 2003; Engel, 2014). In their analysis of global citizenship education in South Korea, Cho and Mosselson (2017) demonstrate how, despite explicit national commitment to a social justice agenda, teacher guidebooks and practices with respect to global citizenship education tend to reinforce neoliberal norms and power inequalities both globally and locally. For example, they argue that the 'global citizen' is frequently constructed in teaching materials as a global leader or UN staff member, rather than someone who adopts a particular set of global values or ways of acting in the world. It thus tends to exclude children from poorer families, who are seen as less likely to achieve such positions, and focusses more on the affluent. Studies of national strategies concerning internationalisation of education have drawn similar conclusions (although cf. Engel and Siczek [2017], who found that teachers did hold quite divergent views on this, so that the 'practice' of internationalisation was often out of line with the 'policy'). An analysis of such documents from the US, UK, Canada, Australia and Ireland, conducted by Engel and Siczek (2017), demonstrated that the dominant discourse in all five nations emphasised national interest rather than global citizenship, and was primarily competitive in its orientation (see also Engel and Siczek [2018] with respect to the US particularly). Studies of specific international curricula have developed similar arguments. With respect to the International Baccalaureate (IB), for example, Gardner-McTaggart (2016) has contended that, while in itself the IB does not serve to replicate oppressive inequalities, it is frequently used by elites (particularly among the growing middle classes in the Global South) as a means of acquiring global, rather than national, capital and securing relative social advantage.

Similar themes are evident at the level of higher education. Indeed, Hammond and Keating (2017) have argued that while global citizenship education programmes within UK and Japanese higher education differ in some respects in the two nations, both had 'infused within them an agenda of employability, pointing to the potential co-optation of GC [global citizenship] discourse by neoliberal objectives aimed at the production of globally competent workers' (p. 13). With respect to Japan, this was evident in the way in which the programme was tied to improving the nation's performance in a globalised knowledge economy, while in the UK global citizenship education was promoted as part of a highly marketised approach in which 'global graduates' from the particular institution were positioned as playing an important role in the resolution of global problems.

Nevertheless, there are a small number of studies that have presented a more progressive perspective, suggesting that some forms of internationalisation can contribute towards social justice and are able successfully to resist a neoliberal framing. Reddy (2018), for example, draws on a four-year ethnographic project with college students in the American South who participated in a funded global education programme for young

Americans from low income families. Her participants had been able to take part in short-term global trips, study abroad programmes and overseas work placements. She argues that they made sense of their time abroad, not in terms of instrumental concerns such as future financial gain, but by foregrounding ideas about relations with others and emphasising the importance of dependency, care and love. Moreover, she goes on to maintain that, through their international education, they 'find themselves traversing historical trajectories of oppression' that results in them 'reflecting on their position in the world, engendering feelings of responsibility in terms of addressing historical inequalities and current injustices' (p. 1). These 'alternative' interpretations of internationalisation are important. They point towards a more ethical engagement with international activities and evoke a sense of justice and responsibility through a better understanding of places and their complex interconnections as well as the meaning of difference (Massey, 2012; Pashby, 2011).

This bring us to the question of how international education is entangled within webs of neo-colonial complicity and a Western-centric production of geographical knowledge (Pashby, 2011). Over the past few years, geographers in particular have debated the significance of colonialism, post-coloniality and de-coloniality to understanding how—and by whom—geographical knowledge about the world comes to be produced, disseminated and made into 'truth'. This includes a vibrant discussion about how geography *is taught* and a need, consequently, to de-colonise curricula, both at the level of school learning and higher education. Awkward questions need to be posed about *whose* knowledge curricula are representing and, more importantly, what is being omitted. Esson (2018, p. 2), for example, has considered the 'whiteness' of geography within higher education, concluding:

> The answer is coloniality-induced institutional racism. By coloniality I mean the 'longstanding patterns of power that emerged as a result of colonialism, but that define culture, labour, intersubjective relations, and knowledge production well beyond the strict limits of colonial administrations' (Maldonado-Torres, 2007, p. 243). By institutional racism I mean: 'The collective failure of an organisation to provide an appropriate and professional service to people because of their colour, culture, or ethnic origin. It can be seen or detected in processes, attitudes and behaviour which amount to discrimination through unwitting prejudice, ignorance, thoughtlessness and racist stereotyping which disadvantage minority ethnic people' (Macpherson, 1999, p. 369).

Whilst in our project we are not specifically exploring geography teaching, nor are we concerned with higher education, some of the same claims could arguably be made for international education within schools (in

England). We certainly have lots of examples from our data of uncritical attempts at 'knowledge transfer':

> [Tanzanian school] staff have managed to pick up a lot of learning resources because, of course, they are where we were about 1990, you know.
>
> (Art teacher, School #3)

And philanthropic helping that amounts to the reproduction of neo-colonial developmentalist discourses: 'We sleep well in our beds' (Assistant Head, School #2).

Questionable power relations are sometimes revealed in these exchanges. Debates around decolonising the curriculum have led to a critical use of 'pedagogies that are founded on coexistence and respect, as opposed to domination, separation and assimilation' (Esson, 2018, p. 5; see also Madge et al., 2009). We try, therefore, to consider these important debates in our discussions of how and why schools are internationalising (particularly through their direct engagements with other countries and cultures).

Methods

This project was funded by a Fellowship from the British Educational Research Association, held from 2014 to 2016. Between January and March 2016, we conducted fieldwork in three state-funded secondary schools in different parts of England—in Warwickshire, Oxfordshire and Surrey. Eight schools were contacted by a letter attached to an email, and followed up with a phone call, and, of these, three schools agreed to participate in the project. We had no personal connections with any of the schools we approached. In total, 28 individuals were interviewed for this project, which also included a mix of participant observation, walking interviews (around school sites with staff and pupils), lesson observation, focus groups with pupils and in-depth one-to-one interviews with school staff. In addition to these on-site, in-depth analyses of particular schools, we conducted a web-analysis of 50 state schools in those three counties (using a thematic grid) to get a broader sense of the kinds of international activities schools were engaging in (if any). The focus here was on their 'public face'—that is, the image they are trying to portray on their websites and the extent to which these emphasise 'international' (or local) engagements and interests. In this chapter, we focus mainly on interviews with school staff and head teachers (which have been transcribed in full and analysed thematically), whilst drawing on supplementary materials from the website analysis.

The project received ethical approval from the University of Oxford. We are aware that the schools that responded to our approach and, furthermore, agreed to take part in this study are potentially unusual in a number of ways. It is highly likely that these schools are more 'internationally' active and interested than other schools—schools that did not respond to our letter. We are also aware, having spent time at these schools, that the schools we worked with were located in relatively affluent parts of the UK, although two of them had a mixed, comprehensive intake. All three received an 'Outstanding' grade for their last Ofsted inspection. One of the schools is a state selective grammar school—entry is dependent on success in the 11+ exam—the other two were non-selective. Some schools that declined our request for participation cited lack of time and resources—being too 'stretched' to be able to help. We are not, therefore, making any claims for the representative nature of our sample and in fact believe these schools (state sector but still relatively privileged) might be in many ways 'exceptional'. The interviews that we focus on here have given us particular insight into the motivations for, and practicalities underpinning, schools' involvement with internationalisation.

Discussion of Findings

Paucity of 'Internationalisation' Within Secondary Schools

Our survey analysis of 50 state secondary schools highlighted a number of interesting points, the simplest and most striking of which was the fact that some of the schools made little or no mention of internationalisation or international engagements/activities/interests on their webpages. This stands in stark contrast to what we know about schools in other countries, where internationalisation is seen as a badge or marker of distinction or success (Aguiar & Nogueira, 2012; Hayden, 2011; Yemini, 2014). Our website analysis suggested that the majority of state-funded secondary schools within England are not engaging in any meaningful forms of internationalisation. Instead schools emphasised 'local partnerships' with other proximate schools, supporting 'British values' (mentioned frequently) and local sports fixtures.

It is also interesting that where schools *are* engaging with internationalisation, sometimes this fact was 'buried' rather than 'celebrated' on their website. As an extract from our fieldnotes demonstrates:

> The website makes it [the school] appear very locally oriented and most of the information is about school policies etc. However, if you initiate a search and read through a lot of information you discover that they have a German partner school and have been awarded the British Council International School Award 2015–2018.

This is very much in line with what we found in another project on 'elite' English schools, mentioned previously, where schools were engaging in high levels of internationalisation but were reluctant to demonstrate it (see Brooks & Waters, 2015; Waters & Brooks, 2015).

The general disinclination of state-funded secondary schools to get involved in any meaningful international activities was explained to us during interviews, where an audit culture, time pressures on teachers, and funding cuts were frequently mentioned:

> It's a sad indictment that you live and die by ticking the box: we've done that, we've done that' [in reference to Ofsted]. And when someone changes the boxes, you get, 'oh well, we won't do that anymore'. Community cohesion—that was massive in Ofsted five, six years ago. We don't need to worry about that anymore. So that's gone. . . . And the resources in the school are going to be limited and something. If that's not going to be measured, it [internationalisation] tends to fail, and it's only because of the teachers who still think it's really important [that it might succeed].
>
> (Assistant Head and business studies teacher, previously international coordinator, School # 2)

Another school explained that they frequently received applications from pupils overseas seeking to spend a term or two at the school, but had to turn these requests down (despite assuming they would be 'enriching' for their pupils). They told us: 'We haven't got the resources to be able to do that [accept students temporarily from overseas] because everything is absolutely pared to the bone at the moment' (Head, School #1).

This sense of resources being stretched to their limits with no prospect of additional funding on the horizon (indeed, they were concerned about *further* cuts to their budgets and having to ask parents for 'donations' towards various activities) was repeated time and time again in interviews with different school staff, across the three schools in which we spent time. The point was also made that schools received no additional or allocated money specifically for international activities/engagement, and it required the personal commitment and belief of particular teachers in order to come about. As it happened, in the schools we worked with, internationalisation was important; it was prioritised (by certain teachers) and impressive initiatives were apparent. In what follows, we briefly discuss schools' motivations for engaging in international activities, before interpreting them in light of debates around 'global citizenship' and a more ethical and politically engaged sense of 'responsibility'.

Motivations for International Engagements

All three of our schools had worked for and attained the International School Award. For one school, this rather cynically represented (in their words) 'a logo on the [school] paperwork'. According to the British Council (2018), the International School Award is a 'globally recognised accreditation that helps you enrich learning and improve teaching by guiding your international learning activities, from introducing international education into the curriculum to embedding it within your school's culture' (no pagination). They continue:

> International education enriches teaching and learning. It introduces educators to new practices and perspectives, furthering their professional development and raising teaching standards. It gives young people a window into different cultures and countries, helping them develop as responsible global citizens and preparing them for life and work in a global society. . . . The International School Award provides a supportive and motivational framework to guide your international learning activities and helps you gain recognition for your ongoing international work. It can support schools at any stage of their international journey and can be adapted to any curriculum.
>
> (ibid.)

Finally, the British Council lists the following 'benefits' of achieving the International School Award:

> The International School Award helps schools to: enrich the curriculum and improve teaching by introducing and embedding international activities across the whole school; become part of a global network of international educators open to collaboration and shared learning opportunities; gain recognition for and promote their international work, making it more attractive to students, parents and teachers.

School #1 achieved the International School Award in 2010 and has since had it renewed three times: 'so that's an indication that, you know, we do really value the international perspective in school' (Head, School #1). This head teacher went on to talk about some of the places they take their older pupils, with a view to 'engaging' with local schools overseas:

> We do have, I mean . . . the high-level foreign trips, we do have quite a few of those. Yes. India is the one that Phil[3] [Assistant Head] can talk to you about because he went three times. I went on the first one. There're the photos, under the clock there [gestures to a display of framed photographs]. . . . There's lots of other foreign visits, which Steve ['School Enrichment Coordinator', teaches history and politics] will probably be able to go into more detail with you. He's off to Washington, for example, with the economists and politicians in February. . . . We've had sports tours all over. And that's nicely engaging with the local girls' school—you know—[local] populations, if you

like. So they go and play hockey in Australia and South Africa, and we've got a link with a school in Chile. So we are outward looking.

(Head, School #1)

This outward-looking-ness was surprisingly unconnected to a strategic notion of building a 'global citizen' or future 'global worker' (Mitchell, 2003). Very little of what was said to us could be clearly interpreted in terms of the acquisition, by pupils, of 'cosmopolitan capital' (Weenink, 2008). Rather, what we were told painted a more ambiguous, more sympathetic, caring and 'humanistic' picture of 'the global', as the following quotes from interviews at School #1 revealed:

It's widening their horizons. It's enabling them to see perspectives other than their own. And I think . . . I think any school would be interested in getting their students to, you know, understand where they come from, but also to be empathetic. To look more widely. . . . We're about educating the whole person and giving them those opportunities and putting them through experiences . . . experiences of failure as well . . . making them resilient . . . Developing good human beings in whatever way we can.

(Head, School #1)

It's really hard to pick specifics, but it's that whole experience and it's that life. I always say to the girls it's a life-shaping experience. If you talk to the Year 12s now, who came [to India on a school trip] last year in Year 11, they still say 'we talk about it all the time'. . . . So there's a real legacy to it, and its one of the things you draw on as you develop as a young person into adulthood. . . . And the further down your life story you get, you'll draw different things. So I think there's a real sort of holistic conceptual underpinning to this, which is really quite powerful. And the other thing the India trip particularly did was to—because it is quite arduous in places and quite testing and challenging emotionally, physically, all the rest of it, it's that pushing of your limits. What you perceive your limits are aren't actually your limits. And we talk about realistic educational experiences that build resilience. That build you 'know how'—to get over failure and knockbacks and push through. These sorts of experiences for the lucky ones who can go can be really, really powerful.

(Assistant Head, School #1)

The 'holistic conceptual underpinning' indicated in the second interview extract captures the sense we have, from our data, that international activities are viewed apart from specific curricula goals or attempts to prepare pupils for a workforce; rather they are about developing individuals as open-minded, well rounded people. This last quotation has resonance with Prazeres's (2017) discussion of higher education students' motivations to participate in short-term international exchanges, which they viewed primarily as an opportunity to 'leave their comfort zone'. Prazeres (2017) raises two points in particular: that (a) the notion of the 'comfort zone' has not been sufficiently explored within the international student mobility literature, and (b) whilst the academic literature is dominated by studies of students moving from the Global South to the Global North for study, very few studies consider mobility in the other direction. Fiddian-Qasmiyeh (2015) has written on South–South educational migration, and Brooks and Waters (2009) and Waters and Brooks (2010) on UK students going overseas for higher education, but research on the mobility of younger students moving from the Global North to the Global South remains scarce. Brown (2008, p. 3), quoted in Prazeres (2017), argues that within adventure education literature the comfort zone 'is based on the belief that when placed in a stressful situation people will respond by overcoming their fear and therefore grow as individuals'. And indeed, our interviewees talked about striking a balance, on international trips, between controlling and managing pupils' experiences (with safety primarily in mind) and facilitating pupils' discomfort and unease, with the assumption that this will, longer term, allow them to grow into 'stronger' individuals better able to cope with the demands of life. International excursions, therefore, are not just about pupils' 'exposure' to different cultures and lifestyles (including extremes of poverty and hardship) but are also involved in creating an uneasy, unfamiliar environment for young people, which they can then, through effort, 'overcome'.

In terms of the 'success' of these initiatives, students' university destinations or career prospects were never mentioned. However, success in other spheres (such as charity or international policy work) were emphasised by schools:

> And the students, who have gone on to do excellent things. You know, in five years' time, I'm going to look back and some of these students are going to be doing amazing things through what they've learned or the contacts they've made, or the difference they've made.
> (Assistant Head, teaches business studies, School #2)

Consequently, it has been hard to read off, from the accounts given by schools, straight forward 'strategic' intentions when it comes to engaging with international activities. Schools feel that they are going against what is expected of them (by Ofsted) in order to undertake these activities. They are very aware that school trips can be expensive and exclusionary, but tend to describe the 'benefits' to pupils not in terms of university entrance or career prospects, but in relation to providing an experience that would stay with them 'for life' whilst also being, somehow, life-shaping.

Politics and Igniting Political Imaginaries

> The Chicken Project is a unique, sustainable and replicable enterprise, linking classrooms, communities and countries across the world.
>
> (Assistant Head, School #2)

Philanthropic gestures were commonly described in interviews and occasionally showcased on schools' websites. Many schools seem to attempt to combine 'community projects' with travel experiences and exploring. Painting classrooms, planting trees, building houses and gifting materials were common-place:

> Students, staff and teachers at the Gambia school visit the UK each year where they spend some time teaching, learning and being involved the normal activities of the school. The [Oxfordshire] school annually visits Gambia to repair the building, provide technology, replace books, etc.
>
> (Oxfordshire school website, fieldnotes)

Here we see that pupils visiting from Gambia get to partake in 'the normal activities of the school' as if that, in and of itself, will be beneficial to them. In contrast, pupils from the English context are involved in 'repairing' and 'providing' for the school when they, in turn, visit Gambia. It is hard not to read some neo-colonial narrative onto this—and other similar—depictions. The question remains, to what extent do these kinds of international engagements represent a reigniting of colonial imaginaries or a new kind of politics? School #3 discusses an exchange project they have with Tanzania:

> When staff have come over [here], they've got a small number of computers, so that . . . Staff have managed to pick up a lot of learning resources because, of course, they're where we were about 1990 . . . When staff have come over, because you can't just give them stuff because it might not fit their curriculum. But when the staff have come over, they've gone back with memory sticks full of all sorts of subject stuff and then they can just sort of pick out and adapt what they want to use. So there's that benefit. What we've got to try and manage, I think, is that when we go, we don't just sort of turn up looking like we're, you know, the good guys from Europe with lots of money.
>
> (Art teacher, School #3)

Some schools, then, showed at least *some level* of critical awareness of the potentially problematic nature of post-colonial relationships and how this method of engaging with overseas schools might indicate uneven and damaging relationships. Nevertheless, websites appeared far less reflexive, and mentioned how schools would 'send container loads of items for the school [in Malawi], e.g. books, pens and pencils, bedding and sheets . . . calculators, textbooks and bibles' (Surrey school website) or have been involved in projects including 'repainting and furnishing a classroom, providing electricity to be installed at the school [in Zambia] as well as digging a borehole for the school and local community. In 2015, the students adopted an elephant and receive updates on its welfare and development' (Surrey school website). Another school noted on its website that it had 'helped build a house for an elderly man [in Tanzania]'. These kinds of material projects, involving charity giving, will only result in meaningful, ethical exchanges if their broader geographies are interrogated by the schools involved.

In the last part of this section, we want to focus on one initiative in particular, undertaken by one of our case-study schools, called 'The Chicken Project'. We use this as a lens through which to explore some of the issues discussed previously, in more detail. The Chicken Project began as a link between a school in Oxfordshire, England and a school in the Western Cape, in South Africa. The link was originally set up through BEFSA (Borien Educational Foundation for Southern Africa)—a charity that works to reduce poverty through education (and set up links with 55 schools in South Africa and Oxfordshire). Our particular school initiated 'The Chicken Project' as part of this link. The school conceived it as a form of 'enterprise' that provides schools in South Africa with chickens and then teaches pupils both to take care of the chickens (agriculture) and to sell the eggs and/or meat (business)—developing both their business and agricultural skills. The scheme has now expanded to include many schools throughout South Africa and in the Cameroons. In addition to chickens, the Oxfordshire school has also raised money to provide libraries for schools [in Africa] and are also engaging in environmental projects within those schools: 'In five years, we've put eight libraries in schools . . . through raising money, and three lots of chickens' (Assistant Head, School #2).

The school documents the various fundraising activities it undertakes throughout the year in order to expand this project even further. Pupils are not, however, involved in exchange activities anymore (a consequence of funding cuts and practical concerns):

> We haven't had an exchange. It's a really, it's a very poor, rural area and we did in 2010, the initial students who set this project up, we flew to Cape Town and we spoke at an international conference, but I also raised the money to fly the head teacher and deputy head to Cape Town. They'd never been—these professional people, head teacher and deputy head—had never been in an aeroplane!
>
> (Assistant Head, School #2)

The initial 'culture shock' experienced by the teacher involved in this project was palpable. How the benefits to the pupils at the school in Oxfordshire are described, however, was interesting, and very much framed in terms of 'skills':

> So, the skills, the skills, doing international work is not just fundraising and it's not just working with other schools. It's life skills.
>
> (Assistant Head, School #2)

The interview with this Assistant Head Teacher about the Chicken Project repeatedly emphasised how the project was directly developing the skills of the pupils: artistic skills, business and accounting skills, public speaking, confidence building and so on.

On the one hand, the charity side of the fundraising is very much in line with the well-known proverb 'If you give a man (sic) a fish, he will feed for a day. If you teach him to fish, he will feed for a lifetime'. The idea behind donating chickens is not that the chickens themselves will be of use, but that the pupils and the schools receiving the chickens will learn two new skills: business acumen and agricultural know-how. The idea is that they breed more chickens, they sell chickens for meat and they sell their eggs. And they run a business at the same time, to raise profit for their school, and the cycle continues. At the same time, this Oxfordshire teacher has a very clear view of the specific skills that the Chicken Project is developing in her 'own' children (who also learn about the business and agricultural sides of the project as well as being involved in fundraising and speaking about the project at public events). For this school, internationalisation meant being involved in a deliberate and purposeful exchange and interaction with schools overseas, where *both sides* benefit. Elements of a neo-colonial, potentially patronising attitude are apparent; yet, so too is a clear ethical stance towards when and how the school engages (guided by the other partner and outside charities). The Chicken Project is an example, we contend, of a more 'creative' approach to internationalisation that is open-minded and not framed by an overt narrative of 'global citizenship' nor a neoliberalising creation of *the* global citizen (Mitchell, 2003). The complex reality that the Chicken Project presents enables the development of different—if more messy and less contained—readings of how and why schools are engaging with internationalisation.

Conclusions

Surprisingly little research has, to date, explored the international activities of state-schools in England and their implications, given a broader intellectual interest in the internationalisation of education. In this chapter, we attend to this, focusing on our qualitative research within three state-schools in Oxfordshire, Surrey and Warwickshire and a review of the websites of 50 additional schools in those three areas. Our objective was to ascertain the extent to which schools are engaging with 'inter-nationalisation', how they are engaging, and its implications, in the context of debates around the 'benefits' of internationalisation for edu-cation, in general, and schools, in particular. Whilst schools did justify their 'international' activities in terms of the need to educate pupils to become global citizens, or citizens of the world, there was relatively little articulation of any strategic and instrumental benefits of an international outlook (providing students with a positional advantage when it comes to university entrance and future career paths) (see, for example Mitchell, 2003). Rather, this 'global outlook' was framed in far more humanistic and relational terms than we were anticipating; simply put, it was about creating 'better', more caring people with a greater understanding of the world and its diversity. With one isolated exception, no mention was made of improving chances of university access or career success. There were clear instances of neo-colonial forms of knowledge and resource 'exchange', although some of these were tempered by a critical aware-ness of this and caution was expressed. These neo-colonial narratives tended to be more apparent on the websites than in the schools we vis-ited. However, a final important finding is that so few schools seemed to be involved in any meaningful international activities at all (excluding school trips). The schools we spoke to were very clear about this—that stretched resources barely allowed for additional activities, and interna-tional engagements and exchanges were very much seen as 'additional' to the core requirements demanded by Ofsted. And yet, the current political climate seems to lend some critical urgency to the need for an 'interna-tional' perspective within UK schools. On the one hand, we have the outcomes of 'Brexit' (still uncertain at the time of writing), where discus-sions have been frequently underpinned by an insular, isolationist and nationalist narrative (indicated more widely with the rise of far-Right parties in parts of Western Europe). At the same time, young people are articulating for themselves a need for a global narrative on climate change, indicated by the success of the 'school strikes for climate change' and globally coordinated marches. It is at this political moment, where school budgets continue to be 'slashed', that the inclusion of 'interna-tionalisation' in England's schools would seem more pressing than ever. There is the potential, at this moment, to help foster the 'geographies of [international] connection' that Featherstone (2008, p. 2) discusses: 'the forms of political identity and agency they have shaped can animate contemporary political imaginaries' (p. 2), creating meaningful alliances and solidarities.

Notes

1. According to the Independent Schools Council, this sector educates 625,000 children in the UK, which, for England, equates to 7% of all pupils.

2. Ofsted is the UK Office for Standards in Education, Children's Services and Skills. It carries out 'inspections' and aims to regulate services that cater for children and young people, including schools.
3. We use pseudonyms here.

References

Aguiar, A., & Nogueira, M. (2012). Internationalisation strategies of Brazilian private schools. *International Studies in Sociology of Education*, 22(4), 353–368.

British Council. (2018). Retrieved from https://schoolsonline.britishcouncil.org/about-programmes/international-school-award. (accessed 12 October 2018)

Brooks, R., & Waters, J. (2009). A second chance at 'success' UK students and global circuits of higher education. *Sociology*, 43(6), 1085–1102.

Brooks, R., & Waters, J. (2011). *Student mobilities, migration and the internationalization of higher education*. Basingstoke: Palgrave Macmillan.

Brooks, R., & Waters, J. (2015). The hidden internationalism of elite English schools. *Sociology*, 49(2), 212–228.

Brown, M. (2008). Comfort zone: Model or metaphor? *Journal of Outdoor and Environmental Education*, 12(1), 3–12.

Brown, S., & Jones, E. (2007). Introduction: Values, valuing and value in an internationalised higher education context. In E. Jones & S. Brown (Eds.), *Internationalising higher education* (pp. 1–6). London: Routledge.

Cheng, Y. E. (2015a). Biopolitical geographies of student life: Private higher education and citizenship life-making in Singapore. *Annals of the Association of American Geographers*, 105(5), 1078–1093.

Cheng, Y. E. (2015b). Cultural politics of education and human capital formation: Learning to labor in Singapore. *Labouring and Learning*, 1–20.

Cho, H. S., & Mosselson, J. (2017). Neoliberal practices amidst social justice orientations: Global citizenship education in South Korea. *Compare*, Advance online access.

Engel, L. C. (2014). Citizenship education and national (re)formations: Reflections from Spain. *Education, Citizenship, and Social Justice*, 9(3), 239–254.

Engel, L. C., Fundalinski, J., & Cannon, T. (2016). Global citizenship education at a local level: A comparative analysis of four U.S. urban districts. *Revista de Educación Comparativa Espanola* [Journal of Spanish Comparative Education], 28, 23–51.

Engel, L. C., & Siczek, M. M. (2017). A cross-national comparison of international strategies: Global citizenship and the advancement of national competitiveness. *Compare: A Journal of Comparative and International Education*, online 28 July.

Engel, L. C., & Siczek, M. M. (2018). Framing global education in the United States: Policy perspectives. In L. D. Hill & F. J. Levine (Eds.), *Global perspectives on education research* (pp. 26–47). New York: Routledge.

Esson, J. (2018). 'The why and the white': Racism and curriculum reform in British geography. *Area*. doi:10.1111/area.12475

Featherstone, D. (2008). *Resistance, space and political identities: The making of counter-global networks*. Chichester: Wiley-Blackwell.

Ferguson, D. (2014). *The parents expected to pay £3,000 for a state school trip*. Retrieved www.theguardian.com/money/2014/feb/01/parents-pay-state-school-trip

Fiddian-Qasmiyeh, E. (2015). *South-South educational migration, humanitarianism and development: Views from the Caribbean, North Africa and the Middle East.* London: Routledge.

Gardner-McTaggart, A. (2016). International elite, or global citizens? Equity, distinction and power: The International Baccalaureate and the rise of the South. *Globalisation, Societies and Education, 14*(1), 1–29.

Geddie, K. (2012). Constructing transnational higher education spaces: International branch campus developments in the United Arab Emirates. In R. Brooks, A. Fuller, & J. Waters (Eds.). *Changing Spaces of Education: New Perspectives on the Nature of Learning.* London: Routledge.

Hammond, C., & Keating, A. (2017). Global citizens or global workers? Comparing university programmes for global citizenship education in Japan and the UK. *Compare,* Advance online access.

Harrison, N. (2015). Practice, problems and power in 'internationalisation at home': Critical reflections on recent research evidence. *Teaching in Higher Education, 20*(4), 412–430. Hayden, M. (2011). Transnational spaces of education: The growth of the international schools sector. *Globalisation, Societies and Education, 9*(2), 211–224.

Knight, J. (2008). *Higher education in turmoil: The changing world of internationalisation.* Rotterdam: Sense Publishers.

Madge, C., Raghuram, P., & Noxolo, P. (2009). Engaged pedagogy and responsibility: A postcolonial analysis of international students. *Geoforum, 40*(1), 34–45.

Massey, D. (2012). Power-geometry and a progressive sense of place. In J. Bird, B. Curtis, T. Putnam, & L. Tickner (Eds.), *Mapping the futures: Local Cultures, Global Change* (pp. 75–85). London: Routledge.

Maxwell, C. (2018). 'Changing spaces—The re-shaping of (elite) education through internationalisation'. In C. Maxwell, U. Deppe, H. H. Krüger, & W. Helsper (Eds.), *Elite education and internationalisation: From the early years into higher education* (pp. 347–367). Basingstoke: Palgrave Macmillan,.

Mitchell, K. (2003). Educating the national citizen in neoliberal times: From the multicultural self to the strategic cosmopolitan. *Transactions of the Institute of British Geographers, 28*(4), 387–403.

Ong, A. (1999). *Flexible citizenship: The cultural logics of transnationality,* Durham: Duke University Press.

Pais, A., & Costa, M. (2017). An ideology critique of global citizenship education. *Critical Studies in Education,* Advance online access. https://www.tandfonline.com/action/showCitFormats?doi=10.1080%2F17508487.2017.1318772

Pashby, K. (2011). Cultivating global citizens: Planting new seeds or pruning the perennials? Looking for the citizen-subject in global citizenship education theory. *Globalisation, Societies and Education, 9*(3–4), 427–442.

Prazeres, L. (2017). Challenging the comfort zone: Self-discovery, everyday practices and international student mobility to the Global South. *Mobilities, 12*(6), 908–923.

Reddy, S. (2018). Going global: Internationally mobile young people as caring citizens in higher education. *Area,* 1–9.

The Macpherson Report (1999). Retrieved from https://www.gov.uk/government/publications/the-stephen-lawrence-inquiry

Waters, J. (2006). Geographies of cultural capital: Education, international migration and family strategies between Hong Kong and Canada. *Transactions of the Institute of British Geographers, 31*(2), 179–192.

Waters, J., & Brooks, R. (2010). Accidental achievers? International higher education, class reproduction and privilege in the experiences of UK students overseas. *British Journal of Sociology of Education, 31*(2), 217–228.

Waters, J., & Brooks, R. (2015). 'The magical operations of separation': English elite schools' on-line geographies, internationalisation and functional isolation. *Geoforum, 58*, 86–94.

Waters, J. L., & Leung, M. (2012). Young people and the reproduction of disadvantage through transnational higher education in Hong Kong. *Sociological Research Online, 17*(3), 1–8.Weale, S. (2018). www.theguardian.com/education/2018/nov/22/3000-pounds-for-a-school-trip-you-must-be-joking.

Weenink, D. (2008). Cosmopolitanism as a form of capital: Parents preparing their children for a globalizing world. *Sociology, 42*(6), 1089–1106.

Yang, P. (2018). Compromise and complicity in international student mobility: The ethnographic case of Indian medical students at a Chinese university. *Discourse: Studies in the Cultural Politics of Education*, 1–15.

Yemini, M. (2014). Internationalization of secondary education— Lessons from Israeli Palestinian-Arab schools in Tel Aviv-Jaffa. *Urban Education, 49*(5), 471–498.

Yemini, M., & Fulop, A. (2015). The international, global and intercultural dimensions in schools: An analysis of four internationalised Israeli schools. *Globalisation, Societies and Education, 13*(4), 528–552.

3   The 'Internationalisation of Public Schooling' in Practice

A 'Skeptical Reality' Approach

Tristan Bunnell

Introduction and Context

The 'Internationalisation of Higher Education' is well discussed, and relatively well theorised. An established model (e.g. Knight, 2004) identifies four distinct strategies, in practice. These involve governance, operations, support services, and human resource development. Yemini (2014, p. 475) has offered an adjusted model for application in the context of 'public schooling': governance, curriculum, operations (activities), and support services.

This chapter will deal specifically with the 'curriculum' aspect of this broad framework and the somewhat unexpected and largely under-reported entry into the public schooling sphere, in some nation-states, of the programmes of the International Baccalaureate (IB), beyond the traditional, core base of 'pioneer' private international schools' (see Bunnell, 2013). This phenomenon has particularly involved the IB's 'flagship' Diploma Programme (IBDP), but the Middle Years Programme (MYP) and the Primary Years Programme (PYP) are also involved.

It is worth saying a little more at this point about the IB. At the heart of all the IB programmes lies the under-researched concept of 'International Mindedness' (IM: see Hill, 2012). IM is a key and deliberately-placed component of international curricula such as the International Primary Curriculum (IPC), the first curriculum designed to incorporate IM (See Bunnell, 2010a), but especially the programmes of the IB which encapsulate IM in practice (see Barratt Hacking, Blackmore, Bullock, Bunnell, Donnelly, & Martin, 2018) alongside other 'useful' 21st century skills and attitudes such as inquiry, critical-thinking, and risk-taking (the essence of the ten-attribute 'IB Learner Profile').

The strength of the IB programmes is shown by Carder's (2009, p. 101) proposal that 'the IB student profile may be an important preliminary consideration for any school aspiring to an international identity'. The IB, with an ambitious irenic-based mission dating its origins back to a peak–Cold War period, celebrated its 50th anniversary as a Geneva-registered entity in 2018, and its continued global dominance as a provider of educational services (assessment, curricula, research, resources, and teacher training) adds to the substantial argument that 'current internationalisation practices continue to embed the North/South divide' (Maxwell, 2018, p. 347).

This chapter will use the growth of the IB programmes in public schools in areas as diverse as Chicago, Ecuador, and Japan to empirically show that although it is argued (Yemini, 2015) that internationalisation practices across the world will lead to different outcomes, and there is 'no one consensual path' (Yemini & Fulop, 2015, p. 531) to accomplish it, one can, in fact, identify certain trends. The distribution of scarce educational resources to benefit mainly the urbanised middle-class is a key aspect of IB programme implementation in public schools, and this presents a critical issue requiring on-going investigation. Does any process of internationalisation directly benefit or involve rural public schools?

In particular, this chapter will offer an original, skeptical perspective, building upon Maxwell's (2018, p. 353) view that a critical lens of analysis is required when viewing how 'effectively and deeply internationalisation is seeping into national (or sub-national) educational spaces'. It will seek to show that in practice the extent of contact between the IB and public schooling is relatively scarce, small-scale, and minimally funded and prioritised (I have called it 'triaged' before: see Bunnell, 2011).

The story of the implementation of the IB programmes in general, across various parts of the world, shows that the 'internationalisation of public schooling' seems, on paper, as being a 'massification' process, yet in reality contact is focused and filtered to directly benefit a relatively small number of (urban-based) children who can potentially, and quickly, become 'globalised workers'. At the same time, there is scope for a filtering-down, perhaps unintentionally, of indirect benefits across the education system more generally. I offer this two-tiered framework for further investigation, and comparative research. In particular, I will also develop a 'Skeptical Reality' framework, which could be utilised in other contexts beyond the scope of the IB, to be explored next.

The 'Skeptical Reality' Framework

This prioritizing of resources, benefitting and involving a minority of society, offers scope for a 'Skeptical' approach to be deployed. Several globalisation models appeared in the 1980s and 1990s, based on the notion that there have been 'waves' of thought (Martell, 2007). It became normal in globalisation literature (e.g. Holton, 2005) to identify three distinct waves of thought, as developed in 'The Three Approach Model' (Held, McGrew, Goldblatt, & Perraton, 1999), where a 'Skeptical' approach can be seen as the second wave, following on from the initial 'Hyperglobalist' approach. A third, 'Transformationalist' view subsequently appeared, offering a view that was middle-way.

This well-established globalisation framework offers a useful reference point for studying the topic of the growth of the IB programmes in public schools. It has previously been used by commentators on the growth and development of the IB programmes (e.g. Walker, 2000). It is commented that the three approaches 'serve as a useful analytical tool' for analysing globalisation trends in education (Tikly, 2001, p. 152).

The 'Hyperglobalist' approach would see the movement of the Geneva-registered IB into public schooling as a process of the 'Westernisation of education', imposing Western-Liberal-Humanistic values and potentially undermining the nation-state, where the educating of the national-citizen is normally viewed as a priority. The 'Transformationalist' approach would identify the spread of the IB in public schooling as a process of indoctrination, aiming to impose universal-values and deliberately transform the national-citizen into a global-citizen. This is the essence of the 'culture war' attack on the IB in the United States (see Bunnell, 2009).

The 'Skeptical' approach identifies regional rather than global trends, and rejects the notion (myth) that national-identity or sovereignty is under threat, or a mass process of indoctrination is occurring. Instead, this approach identifies how nation-states are harnessing globalising trends and developments in order to deliberately promote nationally set goals. In other words, the IB has not imposed or forced itself into public schools but has been selected and invited to enter the national arena. For instance, the IB has been proposed as a possible 'rescuer' of Thai public schooling, especially as plans in 2015 were put forward there to focus on social studies and history, strong elements of the IBDP (Daniel Maxwell, 2015). A framework for identifying this approach in practice comes from the comment that 'it has been acknowledged that the role of the nation-state remains central to global education initiatives' (Engel & Siczek, 2017, p. 2). In other words, the nation-state remains in control and usually operates a policy of directing and prioritizing the action.

Further, the 'Skeptical' approach would identify a small-scale level of activity, rejecting the notion that the whole of society is being affected. In particular, it would see developments as being mainly aimed at, and involving, urbanised areas with large swathes of the nation being un-affected or un-involved. This gives the 'Skeptical' approach an arguably more realistic dimension when studying the expansion of the IB in public schooling where it largely occupies an urbanised-space. This requires a prioritizing, or rationing, of resources which inevitably will lead to challenges and tensions, favouring particular sections of society who are well-positioned to benefit from it. As noted by Claire Maxwell (2018, p. 348): 'Internationalisation practices within education are shown to offer yet a further mechanism for distinction-making and positively privileged particularly those who are economically-wealthy'.

I will next apply this 'Skeptical Reality' approach to study the effects of the imposition of the IB in several countries where growth in public schooling has been quite prevalent, involving what seems, at first glance, to be a mass process involving many children, yet in reality lacks depth both within and across nation-states, and involves relatively little financial support.

The Lack of Access in Reality

The Enormous Global Disparities

The bedrock of my application of the 'Skeptical Reality' approach is the fact that the IB does not have the scope of global exposure to public schooling that many observers might believe or sense. At first glance, the IB seems well-entrenched in public schools globally, yet the truth of the matter is that access is heavily skewered towards the United States and Canada. In October 2018, the IB had 5,251 fully authorised schools worldwide. Of these, 55% (2,882) were public schools. This was down slightly from 57% in 2010 (Hill, 2011, p. 122). Of the public ones, 61% (1,758) were in the USA, and Canada had a further 11 % (315). In other words, North America accounted for 72% of the IB's public schools. Moreover, 89% of the IB schools in the USA were public. This was down slightly from 91% in 2010 (Hill, 2011, p. 123). Ecuador had a further bloc of 204 public schools, and Australia had 69 public schools delivering IB programmes.

In stark contrast, my paper on the dearth of the IB across Africa (Bunnell, 2016) revealed how the IB at that time had just 77 member-schools in only 25 African nations, which represented together a mere 1.8% of world activity. Moreover, the entire Continent of Africa has no public schools delivering IB programmes, as acknowledged by the IB itself: 'Where governments are struggling to meet millennium development goals, there is no access to IB programmes in state schools at all; this is the case in Africa' (Guy, 2011, p. 149).

Of the biggest localities in terms of IB activity in 2018, India also had zero public schools delivering IB programmes, China had 23, and the United Kingdom (UK: although mainly in England) had 33, revealing that in most nation-states the IB operated largely in private/independent school settings. By contrast, California had 185 public schools delivering an IB programme, Texas had 176, whilst Florida had 153. There are other small 'pockets' of public schooling activity, e.g. Sweden had 35, and Peru had 27. At the other extreme, France had two public schools and Italy had another two. Mexico had four.

In addition, areas within some nation-states have no IB public schooling activity. For example, New South Wales, Northern Territory, and Tasmania in Australia had no IB public schools. Northern Ireland had no IB activity at all. A number of other nations had a solitary IB public school, including Chile, Iceland, Iran, Israel, Serbia, and Slovakia. Alongside

India (and Africa), several more nations had zero public schools involved in IB delivery, including Albania, Armenia, Bangladesh, Belgium, Bolivia, Brazil, Colombia, Czech Republic, Indonesia, Korea, Kuwait, Lebanon, Malta, Myanmar, Nigeria, Panama, Philippines, Portugal, Romania, Sri Lanka, Thailand, Ukraine, United Arab Emirates, Uruguay, Venezuela, and Vietnam.

Put simply, in 2018 there were at least 53 nations where there existed authorised 'IB World Schools' yet zero public schooling activity, whilst four nations (Australia, Canada, Ecuador, and the United States) accounted for 81% (2,346 schools) of the IB's overall body of public schools. This is an enormous, and widening, polarisation. In most parts of the world, the IB (still) operates out of a traditional, private and relatively elite schooling mode of activity.

The key point to observe here is that large areas of the world are seemingly focused on delivering a wholly national-focused education for their national-citizens, and delivering a national curriculum. Put another way, in many nation-states access to an 'internationalised' form of education seemingly remains the preserve of (elite, expensive, selective) private schooling, and involves those who presumably can most afford it.

The Distribution Within Nations

The 'Skeptical Reality' approach can be applied within a nation. The story of the huge, sudden growth of the IB in Ecuador acts as a good example of how distribution within national contexts tends to be rationed. The first IB public school had appeared in December 2003 in the capital city, Quito. The subsequent growth can be broken down into two phases, beginning when the Ecuadorian Ministry of Education drew up the *Ten Year Education Plan in Ecuador 2006–2015*, aimed at increasing high school enrolment to 75% (Barnett, 2013). In February 2006 the Ministry signed the Memorandum of Mutual Commitments with the IB, which agreed to support having one IBDP school in each of the nation's 24 administrative provinces ('provincias'). Schools were 'hand-selected as having strengths that would allow them to be educational leaders' (Barnett, 2013, p. 12).

The goal was to 'elevate the academic and humanistic preparation of young people' (Barnett, 2013, p. 12). Critically speaking, this sentence might have added '*some* young people spread *across* the nation' rather than implying an inclusive, broad-based process. The phenomenon of IB public schools being rationed within a nation was exemplified by the initial developments in Ecuador. Consequently, it was said in 2011 that '15 state schools now offer the IBDP in 15 different provinces throughout the country' (Hill, 2011, p. 123).

It is worth noting that all the schools involved in the first phase were distributed evenly across Ecuador, beyond Quito. This fits well with Maxwell's (2018) view that 'internationalisation has led to further stratification of local, national, regional' systems of education. The second phase, beginning in late-2012 was 'on a different scale' (Barnett, 2013, p. 3) but had a similar geographical and stratification theme. The plan was for 120 new IBDP schools each year, of which half would be in the coastal region ('La Costa') and half in the highlands region ('La Sierra'). The selection process was more formal, guided by a set of criteria including 'the presence of stable, experienced directors, geographical distribution and existing infrastructure' (Barnett, 2013, p. 12).

This fragmentation process has been noted elsewhere. Kotzyba et al. (2018) show how secondary education in Germany is being fundamentally re-shaped by 'Internationalisation at Home' (Nilsson, 2003) processes, in particular by the 'promotion of the IB Diploma, usually only found in state-funded institutions based in urban centres'. This issue of dominance in 'urban centres', has been noted in Australia where research has found that 'access to IB schools in Australia is largely limited to families who reside in large cities' (Dickson, Perry, & Ledger, 2017, p. 75). Indeed, it was concluded that 'most IB schools are located in Australia's capital cities' (Dickson, Perry, & Ledger, 2017, p. 71). This evidence from Australia backs my assertion that the 'internationalisation of public schooling' is largely an urban-based phenomenon, spread among cities, and rarely involving rural communities.

It is noted that 'the literature suggests notable tensions in the various rationales for internationalising education' (Engel & Siczek, 2017, p. 2). Here we have another set of tensions, focusing on geographical access in particular: promoting wide access across the entire nation versus prioritizing and rationing access in urban settings.

The Lack of Depth in Reality

The lack of depth in terms of the IB's contact with students in schools, in reality, is well exemplified in Chicago, where the IB has, on paper, a considerable presence. In fact, in 2018 Chicago Public Schools had the United States' largest network of 'IB World Schools', with a total of 56 (22 high schools and 34 elementary schools) serving 16,000 students across the city. The number of students taking the IBDP examinations in Chicago has grown from 740 in 2011, to 2,006 students in 2017 (Office of the Mayor Press Release, 27 March 2018). The growth of the IB programmes in Chicago's public schools is seen as partly a policy reaction to dealing with external factors such as immigration and poverty (Shipps, Kahne, & Smylie, 1999; Lipman, 2004), especially the high drop-out rate in Chicago's high schools. One study (Saavedra, 2014) shows the IBDP in Chicago has been 'a cost-effective way to increase high school graduation rates'.

However, the scale of activity there needs to be put into perspective; Chicago Public Schools serve 371,000 students in 646 schools, and is the United States' third-largest school district. It has been correctly noted that: 'While seven Chicago high schools offer a complete IB curriculum, eight offer a portion of the program. Chicago schools that offer IB serve more than 15,000 students, a fraction of the school system's total enrollment' (Corfman, 2014). Thus, we can deduce that only about 4% of children in Chicago's relatively extensive body of 'IB World Public Schools' have access to any form of IB education. In this context, the process of IB delivery in public schools can still be firmly identified as an 'elitist' one involving severely limited access.

Moreover, many IB schools enter a very small number of students in examinations, showing the extent to which many schools ration the IBDP to involve only a few students. This is particularly telling in the November exam session, delivered by the substantially smaller bloc of 'IB World Schools' in the Global South (whilst the Global North-based schools undertake the May exam session). Official IB statistical bulletins (see www.ibo.org) show that in November 2017, 75% of schools (752 out of 1,079) entered less than 10 candidates. In May 2017, 29% of schools (780 out of 2,666) entered less than 20 candidates. All these figures have been very consistent since 2013. Overall, 30% of all schools in 2017 entered less than 10 candidates.

It is worth focusing on Ecuador, as a case study of this activity in reality. Ecuador in 2017 had 271 'IB World' schools (270 offering the DP), representing the third largest bloc of schools in the world, behind the United States and Canada. In 2017, Ecuador had 2,792 candidates in the November session (out of a total 16,535). This was biggest bloc of candidates in that exam session. Ecuador had a further 3,059 candidates in the May session (out of 157,488). This was the eighth biggest bloc of students submitted for the IB overall in 2017, dwarfed by the United States' 85,508 candidates. Thus overall, Ecuador in 2017 had 5,851 candidates out of a combined examination session 174,023 (i.e. Ecuador 'housed' only 3.4% of the global total, yet had 8% of all DP schools). Put another way, Ecuador's 270 schools offered an average of 22 candidates per school (with the rest doing solely the Bachillerato High School Programme).

However, not all these candidates were sat in public schools. Of the 270 schools in Ecuador, 66 are private/'international' schools. In other words, 204 public schools delivered the IBDP. The point to observe here is that many of the 5,851 candidates that sat the DP exams in both sessions in 2017 were 'housed' in private schools such as Academia Cotopaxi American International School, the first school in Ecuador to deliver the IB, in 1981. Another way of viewing this data is to identify that the UK's dwindling bloc of 110 DP schools 'offered' 4,728 candidates in the May 2017 exam session (i.e. an average of about 40 candidates per school). In other words, the UK-based schools offered more candidates than Ecuador (overall, and per school), yet had 160 fewer schools. Put simply, beneath the surface in Ecuador's public schools there is a lot less activity than at first envisaged.

The Mechanisms of Implementation

The Low Levels of Funding

The 'Skeptical Reality' analysis can be continued in terms of public-funding. Comparative education studies (e.g. Resnik, 2016) show that the introduction of the IB programmes differs from country to country and is dependent upon the prevailing 'institutional assemblage'; in Argentina and Chile, for example, the growth is led by IB-private school assemblage, but in Ecuador, Japan, and the United States it is led by an IB-government assemblage.

In fact, very few governments directly support the IB, and it tends to involve relatively small grants of money. Data can be garnered from the IB's *Annual Reviews* (available at www.ibo.org/about-the-ib/facts-and-figures/ib-annual-review/). In 2015, four nations financially directly supported the IB: Germany, Norway, Japan, and Malaysia. However, in 2016 and 2017 only Germany and Japan had supported the IB. The Malaysian Government (AIM Agency) in 2014 gave the IB a fund of USD 0.8 million, to help prepare 10 government secondary schools in Malaysia to successfully implement the IB Middle Years Programme (IBMYP). Malaysia had given USD 1.5 million in 2013 to support the same project. Japan in 2014 had given USD 0.5 million.

The United States began tax-payer funding the IB programmes in 2003, when a sum of USD 1.17 million was given to six middle-years schools in Arizona, Massachusetts, and New York to become 'feeder schools' for the Diploma Programme in low-income schools. This was supplemented in September 2006 with a further grant of USD 1.08 million targeted at 50 DP schools (Bunnell, 2012, p. 70.). In 2006 UK Prime Minister Blair had announced GBP 2.5 million worth of funding, for which 124 state schools in England could apply through their Local Education Authorities (LEAs) to help them cover the costs of applying for the two-year IBDP accreditation process. In fact, the aforementioned examples reveal that the funding is usually merely to cover the basic costs of applying for the accreditation process, i.e. there is no long-term funding available.

The Support of Political 'Champions'

The lack of depth of the IB programmes in the sphere of public schooling has very practical roots. It is acknowledged that 'internationalisation within local schools is a complex process that poses many challenges'

(Yemini & Fulop, 2015, p. 531). Barriers can occur at the institutional level, such as a lack of funding. Other barriers can occur at the individual level, such as teachers' lacking the necessary training. The latter barrier can also be *political*, and there is much evidence to show that the IB depends very heavily on garnering the support of key individual politicians or public advocates. In other words, the support can often lack political depth.

The IB's large presence in CPS comes through the support of Mayor Rahm Emanuel (Democratic Mayor of Chicago since 2011), 'who likes to tout that Chicago has more IB schools than any school district in the county' (Corfman, 2014). The huge growth in public schools in Ecuador occurred after the head of a private IB school who had 'fallen in love with the IB' became Ecuador's Minister for Education (Hill, 2011, p. 123). The support of the ex-President (Rafael Correa) was also instrumental in promoting growth: 'Until the 2000s the majority of IB schools in Ecuador were private elite schools following the socio-education cleavage characteristic to South America. It was Correa's administration that changed this pattern and today IB public schools outnumber the private ones' (Resnik, 2016 p. 306).

The IB in 2006 had garnered the support in the United Kingdom of Prime Minister Blair. The ultimate aim was for 124 of England's 150 LEAs, to have *one* IBDP school each (Bunnell, 2015, p. 392), offering a remarkably similar story to Ecuador's first phase of growth (2006–2012). After Blair's political departure in 2006, the IB began a 'spiral of death', falling from a peak of 230 schools in November 2010 to just 110 in October 2018, of which only 33 were public schools. In 2014 the IB formed a partnership project with the King Faisal Foundation (KFF) to bring programmes to almost 40 primary and secondary schools across the Kingdom of Saudi Arabia.

The 'Ripple-Effect'

Within this framework of low-levels of funding and shallow, often unsustainable political support, the introduction of the IBDP in public schools can still act as an internal catalyst for change. Research among IB public school schools in Spain (Valle, Menendez, Thoilliez, Garrido, Rappoport, & Manso, 2017) revealed numerous and substantial 'secondary effects' including a 'contagious' learning environment where even the non-IB students began to undergo, for example, more extra-curricular activity, even though this is not compulsory for that set of children. Overall, Valle et al. (2017) noted a 'positive shift in school culture'. Referring to Thailand, it is said that: 'Implementing the IB in selected government schools, such as leading provincial schools would not only benefit those students directly but could also become a catalyst for wider changes' (D. Maxwell, 2015).

Here we can identify two major aims. First, the entry of the IBDP into public schools is believed to provide better opportunities at high school-level for those fortunate enough to undertake it; plus it is meant to raise the level and standard of secondary education across a nation more generally with the schools acting as showcases of leading educational practice. This is a common theme regarding IB programmes, with the chosen public schools acting as both incubators and models of promising practice. It is said that: 'Ecuadorian state schools offer the IBDP to academic high achievers, but despite limiting the programme to select groups the IB has influenced the larger education system by providing examples of how things can be done better' (Maxwell, 2015). This point is backed by research (see Barnett, 2013).

It is said that 'the rationales underlying global education across—and even within—settings can vary considerably' (Engel & Siczek, 2017, p. 2). However, one can identify a definite desire to use the IB programmes, especially the DP, as a catalyst for greater change both at a teaching and social level. Japan offers a further good example of this, in practice. In June 2012 the Japanese Ministry of Education (MEXT) announced its highly ambitious intention to 'bring the IB into the wider school system' (Kosaka, 2014) by offering a dual-language IBDP in 200 public schools by 2020; in fact, most subjects will be taught in Japanese. There were 16 IBDP schools in Japan at that point in time, of which 11 were traditional 'international schools'.

Comment appeared in Japan saying there exists a hope that 'its internationally minded philosophy will become the talking point in the scholastic community' (Kosaka, 2014) so that this type of education 'would begin to spread to other areas of education'. In other words, MEXT is looking for a catalyst for change that will benefit the entire education system. In particular, MEXT is seeking educational initiatives that will help deliver the goal of fostering *ikiru chikara (English: Zest for Living)*, the capacity to lead a fulfilling life as an independent and productive member of society, which was demanded partly as a policy response to poor OECD-PISA test results (Tasaki, 2017). In this context, Claire Maxwell (2018) seems correct to assert that 'pragmatic articulations of internationalisation predominate'.

Conclusions and Discussion

At first glance, the IB seems to be a global player, and now deeply entrenched in public schooling. However, this chapter has utilised three sets of data to show the 'Skeptical Reality'. The 'geographical data' reveals quite clearly that the IB exists in public schools largely in Western, urbanised contexts, spread across a nation. The 'funding data' shows that relatively very little public money is used to implement the IBDP, and in only an ad-hoc manner. The 'exposure data' shows that each public school has few IBDP students and enters few candidates for exams in either the May or November exam sessions. This all seems to vindicate Claire Maxwell's (2018) assertion that the internationalisation of education in a stratified geographical context should *always* be viewed as a process of elite-making.

I have used three significant growth arenas (Chicago, Ecuador, and Japan) to reveal that the implementation of the IB programmes into the public schooling sphere in practice lacks depth, scope, access, funding, and relies on what might become in the long-run rather flimsy political support. The mechanisms of implementation and delivery are seemingly based upon rationing direct access to those young people (in cities) who are potentially best-situated to benefit from it whilst hoping that the implementation of the IB programmes will cause an indirect 'ripple-effect' through education in general, thus giving benefits to the wider base of electorate/tax-payers. Economically this is the most cost-effective set of outcomes.

A critical observation therefore to be made with the current academic literature and dominant discourse on the topic of the 'internationalisation of public schooling' is the generalisation made about access; i.e. there is normally an assumption implicit in the literature that makes it seem as though there does exist a massification process involving *many* schools aimed at educating a *large* number of young people. For example, it is said in the context of internationalising American public schools that the process is a 'key and desirable development to cultivate globally competent citizens and benefit from the global education marketplace' (Engel & Siczek, 2018, p. 26). In reality, the aim is to develop and cultivate *some/a few* globally competent citizens (i.e. it involves the formation of a discreet *cadre*). It is not, in reality, an inclusive process involving the masses, unlike access to higher education.

A much bigger picture now starts to emerge. There exists in practice a rather precarious process of filtering and focusing scarce resources so that only a relatively few 'globalised workers' emerges. This in turn becomes an elite and exclusive process focused on the urban elite who have the propensity to compete and work (trade) at a global level. The internationalisation of public schooling is not a large-scale process aimed at the 'masses'. It becomes, in reality, merely the small-scale de-nationalisation of urban public schooling.

There are several logical reasons behind this. First, national policy-making demands public schooling produces mainly 'national citizens'. Second, the demands of Global Capital can well be served by the emergence of only a small group of urbanised 'globalised workers'. Third, governments have a limited amount of monies to spend in this area and are also unwilling to spend more; i.e. they are looking at high-returns for a small-investment. Fourth, governments do not engage in long-term education policy-making; they want quick returns.

I have offered a Skeptical approach, but other approaches can be developed. The Hyperglobalist approach would identify a form of neo-imperialism (the IB being largely an English-speaking Western-Liberal-Humanistic and Global North–based educational force), yet the examples of policy-making from Japan and Ecuador show that nations, including some in the Global South, are seeking an adapted form that will facilitate economic growth. They have approached the IB; it has not been imposed. The Transformationalist approach would identify a massified process of indoctrination (see Bunnell, 2012), yet my figures show that most young people remain untouched by the IB's tentacles.

At the same time, the OECD's much vaunted Programme for International Student Assessment (PISA) tests in 2018 included 'global competency', and the test in 2021 will include 'creativity', which could put some nations under pressure to further bring in IB programmes, alongside the IB Learner Profile and the associated attributes, skills, and competencies linked with 'IM'. As noted by Engel and Siczek (2018), much of the focus in the United States is already on attaining success in such system-wide assessments. It is significant to note how on 12 December 2017 the IB Director General joined a panel discussion at the Harvard Graduate School of Education for the launch of a new 'global competence framework' developed by OECD-PISA (www.ibo.org). Here lie clues as to the next possible growth phase of the IB programmes in public schools, especially further growth in the United States, where it already has a disproportionate share of activity.

Moreover, the advent in 2018 of the PISA 'global competency' tests, could potentially spur a broader interest in the 'internationalising' of public education, especially among developing and highly competitive nation-states in areas of the world such as Southeast Asia or the Gulf region, where testing of 15-year-olds in other PISA domains, since 2012, has been quite rivalrous. My 'Skeptical Reality' framework offered in this chapter could be useful for analysing, and discussing, the scope, depth, and geography of funding towards the goal of high-achievement in the 'global competency' and 'creativity' testing. The evidence from the growth of the IB programmes in the realm of public schooling shows that the testing will probably involve a select grouping of young people situated in urban, metropolitan/cosmopolitan settings. The scene is now set for further investigation, beyond the 'IB World'.

References

Barnett, E. (2013). *Research on the implementation of the diploma programme in Ecuador's State schools* (Final Report, May 2013). Teachers College, Colombia University, New York. Bunnell, T. (2009). The international baccalaureate in the USA and the emerging 'culture war'. *Discourse: Studies in the Cultural Politics of Education*, 30(1), 61–72.

Bunnell, T. (2010a). The momentum behind the international primary curriculum in schools in England. *Journal of Curriculum Studies, 42*(4), 471–486.

Bunnell, T. (2011). Post-16 curriculum provision in England: The emerging functional 'triage' serving capital's needs. *Journal for Critical Education Policy Studies, 9*(1), 149–187.

Bunnell, T. (2012). *Global education under attack: International baccalaureate in America*. Peter Lang: Frankfurt.

Bunnell, T. (2013). The role of the pioneer International Schools and the growth of the international baccalaureate. In R. Pearce (Ed.), *International education and schools: Taking the first forty years forward* (pp. 167–189). London: Bloomsbury.

Bunnell, T. (2015). The rise and decline of the international baccalaureate diploma programme in the United Kingdom. *Oxford Review of Education, 41*(3), 387–403.

Bunnell, T. (2016). The dearth of international baccalaureate schools across Africa. *Africa Education Review, 13*(2), 181–195.

Carder, S. (2009). What will characterize international education in US public schools? *Journal of Research in International Education, 8*(1), 99–109.

Corfman, T. (2014, April 21). Which Chicago elementary schools are going International Baccalaureate? *Chicagobusiness.com*

Dickson, A., Perry, L. B., & Ledger, S. (2017). How accessible is IB schooling? Evidence from Australia. *Journal of Research in International Education, 16*(1), 65–79.

Engel, L., & Siczek, M. (2017). A cross-national comparison of international strategies: Global citizenship and the advancement of national competitiveness. *Compare: A Journal of Comparative and International Education, 48*(5), 749–767.

Engel, L., & Siczek, M. (2018). Framing global education in the United States: Policy perspectives. In L. Hill & F. Levine (Eds.), *Global perspectives on education research* (pp. 26–47). New York: Routledge.

Guy, J. (2011). Challenges to access. In G. Walker (Ed.), *The Changing Face of International Education* (pp. 139–158). Cardiff: IBO.

Hacking, E. B., Blackmore, C., Bullock, K., Bunnell, T., Donnelly, M., & Martin, S. (2018). International mindedness in practice: The evidence from international baccalaureate schools. *Journal of Research in International Education, 17*(1), 3–16.

Held, D., McGrew, A., Goldblatt, D., & Perraton, J. (1999). Global transformations. *ReVision, 22*(2), 7–7.

Hill, I. 2011. Working with governments. In Walker (Ed.), *The changing face of international education: Challenges for the IB* (pp. 121–138). Cardiff: IBO.

Hill, I. (2012). Evolution of education for international mindedness. *Journal of Research in International Education, 11*(3), 245–261.

Holton, R. (2005). *Making globalisation*. Basingstoke: Palgrave Macmillan.

Knight, J. (2004). Internationalisation remodelled: Definition, approaches, and rationales. *Journal of Studies in International Education, 8*, 5–31.

Kosaka, K. (2014, February 9). Globally focused International Baccalaureate diploma needs local-level support, *The Japan Times*.

Kotzyba, K., Dreier, L., Niemann, M., & Helsper, W. (2018). Processes of Internationalisation in Germany's secondary education system: A case study on

Internationality in the Gymnasium. In C. Maxwell, U. Deppe, H. H. Krüger, & W. Helsper (Eds.), *Elite education and internationalisation: From the early years into higher education* (pp. 191–208). Basingstoke: Palgrave Macmillan.

Lipman, P. (2004). *High stakes education: Inequality, globalization, and Urban school reform.* New York: Routledge Falmer.

Martell, L. (2007). The third wave in globalization theory. *International Studies Review*, 9(2), 173–196.

Maxwell, C. (2018). Changing spaces—The re-shaping of (elite) education through internationalisation. In C. Maxwell, U. Deppe, H. H. Krüger, & W. Helsper (Eds.), *Elite education and internationalisation: From the early years into higher education* (pp. 347–367). Basingstoke: Palgrave Macmillan.

Maxwell, D. (2015, August 5). The international baccalaureate—Could it rescue Thai education? *Asiancorrespondent.com*Nilsson, B. (2003). Internationalisation at home from a Swedish perspective: The case of Malmö. *Journal of Studies in International Education*, 7(1), 27–40.

Resnik, J. (2016). The development of the IB in Spanish-speaking countries: A global comparative approach. *Globalisation, Societies and Education*, 14(2), 298–325.

Saavedra, A. (2014). The academic impact of enrolment in IBD programs: A case study of Chicago public schools. *Teachers College Record*, 116(4).

Shipps, D., Kahne, J., & Smylie, M. (1999). The politics of urban school reform: Legitimacy, city growth, and school improvement in Chicago. *Educational Policy*, 13(4), 518–545.

Tasaki, N. (2017). The impact of OECD-PISA results on Japanese educational policy. *European Journal of Education*, 52(2), 145–153.

Tikly, L. (2001). Globalisation and education in the postcolonial world: Towards a conceptual framework. *Comparative Education*, 37(2), 151–171.

Valle, J., Menendez, M., Thoilliez, B., Garrido, R., Rappoport, S., & Manso, J. (2017). *Implementation and impact of the IBDP in Spanish state schools: Research summary.* IBO, March 2017.

Walker, G. (2000). Connecting the national to the global. In M. Hayden & J. Thompson (Eds.), *International schools and international education: Improving teaching, management and quality* (pp. 193–204). London: Kogan Page.

Yemini, M. (2014). Internationalisation of secondary education—Lessons from Israeli Palestinian-Arab Schools in Tel Aviv-Jaffa. *Urban Education*, 49(5), 471–498.

Yemini, M., & Fulop, A. (2015). The international, global and intercultural dimensions in schools: An analysis of four internationalised Israeli schools. *Globalisation, Societies and Education*, 13(4), 528–552.

4 Equal Global Futures? Pathways of Internationalisation in US Schooling

Laura C. Engel and Heidi Gibson

Chapter 4 is adapted from an article by Engel (2019) published in *Policy Futures in Education*, titled 'Pathways of Internationalisation in US Schooling: Local Innovations in Inclusive Global Education'.

Introduction

Internationally, there has been a growing interest within educational systems in re-assessing the knowledge, attitudes, and skills necessary for success in the 21st century global world. Both the United Nations (UN) 2030 Agenda for Sustainable Development and the Organisation for Economic Co-operation and Development (OECD) articulate the need for international education initiatives aimed at building global competence and global citizenship. However, several studies pointed out the possibly unequal consequences when internationalisation is implemented in schools, both nationally and locally (see e.g. Aguiar & Nogueira, 2012; Goren & Yemini, 2017; Maxwell & Aggleton, 2016).

Much is still unknown about how internationalisation gets leveraged in different contexts. There is no common understanding of what this involves and necessitates in different educational settings, particularly when considering different organisational and governance structures that may support and/or impede internationalisation. This lack of uniformity is particularly evident in federal contexts, where power is located away from the federal government, leaving considerable autonomy to states, local districts, and schools to act as 'laboratories of innovation' for the internationalisation of schools (Engel, 2019; Wallner, Savage, Hartong, & Engel, 2018). The focus of this chapter is on internationalisation of public schooling systems in the United States (US), which is a disjointed space in terms of school-level internationalisation (Engel & Siczek, 2018).

The decentralised nature of the US education system means that internationalisation is more of a grassroots, bottom-up movement of particular states, districts, or individual schools and classrooms. Building on previous research on *why* US school districts engage in internationalisation

(Engel, Fundalinski, & Cannon, 2016), this chapter aims to show *how* the US has approached the internationalisation of public schooling. We examine evidence of internationalisation initiatives in three settings: North Carolina; Washington, DC; and Illinois. The diverse patterns and pathways of internationalisation found across these examples suggest that there is no 'one size fits all' model of internationalisation in the US. Yet, at the same time, we see common driving factors influencing internationalisation initiatives across the three contexts. Notably we see a convergence around the need to produce the 'globally competent' and 'globally ready' US graduate, but these ideas have yet to materialise for all students in all contexts. These efforts reflect more of a skills-based, pragmatic, or instrumentalist orientation (Engel, 2014; Yemini & Fulop, 2015), loosely referring to dispositions, knowledge, and behaviours that students must embody to succeed in the 21st century highly competitive and diverse global world. In this way, global competence and global readiness are rooted in a larger set of imperatives to revamp the US education system to enhance individual and national competitiveness in a global marketplace.

We argue that because internationalisation initiatives have been framed in a more pragmatic, skills-based orientation and less ideological, values-based ways (Engel, 2014; Yemini & Fulop, 2015), they have garnered policy support in US states and districts, allowing them to be sustained even in the more nationalistic, 'America First' era. Moreover, we contend that schools, districts, and states that feature global readiness are becoming increasingly attractive in the hyper-competitive, often chaotic, and largely segregated US educational marketplace. And while such pragmatic ideas help 'sell' internationalisation, there are risks in (1) instilling in US students a foundational perspective of viewing the rest of the world as competitors rather than potential collaborative partners; (2) overlooking the relationship between internationalisation and elitism (Maxwell et al., 2018), where internationalisation may in fact deepen inequality in an already unequal US education system; and (3) overshadowing more critical knowledge and global education approaches that could productively help students make sense of the increasingly divided and diverse US society. To that end, we conclude that the Washington, DC case of internationalisation may offer important lessons for many systems in highlighting how internationalisation can facilitate the leveraging of greater equity of access for marginalised and minoritised students to valuable global learning opportunities.

Internationalisation of Schooling

Internationalisation refers to a set of processes and approaches that contain intercultural, international, and global dimensions (Knight, 2015; Yemini, 2012). It emphasises cross-national and cross-cultural relationships across systems and spaces, while maintaining a 'sense of worldwide scope' (Knight, 2015, p. 3). Its primary outputs are considered to be a set of cognitive, social emotional, and behavioural indicators of global citizenship education (UNESCO, 2015) and global and intercultural competency (Cantu, 2013). While not necessarily new ideas, there is an increasing energy at national and international levels in fostering frameworks targeting global citizenship and global competence (Engel & Siczek, 2017). The OECD's Programme for International Student Assessment (PISA) 2018, for example, launched a cross-national assessment of global competence, positioning itself as the major global agency responsible for measuring global citizenship (Auld & Morris, 2019; Engel, Rutkowski & Thompson, 2019; OECD, 2018).

Revealed in these initiatives are a variety of rationales for internationalisation (e.g. economic, political, socio-cultural, academic), from justice-oriented social transformation and solidarity (known as ideological or values-based) to more market-oriented ideas of economic competitiveness (referred to as pragmatic, instrumentalist, or skills-based) (Engel, 2014; Torres, 2015; Yemini & Fulop, 2015). As argued by Engel and Siczek (2017), these different rationales reveal an endemic tension. On the one hand, internationalisation is framed as a means to advance individual and national economic competitiveness, as well as national security in response to risks facing the individual and the nation, thus reinforcing more isolationist tendencies. On the other hand, global education approaches include values-oriented concepts—such as teaching respect for diversity—and aim to be action-oriented in order to target 'social injustice', an orientation to citizenship that extends beyond national borders.

National strategies of internationalisation tend to favour more instrumentalist approaches, what Mitchell (2003) referred to as the rise of strategic cosmopolitanism. To that end, studies have found that more elite classes tend to pursue international education opportunities to gain competitive advantages (Aguiar & Nogueira, 2012; Engel, 2017; Goren & Yemini, 2017; Maxwell & Aggleton, 2016; Weenink, 2008). Research in Israel and England (Goren & Yemini, 2017; Yemini, 2014), for example, suggests that schools curate internationalisation strategies specifically tailored to the socio-economic and cultural backgrounds of the students served in the school. In Brazil, international education is marketed and branded by particular schools as an outreach tool to recruit middle class families (Aguiar & Nogueira, 2012). In the US, mobility opportunities are more frequently offered in schools serving White students from more affluent backgrounds (Engel, 2017). Collectively, this research points to (1) different school-level internationalisation strategies, approaches, and practices within a single national space, and (2) the larger relationship between internationalisation and elitism (Maxwell, Deppe, Krüger, & Helsper, 2018).

Internationalisation Pathways in the Federal US System

Among federal systems of education (e.g. Australia, Canada, Germany), in which governance is decentralised to sub-national units, the US system is unique in the power held by local authorities, as well as the influential role that non-governmental actors play in policy formation (Wallner et al., 2018). The US is therefore a critical space to examine the governance and management structures facilitating and impeding internationalisation pathways.

The federal government has long had a controversial and changing role in education and education policy formation (Harris, Ladd, Smith, & West, 2016). Over the past several decades of educational reform, the federal government has become more influential in education policy formation at state and local levels, with new developments in test-based accountability and standards-based reforms (see e.g. Engel & Olden, 2012; Manna, 2011). This evolving role is largely a response to shifts—both economic and demographic—that have shaped the US societal landscape since the 1980s (Fowler, 2004), as well as fervent concerns over the stagnation of US students' global competitiveness spurred by the 1983 *A Nation at Risk* report and continued in the 2002 *No Child Left Behind* Act, as well as more recent reforms (Engel & Siczek, 2018).

US states, which each have their own state-level departments of education, are largely responsible for educational governance including financial, political, and administrative aspects. Adding to the complexity, each individual state's educational governance model varies, where some states are more centralized than others. Additionally, local levels in the US carry considerable power over educational decision-making, both at the school and district level. At the local level, in addition to school-level leadership, there is a school board comprised of members, usually publicly elected, a superintendent, and staff within a school district. Washington, DC occupies a unique place in the US political landscape, resulting in a hybrid model of educational governance that differs from the 50 states. Although the city is not a state in its own right, it also does not fall under the jurisdiction of any state. DC City Council, DC Mayor, and the DC State Board of Education in some ways function just like representatives in any US city, but also take on some roles usually reserved for the state-level of government. For the DC State Board of Education, one of these roles is in education policy leadership, where the Board functions both as state and school district leadership for DC.

Important in the context of US internationalisation is the role that cross-state organisations, non-governmental organisations, think tanks, and interest groups play in guiding US educational policy formation both vertically and horizontally (Savage & O'Conner, 2015). In the past two decades, many organisations have released statements advocating for advancing global perspectives in US schools (see, e.g. Committee for Economic Development, 2006; Council on Foreign Relations, 2012; National Research Council, 2007). These organisations range from advocacy organisations, like Partnership for 21st Century Skills, which helped inspire the reestablishment of the bipartisan Congressional 21st Century Skills Caucus; to powerful teacher unions, like the National Education Association, which has supported global competence education; to philanthropic entities, which financially support internationalisation activities.

In response to building momentum around the importance of global competence since the turn of the century, the US Department of Education, in 2018 re-released its first-ever international education strategy, initially published in 2012, entitled *Succeeding Globally through International Education and Engagement*. The strategy outlines three objectives: Increase global competencies; learn from and with other countries to improve US education; and engage in education diplomacy. The strategy focuses on education for global and cultural competence, framed as encompassing skills and knowledge for understanding and action, with emphasis to 'expanding access to international education and training, especially for traditionally underrepresented students' (US Department of Education, 2018, p. 4). Despite these articulated interests, analysis of the 2012 strategy suggests an overarching 'nationalistic perspective . . . one that seems more concerned with economic and educational competition over broader goals of global citizenship' (Engel & Siczek, 2018, p. 28). In short, global competence is a vehicle for enhancing individual and national competitiveness, taking precedence over other values, such as collaboration both within an increasingly diverse US society and with other people/countries around the world.

Literature on internationalisation of US schooling frequently frames the US context as fragmented (Frey & Whitehead, 2009; Ortloff & Shonia, 2015; Rapaport, 2010). In part this fragmentation is symbolic of the decentralised governance of the US system, designed to keep authority at local and state levels. Yet, it is also reflective of the deep inequities within the US education system, which bolsters widely varying access to educational opportunities (Reardon, Kalogrides, & Shores, 2016). Indicating a lack of inclusive internationalisation across the US, access to world languages, the International Baccalaureate program, experiential international education programs, and study abroad are frequently not as widely accessible to underrepresented and minoritised student groups. The US system therefore presents an important context for examining internationalisation of compulsory schooling with questions about whether and to what extent school systems are embracing internationalisation and in what forms.

Methods

This chapter draws on data from a National Geographic Society funded research project focused on an extended case study of the DC Public Schools' Study Abroad Program, discussed subsequently in further detail, as well as global education policies and practices in different settings in the US. As part of that project, we (the authors) helped to form the K12 Global Forum, a coalition of district and state leaders interested in equitable access to global learning and research. The K12 Global Forum convenes practitioners, government stakeholders, and organisations working at district, state, and federal levels, as well as researchers to examine and share the ways that different settings are pursuing global education policies and practices. In 2017–2018, our project team (comprising representatives of the DC Public Schools and us as researchers) made a series of virtual and in-person site visits to K12 Global Forum partners in North Carolina, Virginia, Pennsylvania, and Illinois, convening teachers, administrators, government officials, university researchers, thought leaders, and representatives of international education organisations. In September 2018, we held an official launch of the K12 Global Forum in Washington, DC, to also include representatives from other states, including California, Connecticut, Georgia, North Dakota, and key organisations in the international/global education space.

We focus our chapter on three different US settings that have pursued internationalisation, including a well-established state-level policy of internationalisation (North Carolina), a newer grassroots policy initiative formed by a state-wide coalition (Illinois), and a site that represents a multi-pronged approach with more equity-based or inclusive internationalisation programming (DC Public Schools). We focus on the governance of internationalisation initiatives at a systems level, asking:

1. How did they develop?
2. What initiated the process and based on what rationales?
3. What factors facilitated and constrained them?
4. What is the focus of the internationalisation initiatives?

We draw on state- and district-level policy documents related to internationalisation, as well as documents and public statements made by key stakeholders during site visit meetings, interviews with stakeholders, and a set of K12 Global Forum 'Global Education Talks' made by district and state leaders at the launch convening.

Three Systems, Three Models

North Carolina: State Policy Leadership

North Carolina is located in the South Atlantic. Similar to Illinois, North Carolina is divided politically along urban (often Democratic) and rural (often Republican) lines; North Carolina has tended to vote Republican in Presidential elections, while electing Democratic governors, with Democrats increasingly dominating urban areas. Demographically, North Carolina public schools serve higher proportions of Black students (25%) and lower proportions of Hispanic students (16%) than the national US average (50% White, 15% Black, 26% Hispanic, [US Department of Education, 2019]) and about 60% of North Carolina public school students are classified as low income, compared to the US average of 50% (www.publicschoolreview.com/north-carolina). It shares similar educational challenges with other states in the US, with persistent gaps in academic achievement and lower secondary school graduation rates among Black and Hispanic students, English Language Learners, and students with special education needs.

North Carolina's global education approach uses state-level policy leadership focused on providing professional development resources, frameworks, and incentives needed for districts and schools to internationalise. The state-level leadership related to internationalisation in North Carolina makes it arguably the most mature and developed state-level global education policy in the US, aimed at creating 'global-ready' schools, educators, and students. State-level supports target districts, schools, and individual educators, and can be loosely characterised as sharing information about global education, recognising outstanding practice, facilitating access to resources, and providing professional development opportunities.

Emerging from a State Board of Education Task Force, the rationale behind this move towards global education was largely based on preparing students for a more globalised economy. Specifically, interacting with foreign co-workers and companies, using global supply chains, and supporting the ability to export goods are cited as reasons for needing a focus on global education (State Board of Education of North Carolina, 2013). The focus for the Task Force was to submit recommendations that would make North Carolina's students globally competitive. The 2013 final report suggested recommendations focused on five areas: Teacher development and support, language instruction, innovative school models, networking and recognising districts engaging in global education, and international relationships.

In response to these recommendations, the North Carolina Department of Public Instruction (NCDPI) undertook a number of actions directly related to encouraging classroom change. They created a dedicated position at the NCDPI, the Special Assistant for Global Education, to concentrate on internationalisation efforts (a position that was subsequently eliminated in 2018). The NCDPI worked with local partners to develop an extensive online, self-paced professional development course for teachers and established a State Board of Education Global Educator Digital Badge. NCDPI also collaborated with local teacher training programs to increase the number of trained world/foreign language teachers in the state, increased dual language immersion, and established programs to bring foreign teachers into North Carolina classrooms.

In addition, in accordance with the Task Force recommendations, NCDPI adopted a framework defining the key attributes of global-ready schools and districts and created a process to assess and recognise these efforts. The global-ready assessment is based around three overarching principles for schools and districts: Strategic planning, curriculum integration, and partnerships (local, global, business, and community). Each principle has multiple attributes, detailing different aspects, and each attribute itself has key elements. A rubric of how practice looks at the early, developing, prepared, and model stages is the basis of the assessment. Key elements are mostly similar for both districts and schools, with differences based on the situational context. For example, district professional development (PD) key elements look at the PD needs of administrators, and school-level PD is aimed at teachers. In addition, there are some key elements that exist only for districts, such as the number of global-ready schools in their district, or only for schools, such as detailed curriculum integration measures. Schools and districts complete a self-assessment, along with a narrative for each key element. They are also required to submit evidence (data, documents, videos, etc.) to show their practice. If the schools are found to be at the prepared or model stage, a site visit by state staff confirms their final designation.

This process is potentially useful for schools for two reasons. First, the process allows schools to understand how they fall on a continuum of 'early' to 'model' practice. The detailed rubrics help break down the progression to make it easier for schools to visualize the structures and practices of global-ready schools. Second, the rubrics offer the state the opportunity to incentivize the move towards global readiness through the use of designations. Although the designation of 'global-ready' school or district contains no tied financial incentive, the award is significant. Not only does it signal to educators and administrators that the state sees the school's work as important, but it also sends the same signal to community members.

Illinois: Grassroots Initiative and Coalition

Illinois is situated in the Midwest. It is divided politically in fairly similar ways to North Carolina. As a state, Illinois has tended to vote Democratic due to the voting patterns in the city of Chicago and its surrounding suburbs, while the rest of the state generally tends to vote Republican. About half of Illinois public school students are classified as low income, which is similar to the US national average. Public school students in Illinois in 2016–2017 were 50% White, 16% Black, and 29% Hispanic, similar to the US national average (US Department of Education, n.d.).

In Illinois, our focus is on the new Illinois Global Scholar diploma seal, one of the newest state-wide global education developments. Illinois joins a handful of other states and districts from across the US in offering a global certificate (e.g. Kentucky, Wisconsin, Ohio, Washington, DC Public Schools, among others) (Manise, 2018). The certificate is aimed primarily at creating a pathway for high school students in Illinois to develop global skills and knowledge through a competency-based approach. According to the certificate website, the broader articulated goal is the cultivation of global competencies among students:

> In order to best prepare Illinois students for career and citizenship, they must learn to navigate and achieve in an increasingly competitive and globalized world. The Global Scholar Certificate responds to a growing body of research and data that suggest future careers will depend heavily upon the ability of students to work and collaborate in multiple cultural contexts. . . . The time has come to reward Illinois students for achieving the skills and knowledge that will be crucial to succeeding in a rapidly changing, globalized world.
>
> (www.global-illinois.org/)

The formal diploma designation allows students to stand out from peers as they enter the workforce or pursue college admission.

The Illinois Global Scholar Certificate offers a diploma seal to students who complete certain criteria, including

1. taking specific globally-oriented classes as part of their regular curriculum,
2. engaging in service learning that has a global focus or reach,
3. participating in cross-national dialogue with peers, and
4. completing an independent and globally-focused capstone project that requires students to take action to affect change.

While it primarily recognises efforts by specific students, it also encourages a school- or district-wide investment in internationalisation through the course offerings and teachers for the capstone course.

The new certificate emerged from more of a grassroots effort. A coalition of educators from across the state looked at the new Global Education Achievement Certificate (GEAC) offered in the neighbouring state of Wisconsin and was interested in offering something similar to their students. The proposal for the Illinois Global Scholar Certificate was originally envisioned as a district-level initiative that would later be scaled to the state. Funding from the Longview Foundation and the European Union Center at the University of Illinois helped to convene a coalition of leaders from across the state allowing the certificate to be developed, which in turn led to its ultimate approval as state law (HB 4983).

Overseen by the Illinois State Board of Education, this state law (effective 2016) meant that secondary public education students whose school district had adopted the Illinois Global Scholar programme could earn the certification and have it formally included on the student's high school transcript and diploma. Since the bill was approved, a state-wide global education network launched by global learning advocates has focused largely on implementation, which is based on local district consideration and approval. In its first year, four schools are currently offering the certificate, with four more coming online in 2019–2020.

Student global engagement is a critical component of the certificate. For example, students are required to take action, such as in local service-learning projects (e.g. the Illinois Waterway Cleanup Week, a state-wide initiative), and engage globally with peers. In the capstone project, students ask a question about a global issue that is significant to them. Questions can range widely, but must go beyond theoretical inquiry and be actionable, and students must create an artefact as an outcome. For example, one student, interested in fashion, was inspired to examine the impacts of the fast fashion industry on workers in Bangladesh. Although there were multiple labour rights concerns associated with some garment factories, she discovered that the workers did not want consumers to be encouraged to stop buying the goods they created, as they would lose their livelihood. Instead she approached on the problem at a different level, by creating and distributing a public service announcement in Bangla about the Bangladeshi workers' right to join labour movements. Throughout the process, students work closely with an educator teaching the capstone course, and they must also work with two individuals overseas with expertise on the subject matter of the capstone, encouraging global dialogue. The capstone project is ultimately graded by teachers according to specific state-wide assessment criteria, and long-term plans include peer scoring among educators.

DC Public Schools (DCPS): Equity-focused Programs

In contrast to North Carolina and Illinois, Washington, DC is a unique political context. Its citizens have no voting representatives in the US Congress, though residents are able to vote in presidential elections and overwhelmingly vote Democratic. DC Public Schools bolster significantly lower proportions of White students (15%) and higher proportions of Black (60%) and Hispanic (20%) students than the US average.[1] It also serves a higher proportion of students classified as low income (77%) than the national average (50%). In comparison to Illinois and North Carolina, DC Public Schools has the lowest graduation rate of 68%, compared to a national average of 85%, a rate that disproportionately affects students of colour. In DCPS, for instance, Black students' 2015 graduation rates (61.7%) were significantly lower than White students

(85.6%). Along with having one of the largest Black–White achievement gaps, DC also has a wide Hispanic–White achievement gap (Reardon, Kalogrides, & Shores, 2016).

The current focus on global education in DC Public Schools (DCPS) represents a multi-pronged and equity-focused set of internationalisation initiatives. The approach encompasses actions taken to support schools and classrooms, such as Global Studies or Embassy Adoption, but also focuses on targeting individuals, such as the study abroad programme or the diploma seal. With a core focus on providing *all* students access to global learning opportunities, in 2014, under the leadership of Chancellor Kaya Henderson, DCPS formed its current Global Education unit. This six-member team, situated within the DCPS Central Office, provides ongoing but intermittent programs such as Embassy Adoption Program and International Food Days; Curricular and pedagogical initiatives, such as World Languages, International Baccalaureate, and Global Studies Program Schools; and transformative out-of-school programs such as DCPS Study Abroad Program. In addition, DCPS also offers a Global Scholar Certificate to signal global education achievement for high school graduates. According to a DCPS staff member, these areas were intended to be coherent and comprehensive: 'from the beginning, the way that the Director talked about our work is we're going to have world languages instruction, global programming and global studies', with a vision for a fully funded mobility programme (personal communication).

The justification for internationalisation efforts includes elements from both the social justice orientation and economic competitiveness (Engel & Siczek, 2018). Together the DCPS global education activities reflect larger aims of equity and quality learning for all students, suggesting a model of inclusive internationalisation (de Wit & Jones, 2018; Engel, 2019). For example, there are frequent statements of' 'all students can be global citizens' and 'all teachers can be global educators' (DCPS Global Education, n.d.-a). According to a DCPS staff member,

> DCPS has always been committed to equity . . . it's always been part of our core values, a recognition of DC's unique identity as a global city, the responsibility this city has to its citizens and its young people, to prepare them for the careers that are waiting for them in their backyard and beyond, to prepare them for the diversity in the world, and offer them a million more opportunities than they might have even dreamed of as possible.
>
> (personal communication)

DCPS Global Education programming takes advantage of the opportunities inherent in Washington, DC's local situation, a city filled with international entities. One of the older global education programs unique to DCPS is the Embassy Adoption Program, established in 1974 to 'expose

DCPS students to international perspectives and cross-cultural lessons' (DCPS, n.d.-b) via communication with diplomats. Over 50,000 students have participated in the program, interacting with over 100 embassies (DCPS Global Ed, n.d.-c). Classrooms of students approximately 10–12 years old (5th and 6th grade) are paired with volunteer embassies and other global entities, in order to learn about the represented country by exploring its food, culture, arts, history, and government. As a reflection of intercultural dimensions of internationalisation, DCPS also manages an International Food Day program, where each year DCPS partners with local embassies to have DCPS Food and Nutrition Services create and prepare a menu reflecting food from a represented country, reaching the whole DCPS student population (DCPS Global Ed, n.d.-d). In addition, a DCPS Global Education partnership with the US Peace Corps has led to the recruiting of returning Peace Corps volunteers as world language teachers—an innovative attempt to increase student access to world language instruction, an ongoing challenge to global education efforts in DC. This programme operates as an alternative route to teacher licensure, leveraging the skills of individuals with considerable linguistic and global competencies.

The mission of equitable access to global learning opportunities is at the heart of the design and implementation of the DCPS Study Abroad Program, with its aim to make study abroad 'the expectation, not the exception' for all students (DCPS Global Education, n.d.-a). The Study Abroad Program launched in 2015–2016 and, according to a DCPS Global Education staff member, stemmed from the 'vision of Chancellor Henderson to send all 8th and 11th graders abroad' (personal communication). The DCPS Study Abroad Program supports short-term global trips during the summer for selected eligible DCPS students in middle and high school and is weighted individually towards those who do not have previous travel experiences. The programme is the first fully funded K–12 global travel programme in the US, sending students to locations representing 15 countries (it also includes New York City for students who are unable to travel outside of the US). To date, over 1,400 DCPS students have studied abroad through this program, which required that 800 of these students get passports to enable them to do so—an indicator of the kinds of young people who have benefitted from this initiative. The study abroad program, now in its fourth year of operation, is a model initiative building equitable access to overseas experiences, shifting the narrative around who can and ought to be global citizens (Engel, 2019).

Reflecting more of a whole school internationalisation approach, there are currently eight schools using the IB program, offering a globally oriented curriculum and inquiry-based projects (DCPS, 2017). Additionally, in 2016, DCPS opened three Global Studies schools: One elementary, one middle school, and one high school. Each of the schools has high percentages of low income students of colour. Pedagogy at the Global Studies schools flows from a collaboration between DCPS and Harvard's Project Zero, supporting selected Teacher Fellows in globally oriented teacher professional development. The aim is to infuse global themes throughout the curriculum and the K–12 pathway of the Global Studies schools, from elementary to high school. Similar to North Carolina and Illinois, DCPS Global Education offers the Global Scholars Certificate, allowing students beginning in 10th grade an opportunity to earn a certificate in recognition of their global understanding and competence gained through globally-oriented coursework and experiences.

Discussion

Featuring the examples of these three cases raises two main arguments about internationalisation of US schooling: (1) Internationalisation is not a 'one size fits all', but rather reflects a multitude of practices and an interplay of multiple pathways; (2) Despite this local differentiation, there is a kind of convergence in the US around imperatives of schools to impart global readiness. This section discusses each of these points and the implications.

First, internationalisation of higher education has repeatedly favoured comprehensive internationalisation, considered the ideal model of marrying 'at home' and 'abroad' approaches (Knight, 2008). For example, comprehensive internationalisation emphasizes combining globally-relevant curriculum and pedagogy, a global ethos of inclusion and belonging, and global experiences (de Wit & Engel, 2015; Helms & Brajkovic, 2017; Hudzik, 2011). Yet, in the US school system there is little coherency in internationalisation. From North Carolina's state-wide focus on professional development resources and global-ready frameworks, to Illinois' recent launch of a formal diploma recognition, to the wide-ranging internationalisation approach of Washington, DC, targeting schools and cross-district initiatives, there is no 'one size fits all' to US internationalisation.

Yet, demarcating the internationalisation pathways in these three contexts had much to do with the interplay of different stakeholders and networks, both horizontal and vertical. One common sub-national lever of internationalisation was a 'champion' stakeholder, a person with the power and capacity to leverage change and the commitment to global forms of education. In the case of Illinois, a network of educators spurred a grassroots state-wide movement. In North Carolina, global education leadership came first from a motivated leader of the State Board of Education and then devolved to an engaged state-level administrator. In DC, long-standing programs, such as Embassy Adoption, were re-energized by a Chancellor's establishment of a Global Education unit to focus on equitable access to both 'at home' and 'abroad' internationalisation, particularly for lower income students of colour. Additionally, vertical, horizontal, and multi-scalar networks of champions were frequently formed of different stakeholders, including the business community, schools and districts, non-profit organisations, philanthropic organisations, and the higher education community.

In some sense, these examples of internationalisation may suggest the critical roles that local districts and states play in the development of 'systems-level' internationalisation in the US. In the current America First political landscape, in which terms like global citizenship can be highly politicised (Engel & Siczek, 2017), local actors may perhaps be the leading policy agents able to leverage internationalisation initiatives in ways that the federal government, both structurally, but also politically, is unable to do. This finding suggests that within a single system, governments can promote internationalisation while also simultaneously focusing on more nationalist-oriented policies. Given the autonomy held by local and state levels, it also suggests that there is considerable policy space to develop models of internationalisation that are less instrumentalist, more locally bound, and more equitable or inclusive.

Our second main argument relates to the convergence in the ways in which global competence and global readiness are positioned as positive features of certain public school systems. In the chaotic US educational marketplace, excellent schools are a key component to attracting elite individuals to live and pay taxes in certain areas. For the most part, US school attendance zones are based on residency. Therefore, having 'good' schools affects the whole community. Elite individuals with financial means tend to move to these places, property values increase, and along with them property taxes paid to the locality. Having a school district highlighted as outstanding is one way to grow and develop a community (Dhar & Ross, 2012; Mathur, 2017). Therefore, it is well worth the while of districts and schools to invest in ways that will make them seem more desirable. This is one reason why a designation such as 'global-ready' can become so important.

Undoubtedly, pragmatic, skills-based orientations assist in mobilising internationalisation, including in spaces that politically may resist the idea of international education in public schooling. However, featuring global readiness may in fact prioritise individual social mobility—the strategic cosmopolitan (Mitchell, 2003)—over other purposes of schooling as a civic good. In an increasingly divided and diversifying US society, preparing students to participate in creating a more democratic, peaceful, and inclusive society at home and abroad is essential. However, the attractiveness of global readiness, as both a student and school designation, may in fact result in fostering elitism and inequality in an already unequal US education space. International education already reflects the existing socio-economic and racial gaps within the US, therefore new initiatives in internationalisation are required which foster greater equity of access to global learning opportunities (Engel, 2017). To that end, there is much to learn from the equity-focused approach to internation-alisation in the case of DC Public Schools. Public schools in DC repre-sent a magnified context of the larger US struggle with unequal access to educational opportunities. Yet in DC, internationalisation is purposefully facilitated to leverage greater equity of access of marginalised and minor-itised students to valuable global learning opportunities, thereby provid-ing opportunities to develop global perspectives to a wider swath of the student population and shifting the narrative of who can and ought to become a global citizen.

Acknowledgements

This chapter was adapted from Engel's (2019) article published in *Pol-icy Futures in Education*, titled Pathways of Internationalization in US Schooling: Local Innovations in Inclusive Global Education, and from an Education Week blog post authored by Laura C. Engel, Heidi Gibson, and Kayla Gatalica. We wish to thank the National Geographic Society and members of the K12 Global Forum for their insights and perspectives on internationalisation of US schools.

Note

1. https://dcps.dc.gov/page/dcps-glance-enrollment

References

Aguiar, A., & Nogueira, M. (2012). Internationalisation strategies of Brazil-ian private schools. *International Studies in Sociology of Education*, 22(4), 353–368.

Auld, E., & Morris, P. (2019). Science by streetlight and the OECD's measure of global competence: A new yardstick for internationalisation? *Policy Futures in Education*, 17(6), 677–698.

Cantu, M. P. (2013). Three effective strategies of internationalization in American universities. *Journal of International Education and Leadership*, 3(3), 1–12.

Committee for Economic Development. (2006). *Education for global leadership: The importance of international studies and foreign language education for US economic and national security*. Retrieved from www.ced.org/pdf/Education-for-Global-Leadership.pdf (accessed 20 October 2018).

Council on Foreign Relations. (2012). *US education reform and national secu-rity*. Report, Washington, DC: Council on Foreign Relations Press.

DCPS. (2017). *Global education year in review, 2016–2017*. Retrieved from https://static1squarespacecom/static/5672c707e0327c81fa94fa8b/t/59971320 3e00be99dedb3e3b/1503073059358/DCPS+Global+Ed+2016_2017compress edpdf (accessed 19 October 2018).

DCPS (n.d.-a). DCPS global education. Retrieved 19 October 2018, from https://dcpsglobaledorg/.

DCPS (n.d.-b). Embassy adoption program. Retrieved 17 October 2018, from https://dcpsdcgov/page/embassy-adoption-program.

DCPS (n.d.-c). Global education: Embassy adoption program. Retrieved 19 October 2018, from https://dcpsglobaledorg/eap/.

DCPS (n.d.-d). Global education: International food days. Retrieved 17 October 2018, from https://dcpsglobaledorg/international-food-days/.de Wit, H., & Engel, L. C. (2015). Building and deepening a comprehensive strategy to internationalise Romanian higher education. In J. Salmi, E. Egron-Polak, R. Pricopie, A. Curaj, & L. Deca (Eds.), *Romania: Between the Bologna process and national challenges/priorities* (pp. 191–204). New York: Springer.

de Wit, H., & Jones, E. (2018). Inclusive internationalization: Improving equity and access. *International Higher Education, 94*, 16–18.

Dhar, P., & Ross, S. L. (2012). School district quality and property values: Examining differences along school district boundaries. *Journal of Urban Economic, 71*(1), 18–25.

Engel, L. C. (2014). Citizenship education and national (re)formations: Reflections from Spain. *Education, Citizenship, and Social Justice, 9*(3), 239–254.

Engel, L. C. (2017). *Underrepresented students in study abroad: Investigating impacts.* Report, Washington, DC: Institute of International Education.

Engel, L. C. (2019). Pathways of internationalization in US schooling: Local innovations in inclusive global education. *Policy Futures in International Education, 17*(6), 699–714.

Engel, L. C., & Olden, K. (2012). One size fits all: Globalization and standardization of US education. In B. Shaklee & S. Bailey (Eds.), *Internationalizing teacher education* (pp. 77–92). Lanham, MD: Rowman and Littlefield.

Engel, L. C., Fundalinski, J., & Cannon, T. (2016). Global citizenship education at a local level: A comparative analysis of four U.S. urban districts. *Revista de Educación Comparativa Española* [Journal of Spanish Comparative Education], *28*, 23–51.

Engel, L. C., Rutkowski, D., & Thompson, G. (2019). Toward an international measure of global competence? A critical look at the PISA 2018 framework. *Globalisation, Societies and Education, 17*(2), 117–131.

Engel, L. C., & Siczek, M. (2017). A cross-national comparison of international strategies: National competitiveness or global citizenship? *Compare: A Journal of Comparative Education, 48*(5), 749–767.

Engel, L. C., & Siczek, M. (2018). Framing global education in the United States: Policy perspectives. In L. D. Hill & F. J. Levine (Eds.), *Global perspectives in education research* (pp. 26–47). London: Routledge.Fowler, F. C. (2004). *Policy studies for educational leaders: An introduction.* London: Pearson.

Frey, C. J., & Whitehead, D. (2009). International education policies and the boundaries of global citizenship in the US. *Journal of Curriculum Studies, 41*, 269–290.

Goren, H., & Yemini, M. (2017). The global citizenship education gap: Teacher perceptions of the relationship between global citizenship education and students' socio-economic status. *Teaching and Teacher Education, 67*, 9–22

Harris, D. N., Ladd, H. F., Smith, M. S., & West, M. R. (2016). A principled federal role in PreK-12 education. *Brookings Institution.* Retrieved 16 October 2018, from, https://wwwbrookingsedu/wp-content/uploads/2016/12/gs_20161206_principled_federal_role_browncenter1pdf

Helms, R. M., & Brajkovic, L. (2017). *Mapping internationalization on US campuses: 2017 edition.* Report, Washington, DC: American Council on Education.

Hudzik, J. (2011). *Comprehensive internationalization: From concept to action.* Report, Washington, DC: NAFSA.

Knight, J. (2008). *Higher education in turmoil: The changing world of internationalization.* Rotterdam: Sense Publishers.

Knight, J. (2015). Updating the definition of internationalization. *International Higher Education, 33,* 2–3.

Manise, J. (2018). Why states, districts, and schools should implement global certificate programs. In EdWeek Blog. Retrieved 20 October 2018, from http://blogsedweekorg/edweek/global_learning/2018/06/why_states_districts_and_schools_should_implement_global_certificate_programshtml.

Manna, P. (2011). *Collision course: Federal education policy meets State and local realities.* Washington, DC: CQ Press.

Mathur, S. (2017). The myth of 'Free' public education : Impact of school quality on house prices in the Fremont unified school district, California. *Journal of Planning Education and Research, 37*(2), 176–194. https://doi.org/10.1177/0739456X16654546

Maxwell, C., & Aggleton, P. (2016). Creating cosmopolitan subjects—The role of families and private schools in England. *Sociology, 50*(4), 780–795.

Maxwell, C., Deppe, U., Krüger, H. H., & Helsper, W. (Eds.). (2018). *Elite education and internationalisation: From the early years into higher education.* Basingstoke: Palgrave Macmillan

Mitchell, K. (2003). Educating the national citizen in neoliberal times: From the multicultural self to the strategic cosmopolitan. *Transactions of the Institute of British Geographers, 28*(4): 387–403.

National Research Council. (2007). International education and foreign languages: Keys to securing America's future, *Report of the committee to review the Title VI and Fulbright-Hayes international education programs.* Washington, DC: National Academies Press.

OECD (2018). *Preparing our youth for an inclusive and sustainable world: The OECD PISA global competence framework.* Retrieved 20 October 2018, from www.oecd.org/education/Global-competency-for-an-inclusive-world.pdf.

Ortloff, D. H., & Shonia, O. N. (2015). Teacher conceptualizations of global citizenship: Global immersion experiences and implications for the empathy/threat dialectic. In B. M. Maguth & J. Hilburn (Eds.), *The state of global education: Learning with the world and its people.* New York: Routledge, Taylor and Francis Friends Group.

Rapaport, A. (2010). We cannot teach what we don't know: Indiana teachers talk about global citizenship education. *Education, Citizenship and Social Justice, 5*(3), 179–190.

Reardon, S. F., Kalogrides, D., & Shores, K. (2016). The geography of racial/ethnic test score gaps. CEPA Working Paper No 16–10: Stanford Center for Education Policy Analysis. Retrieved 9 August 2018, from http://cepastanfordedu/wp16-10.

Savage, G., & O'Conner, K. (2015). National agendas in global times: Curriculum reforms in Australia and the USA since the 1980s. *Journal of Education Policy, 30*(5), 609–630.

The State Board of Education of North Carolina. (2013). Preparing Students for the World: Final Report of the State Board of Education ' s Task Force on Global Education, (January). Retrieved from www.ncpublicschools.org/docs/globaled/final-report.pdf

Torres, C. A. (2015). Solidarity and competitiveness in a global context: Comparable concepts in global citizenship education? *The International Education Journal: Comparative Perspectives, 14*(2), 22–29.

UNESCO. (2015). *Global citizenship education: Topics and learning objectives.* Paris: UNESCO.

US Department of Education. (2018). *Succeeding globally through international education and engagement.* Report, Washington, DC: US Department of Education.

US Department of Education (2019). *Status and trends in the education of racial and ethnic groups 2018.* Retrieved from https://nces.ed.gov/pubs2019/2019038.pdf

US Department of Education. (n.d.). *Illinois demographics, 2016–17.* Retrieved from www.nationsreportcard.gov/profiles/stateprofile/overview/IL?cti=PgTab_Demographics&chort=1&sub=MAT&sj=IL&fs=Grade&st=MN&year=2017R3&sg=Gender%3A+Male+vs.+Female&sgv=Difference&ts=Single+Year&tss=2015R3–2017R3&sfj=NP

Wallner, J., Savage, G., Hartong, S., & Engel, L. C. (2018). *Laboratories, co-producers and venues: Illuminating the varying roles of subnational governments in the formation of standards-based assessments in federations.* Paper presented at the Comparative and International Education Society, Mexico City, Mexico.

Weenink, D. (2008). Cosmopolitanism as a form of capital: Parents preparing their children for a globalizing world. *Sociology, 42,* 1089–1106.

Yemini, M. (2012). Internationalization assessment in schools: Theoretical contributions and practical implications. *Journal of Research in International Education, 11*(2), 152–164.

Yemini, M. (2014). Internationalization of secondary education— Lessons from Israeli Palestinian-Arab schools in Tel Aviv-Jaffa. *Urban Education, 49*(5), 471–498.

Yemini, M., & Fulop, A. (2015). The international, global and intercultural dimensions in schools: An analysis of four internationalised Israeli schools. *Globalisation, Societies and Education, 13*(4), 528–552.

5 The Pull and Push Forces in the Internationalization of Education in Russia

Katerina Bodovski and
Ruxandra Apostolescu

A Historical Overview of Internationalization in Russia

The pull and push forces in relation to internationalization in Russia go back to the philosophical debates of the mid-19th century between those who wanted Russia to adopt Western ideas and enjoy the fruits of Western civilization (called 'Westerners' or 'zapadniki'), and those who emphasized the unique Russian way and the special place of Russia in the world ('Slavophiles' or 'slavjanofily'). In his analysis of Russian education during the nineteenth and twentieth centuries, Robert Harris argued that since Peter the Great, the educational system in Russia has been driven by national defence interests, as well as economic advancement needs, which were necessary to support a competitive military machine (Harris, 2010, p. 18). At each critical historical point, Russia was opening itself up to Western ideas as long as they served a military purpose. The curriculum was heavily focused on science and engineering, whereas humanities, social and political studies were largely marginalized. An advancement in mathematics, science and engineering was tightly connected to the State's goals, and the regime dictated and controlled 'who was allowed to access education and in what manner learning should take place' (Harris, 2010, p. 19). Yet, this created a contradiction because the advancement in science requires critical and creative thinking; however, the State wanted to prevent any questioning of the regime. Harris wrote that

> Unswerving loyalty of Russian subjects to the leadership, and reconciliation with the order of society was in part predicated on a minimum of critical thinking and ignorance of other options, especially the liberal democratic political structures of Western Europe. The chronic and irresolvable tension between the necessity to establish a robust international strategic defense policy while preventing the growth of internal questioning and dissent would continue to hold throughout the history of Russian education in the nineteenth and twentieth centuries.
>
> (Harris, 2010, p. 18)

Russian intellectuals have been acutely aware of this contradiction for the last 200 years. One of the most influential Russian philosophers of the 19th century, Peter (Pyotr) Chaadaev wrote in 1829: 'We are neither from the West nor the East, nor do we possess either of their traditions. We are situated, as it were, outside of time, and the universal education of humanity has not reached us'. Interestingly, while the Communist Revolution of 1917 did question and dramatically change the social order of the Russian Empire, once the new social order was established, education was once again used to legitimize the (new) State regime, to keep citizens in order and to advance only those fields directly related to the defence machine. Both the tsarist regime and the Soviet (and, one may argue, the post-Soviet) government maintained control over teachers, curricula and access to educational institutions 'as political instruments to maintain social conformity, to ensure loyalty to ruler and state and to manage modest conservative change, even while increasing numbers of students entering the educational system' (Harris, 2010, p. 39). Thus, there are strong forces in place pushing towards the nationally oriented, State-centred education system.

Such tendencies are only complicated by the fact that, historically, Russia has had strong ties with European culture. Specifically, Germany and France have had a tremendous cultural influence in Russia in general, and on the establishment of its educational system in particular. For example, Russian education has been influenced by the German model since its inception, and these connections go as far back in history as the 18th century. Similarly, the French language, culture and literature has been widely celebrated in Russia—from 1741, due to its association with ideas of progress and European-ness (that were widely, if selectively, welcomed by the nobility)—and its status was well preserved until the Revolution of 1917. In fact the Russian aristocracy used French as their main language of communication throughout the 18th and the first half of 19th century, with Russian language having an inferior status (Offord, Ryazanova-Clarke, Rjéoutski, & Argent, 2015).

Ideological roots of internationalization during the Soviet era were marked by the idea of a world-wide proletarian revolution, which the Soviet leaders hoped would transpire after the Russian revolution (Pevzner, Rakhkochkine, Shirin, & Shaydorova, 2019). When this did not happen, discourse in the 1940s and 1950s swung in the opposite direction, with campaigns against 'rootless cosmopolitanism' and accusations against the intelligentsia for 'kneeling before the West' (Pevzner et al., 2019, p. 3). In the 1960s–1980s, international activities were reintroduced in the form of various student exchanges, youth festivals and the club of international friendship. Those activities mainly involved youth from other socialist countries.

From the standpoint of internationalization, the Soviet Union did not feel isolated on the international arena, in fact it considered itself the leader for education, science and technology, especially across the socialist world. Given the highly centralized education system in the USSR, the school curriculum (textbooks, standards, exams) were prescribed throughout the Soviet Union. The Ministries of Education in the Soviet republics had some influence, particularly in languages and arts, but a significant part of educational provision needed Moscow's approval. The Russian language held special status, becoming in 1938 a mandatory language of instruction across all Soviet republics: 'The Russian language became lingua franca of inter-ethnic communication and understanding in the Soviet Union. After World War II the Russian language became the dominant foreign language in schools in Eastern European countries' (Pevzner et al., 2019, p. 4). Furthermore, many Soviet universities had students from other communist countries in Eastern and Central Europe, as well as from Latin America, Africa and the Middle East (Charon-Cardona, 2013).

Given this historical background, we aim to shed light on the situation around 'internationalization' today in Russia, 25 years after the collapse of the Soviet Union. We think of internationalization as a process of customizing a toolkit of ideas and values that are defined as progressive and/or global (such as human rights, gender equality, civic engagement, democratic leadership, sustainability), as well as facilitating connections to, and relationships with, educational institutions and educators and policy makers from other countries. This definition captures the processes of internationalization we observe in Russia today. Russia desires an equal player status in the international arena, including regaining its strength in science and education (Kapuza, Kersha, Zakharov, & Khavenson, 2017). The Russian National Research universities are encouraged to participate in cutting-edge knowledge production, to attend international conferences and publish in the international journals. Russia participated in the Bologna process aimed at standardizing the higher education curriculum in order to facilitate a cross-national exchange of students and credentials, and is cultivating its position as an educational destination for international students (albeit most come from the former Soviet republics) (Chankseliani, 2015, 2018). Moreover, Russian policy makers in the education field are concerned with Russian student performance in flagship international assessments, such as Trends in International Mathematics and Science Study (TIMSS), Program for International Student Assessment (PISA), and Progress in International Reading Literacy Study (PIRLS), seen to be driving curriculum changes (Kapuza et al., 2017). However, recent political events, such as the annexation of Crimea and the subsequent violent conflict in Eastern Ukraine, have led to the imposition of international sanctions against Russia, to which Russia has responded with placing sanctions on the West. Thus there are multiple, often contradictory factors defining Russia's relationship with 'the outside', in particular 'the West', which directly or indirectly shape (or restrict) the ways in which education system may welcome internationalization.

The developments described previously are reflected in the history textbooks of different periods. In their analysis of the Russian and Soviet history textbooks, Tsyrlina-Spady and Lovorn (2015) note that while the Soviet textbooks presented 'noble government, wholesome people and glorious military past' (p. 54), the textbooks of the 1990s allowed for a more nuanced picture 'showcasing failed or 'less than noble' policies and actions' (p. 54). However, the textbooks of Putin's era returned to the language of the Cold War, emphasizing patriotism and national identity and refraining from any critical analysis of the events. Analysing the two latest history textbooks, published in 2016 for grade 10, Tsyrlina-Spady and Stoskopf (2017) note that Stalin and Putin are depicted using the rhetoric of *savior, unifier* and *leader* (p. 19).

> When Stalin and Putin are portrayed as hero-leaders, they are turned into mythic monuments, as if they were fated to revive the Russian religious spirit, restore the country's military and cultural glory, protect the nation from internal and external enemies, and secure the physical health of its people. The size and significance of these heroic goals and the hubris of national pride justifies any crime against individuals and groups in order to protect the greater public good; this is one of the most important ideological messages conveyed to students.
>
> (p. 29)

History teachers of the Soviet period had a relatively clear task of depicting everything pre-Soviet in negative terms, emphasizing oppression and inequality, while the Soviet era represented freedom and equality. Today, in the post-socialist context, reconciling tsarist and Soviet legacies requires an extensive use of common themes based on national/ist narratives, emphasizing yet again 'us versus them' rhetoric. In the words of the Russian President, Vladimir Putin in 2012 (quoted in Tsyrlina-Spady & Lovorn, 2015, p. 45):

> We should build our future on a solid foundation. And this foundation is patriotism. . . . It is a respect towards our history and traditions, spiritual values of our peoples, our thousand years' long culture and a unique experience of the coexistence of hundreds of peoples and languages on the territory of Russia. . . . A feeling of patriotism, a system of values, moral orientations have their foundation laid in one's childhood and youth. . . . The role of the family and the state is enormous, as well as the educational and cultural policy of the state.

Studies of education in post-socialist spaces reveal the coexistence of multiple, open-ended, often contradictory narratives (Silova, 2009).

Countries previously part of the Soviet system have not necessarily 'adopted' Western, neoliberal discourses that emphasize the benefits of globalization, entrepreneurialism, multiculturalism or problem-solving (Mead & Silova, 2013). Analysing the elementary school textbooks (bukvari) in Ukraine and Latvia during the Soviet times (published in the 1980s) and after the dissolution of the USSR (published during the 1990s and 2000s), Mead and Silova (2013) found significant continuity between Soviet and post-Soviet narratives in their emphasis on national language and history, vastness of nature in the native land, and emphasis on homogenous local space, rather than being a part of the global, multicultural community. Thinking broadly about the education processes in the post-socialist space, Chankseliani and Silova (2018) point out that 'national education systems and practices have shown considerable path dependence, with teachers continuing to teach and leaders continuing to lead the same way they used to do in the Soviet times' (Chankseliani & Silova, 2018, p. 9).

Moreover, the context for internationalization of education is significantly complicated by the 'deliberate marriage between the neoliberal paradigm and democratic ideals' (Chankseliani & Silova, 2018, p. 12). Socialist/Soviet policies based on understanding of education as a public good, equal access to education being the responsibility of the State and the emphasis on moral and social dimensions of education, clash with neoliberal policies, with their emphasis on marketization of education, individual benefits and emphasis on skills and knowledge. As such, not only do strong push and pull forces exist in Russia for its relationship with the 'outside' ideas, but also those ideas are multi-dimensional (market forces and neoliberal policies versus democracy, human rights and civic engagement). In the next section, we propose a theoretical model that is more suitable to capture those nuances in the specific context of Russia.

Proposing a New Theoretical Framework

Is there truly a contradiction between preserving a set of unique 'Russian' values through education, with opening up classrooms to the world? How can an educational system prepare students to be active participants in the world community (through trade, market competition, production, etc.) and yet remain politically isolated? These questions do not just pertain to Russian education. Engel and Siczek (2017) found that even in highly developed, English-medium contexts (US, Australia, Canada and Ireland), discourses of global citizenship and internationalization are largely nation-centric, emphasizing national prosperity and economic growth. In its 175th anniversary issue, *The Economist* published an essay called 'A Manifesto for Renewing Liberalism' saying 'the once barely-questioned link between economic progress and liberal democracy is being severely put to the test' (*The Economist*, 2018, p. 46). This statement shows a potential for de-coupling of the pragmatic or economic aspect of progress from the ideological/political one. The same de-coupling can be applied to understandings of internationalization processes, separating its pragmatic, cultural and political aspects.

Pevzner et al. (2019) proposed the following typology of schools with an international profile in Russia: the global competitiveness type, the human-oriented type, and the language-oriented type.

> Schools of the *global competitiveness type* prepare pupils to be competitive in the globalized society and job market. They introduce an international dimension into study process, using world best practices, participating in joint educational programs and projects, and pay attention to the international standards of quality assessment.
>
> (Pevzner et al., 2019, p. 8)

The second, *human-oriented type*, has the goals of self-development of young people, as well as preparation for their role as citizens in democratic society. The third type is *bilingual schools* or schools with advanced study of foreign languages.

While this typology is useful to describe and understand the working of specific schools, we argue that there is a need to look broadly at the dimensions of internationalization that may co-exist within a specific school or be found across various educational spaces. The current Russian context in which an agreement to internationalize and openness to global forces is fluid and at times ambiguous requires a model that allows such analytical flexibility. Specifically, we propose a model consisting of three dimensions:

(a) **pragmatic dimension** (knowledge, skills, international compatibility of credentials);
(b) **cultural dimension** (borrowing specific content/features from another culture); and
(c) **political dimension** (allowing exchange with a variety of values, beliefs and political/ideological elements).

The pragmatic dimension in our framework corresponds to the 'global competitiveness type' in Pevzner et al.'s (2019) model, focusing on skills and competencies required in the global economy, and the transferability of credentials and diplomas. The language oriented schools in Pevzner et al.'s (2019) typology would fit with both the pragmatic and cultural dimensions in our framework. Foreign language skills may serve as an important tool for pursuing further education abroad and as an instrumental skill in the global job market, as well as representing mastery of cultural knowledge and fluency. The human-oriented type defined by

Pevzner et al.'s model would include all three of the dimensions of our model—pragmatic, cultural and political—allowing for the development of the whole student, including their cognitive, social and emotional needs, as well as preparing them for the role of a global citizen and an active participant in their country's affairs.

Internationalization of education is a multifaceted process. Multi-dimensionality of internationalization allows the actors involved to negotiate its different aspects separately, for instance decoupling political/ideological and cultural dimensions. Given the aforementioned history of Russian 'European-ness', Russian education and educators may be more open to cultural forms of internationalization, such as learning foreign languages, student exchanges, etc. On the other hand, ideas that carry ideological weight (for instance, democratic leadership, human rights, and LGBTQA issues) may not be as welcome. Our model allows for a possibility for *selective internationalization*, a process in which certain aspects of the education system are open to and integrated with the 'borrowed' ideas while other aspects are preserved within the firm national framework. Our model is useful for understanding other post-socialist contexts in which the inheritance of communist past, a unique national character and so-called Western ideas coexist in everyday classroom experience. In the next two sections we will illustrate our model both quantitatively—using a descriptive analysis of the data from two waves of the World Values Survey—and qualitatively, showcasing the examples of two elite private schools in Moscow.

Quantitative Illustration of Internationalization

The data from waves two (1990–1994) and six (2010–2014) of the World Values Survey illustrate the cultural macro context in Russia. The World Values Survey is the largest non-commercial repeated cross-sectional survey of values and attitudes of adults in countries around the world. It is a great source of information on attitudes towards a number of social issues and phenomena, such as globalization, gender equality, environmental protection, and civic participation, as well as attitudes towards raising children. Russia participated in wave two of the survey in 1990 and this information provides an important baseline on the Russian Federation at the very end of the Soviet era. We also analyse the data from wave six and compare it to the data on the US and Germany (as a reference point).[1] The respondents' attitudes regarding the environmental issues, global citizenship and democracy provide a backdrop for the understanding of the processes within the education system (what is allowed in the curriculum, what is assessed, which ideas and topics are promoted). In other words, the data illustrate what cultural and political values are accepted within a society at a particular point in time so that they can be incorporated in the educational process. That being said, the survey findings cannot provide the evidence that these ideas are, in fact, integrated in the education system. Future studies will need to examine that.

Table 5.1 shows the Russian respondents' attitudes towards a number of issues in 1990. Forty-six percent agreed that government should reduce environmental pollution, 71% disagreed or strongly disagreed that all talk about environment makes people more anxious, and 84% disagreed or strongly disagreed that protecting environment and fighting pollution is less urgent than suggested. Ninety-five percent of the respondents approved of the ecology movement or nature protection groups, 90% approved of the human rights movement and 81% approved of the women's movement. These numbers show that on the eve of the dissolution of the Soviet Union, Russian citizens held values largely compatible with those in the Western countries and were open to the topics that are associated with global citizenship education, such as environmental issues, human rights and women's rights.

According to the data from wave six of the World Values Survey, in 2011 56% of the respondents in Russia agreed that protecting the environment should be given priority even at the expense of economic growth. It is a larger proportion than in Germany (49%) or the US (39%). Eighty percent of Russian respondents thought that having a democratic political system is good or fairly good, a compatible number with 82% in US and 96% in Germany. Only 42% in Russia felt that there is enough respect for individual human rights in the country, as opposed to 62% in the US and 86% in Germany. Fifty-one percent of Russian citizens see themselves as world citizens, compared to 62% in Germany and 69% in the US. Only half of Russian respondents strongly disagreed or disagreed that the only acceptable religion is their religion (61% in Germany, 77% in the US). Thirty-seven percent of Russian respondents trust people of another nationality or another religion (52% and 50%, respectively, in Germany; 66% and 69% in the US).

Table 5.1 Attitudes of the respondents in Russia, World Value Survey, wave two

Survey Question	%
Government should reduce environmental pollution (% of the respondents who agree or strongly agree)	46
All talk about the environment makes people anxious (% of the respondents who disagree or strongly disagree)	71
Protecting environment and fighting pollution is less urgent than suggested (% of the respondents who disagree or strongly disagree)	84
Approval of the ecology movement or nature protection group (%)	95
Approval of the human rights movement (%)	90
Approval of the women's movement (%)	81
N = 1,961	

Table 5.2 Attitudes of the respondents in Russia, Germany and the US, World Value Survey, wave six

Survey Questions	Russia	Germany	US
Protecting the environment should be given priority, even if it causes slower economic growth and some loss of jobs (% of the respondents who agree or strongly agree)	56	49	38
Having a democratic political system is very good or fairly good (% of the respondents who agree or strongly agree)	80	96	82
How much respect is there for individual human rights? (% of the respondents who said a great deal or some respect)	42	86	62
I see myself as a world citizen (% of the respondents who agree or strongly agree)	51	62	69
The only acceptable religion is my religion (% of the respondents who disagree or strongly disagree)	50	61	77
How much do you trust people of another nationality? (% of the respondents who trust completely or somewhat)	37	52	66
How much do you trust people of another religion? (% of the respondents who trust completely or somewhat)	37	50	69
N	2,109	1,967	2,171

These data support our proposed framework in the sense that pragmatic aspects of globalization (such as environmental issues) may be acceptable to the larger population, whereas political aspects (such as being a world citizen or trusting people of another religion or nationality) seem to be less internalized. Given the highly centralised nature of Russian education and the current political environment, characterised by strong nationalist discourse and rather antagonistic relationship with the Western countries (specifically, the US and the EU), it seems unlikely that the educational realm would welcome aspects of globalization (such as the emphasis on human rights, democratic participation and civic engagement) that would affect or be perceived as threatening to the ideological or political foundations of the country. At the same time, it seems plausible that the cultural dimension remains fairly open to internationalization. For instance, learning foreign languages or learning about other countries' histories or traditions is quite welcome.

Similarly, as it has been throughout the last 200 years of Russian history and may have only intensified in the last twenty-five years, the pragmatic dimension of internationalization is thriving. Russian educators are concerned with preparing a competitive and knowledgeable labour force, making sure that students in Russian schools are exposed to the same content as their counterparts in other developed countries, partly due to the visibility of the international large-scale assessments. In fact, the Russian government has been paying particular attention to the state of education from the very beginning of its independence after the collapse of the Soviet Union. The legal tools that guide education in post-Soviet Russia are the Constitution of the Russian Federation (1993), the Law on Education (1992 as amended 1996), the Law on Higher Education (1996), the National Doctrine on Education (2000), the Federal Program for the Development of Education (2000), the Federal Program for the Development of Education for 2006–2010 (2005) and National Priority Project Education (2005) (Smolentceva, 2007). In 2008, the Russian government issued a *Concept of long-term socio-economic development of the Russian Federation for the period up to 2020* that declared a crucial role of education in making the economy competitive by developing intellectual and creative abilities of the citizens (Smolentceva, 2017, p. 1100).

Further supporting a commitment to the pragmatic dimension of internationalization in Russia is the consistent participation of the country in all waves of TIMSS (1995–2015) and PISA (2000–2018). Russian students, both fourth and eighth graders, have been performing consistently well on TIMSS, scoring among the top ten countries, well above the international average in math and science.[2] However, the Russian 15-year-olds have consistently performed less well—slightly below the international average—on PISA.[3] TIMSS questionnaires are primarily measuring students' performance in relation to math and science curriculum, whereas PISA is more concerned with the application of knowledge to real life situations and problem solving. Kapuza et al. (2017) examined the trends in academic achievement of Russian students from different backgrounds between 2000 and 2015, using both TIMSS and PISA data. The authors then interviewed the experts and policy makers to make sense of the findings, including supposed stagnation of the academic achievement, particularly for science. The authors and their interviewees agreed that the challenge is to innovate the educational system in a way that allows its graduates to become professionals with the abilities to implement their knowledge and skills in new situations and remain open to learning in the ever-evolving and changing world economy. As such, the pragmatic aspect of internationalization has been evident in the policy discussions of education in Russia.

Qualitative Illustration of Internationalization in Russia

In this section, we will take a brief look at the two elite schools in Moscow[4] and will demonstrate how different aspects of internationalization from our proposed theoretical framework come to play in these specific contexts. The benefit of our model is in its capacity to allow for varying engagements with different dimensions of internationalization. The ways these programs are advertised reflect the 'cosmopolitan tastes and knowledge' that 'serve as symbolic capital in elite competitive games of distinction' (Yemini, 2014, p. 473).

The first school is called Zolotoe Sechenie[5] (Golden Ratio or Golden Section); the title referring to an ideal or divine proportion, a concept in mathematics that has been found in nature, art and sciences. This private school was founded in 1992. The website states that the mission of the school is to 'raise a socially responsible generation and to develop in the students all types of intellect, including social, emotional and practical' (www.theschool. ru/about_school/mission/). The mission statement asserts that Zolotoe Sechenie is a school of multicultural communication, with the emphasis on various international exchange programs with schools and universities both in the US and Europe. Further, the curriculum requires every student to learn English and a second foreign language. The main page contains links to various recent events. One such event is a Thanksgiving Day celebration where the elementary school students discussed the traditions and history of this American holiday. The video depicted various activities that featured the map of the US, the traditional Thanksgiving dishes, and children participating in the 'festival of gratitude'. Furthermore, the school website has a section in which they display the list of graduates and the institutions of higher education to which they matriculated. Among the graduates of 2015, 11 students went on to study at the European or American colleges and universities (two students in 2016, 3 in 2017 and 6 in 2018).

Our second school example is School Letovo,[6] a private school founded in 2017. School Letovo is a boarding school that attracts the brightest students from different regions of the country starting in seventh grade. The school statement declares that the school mission is 'to provide an enabling environment for bright and motivated students to achieve their intellectual and creative potential' (https://en.letovo.ru/about-us/our-mission/). It further elaborates:

> We seek to create a school in which each child will want to grow, achieve high academic, creative and sports results, communicate, be friends and just live while retaining strong Russian educational and cultural traditions. In Letovo we implement state of the art practices offered by top schools globally while retaining the best of established tradition. The best Russian and foreign teachers work on our educational programs. . . . They will develop strong moral principles and become leaders with a deep sense of responsibility towards their nation and the world.

The advertised school model includes skills, knowledge and activities, making sure that every student receives a solid academic training combined with rich and enjoyable extra-curricular participation. The Letovo is currently a candidate school with International Baccalaureate Organization (IBO) for the Diploma Programme and Middle Year Programme. The website asserts that the students wishing to continue their education in the US universities will be prepared for the advanced placement (AP) exams and SATs. In addition to strong academic emphasis, the school celebrates various extra-curricular pursuits of their pupils, including music, dance, theatre and sports. Under the news and events section, the website features a theatre performance based on the novel by British writer David Almond, traditional Spanish Christmas songs and dances, and 'Christmas Jumper Day' following British holiday tradition (not to be confused with the American 'Ugly Christmas Sweater Day').

Both schools' websites provide an illustration of our theoretical framework. The pragmatic aspect of internationalization is clearly welcome in both schools. Both websites advertise the internationally recognised teaching methods and curriculum, and both emphasize learning foreign languages, in particular English. Letovo goes as far as to try and establish the infrastructure for their pupils to prepare for IB and AP exams, thus facilitating their transition to the institutions of higher education in Europe and the US. Zolotoe Sechenie specifically features the post-secondary placements of their graduates, including the ones who go abroad. Similarly, the cultural aspect of internationalization is embedded in both schools as well. Zolotoe Sechenie declares itself as a school of multicultural communication and provides its students with the opportunities to learn about and to practice other cultural traditions (an example being the Thanksgiving celebration). Letovo features the news about Spanish Christmas dance and songs, a British play and Jumper Day that took place in the school, the content that is culturally borrowed and then successfully appropriated. At the same time, Letovo's website makes efforts to reassure that the school follows and retains Russian educational and cultural traditions. Neither of the schools explicitly uses the language of global citizenship or global community, nor focuses on youth participation in and preparation for democratic leadership. As such, the political aspect of internationalization is not evident in these schools.

Yemini (2014) argues that internationalization comes to schools from several directions, one of them being the expectations of the institutions of higher education for globally and internationally fluent applicants. This is consistent with our findings since both schools' websites emphasize the multicultural content and possibilities of continuation of students' education abroad. Further, Yemini and Fulop (2015, p. 536) commented on 'pragmatic versus ideological motives' to internationalize schools. Several principals in their study commented on practical aspects of internationalization such as the image of the graduates, creating a competitive edge, enabling the students to take part in international delegations, conferences and other extra-curricular activities. On the other hand, one of the principals in their study understood internationalization

as 'a cultural tool that helps expand students' horizons and enables introduction of 'the other' (Yemini & Fulop, 2015, p. 537). The respondents
also discussed the recognition they receive for their efforts to internationalize their schools, as well as the fact that internationalization is helpful
for marketing and branding. Yemini and Fulop (2015) write:

> All schools studied exploit their international and intercultural
> dimension for marketing and branding purposes to attract potential
> candidates, to the extent that the stress placed on marketing and
> branding the school as internationalized to attract future students
> and their parents seems to outweigh any real pedagogical value the
> students can receive from internationalization activities.
>
> (p. 538)

Given the current political climate in Russia, it would be interesting to
explore whether the content found in these two elite private schools
spreads to other schools and whether international and intercultural
dimension serves to attract new students.

Conclusion

In this chapter we provided a brief historical account of internationalization in pre-Soviet, Soviet and post-Soviet Russia. We highlighted the pull
and push forces towards 'the global', while proposing a new theoretical
framework of internationalization that distinguishes between pragmatic,
cultural and political dimensions. Our model allows for a possibility of
selective internationalization, a process in which certain aspects of the
education system are open to the 'outside' ideas while others are not. Our
model is useful for understanding other post-socialist contexts in which
the inheritance of communist past, a unique national character and so-
called Western ideas coexist in everyday classroom experience.

We illustrated our theoretical framework both quantitatively—using
a descriptive analysis of the data from two waves of the World Values
Survey—and qualitatively, showcasing the examples of two elite private
schools in Moscow. Indeed, we found that while pragmatic and cultural
dimensions of internationalization are present in the larger discourse,
as well as in the deeply rooted understanding of elite (or high) culture
in Russia, the political aspect is much rarer. These findings highlight
the multidimensionality of internationalization and the need for more
nuanced approaches to measuring the 'global' in the educational realm.

Kelly (2007) finished her seminal work on childhood in Russia by
commenting on the profound sense of difference that was 'imparted by
growing up in a culture where separateness from other nation-states was
always emphasized . . . by insistent use of 'there' and 'here' oppositions
in the literature, art, and propaganda that a child encountered from the

nursery onwards' (p. 598). Echoing similar sentiments, Laruelle (2016) called Russia an 'anti-Western European civilization', and writes that with 'the West' becoming increasingly assimilated to liberalism (political, economic and moral), conservatism is seen as another way of formulating Russia's status as the other Europe, the one that does not follow the Western path of development' (p. 293). The idea of national exceptionalism is philosophically in opposition to the idea of being part of a global community—of cooperation and exchange. It remains to be seen how Russian parents, students and schools will negotiate and reconcile the unique values that have historically characterized the Russian society and culture with the demands and realities of the 21st century.

Notes

1. Russia and the US were surveyed in 2011, Germany in 2013.
2. https://nces.ed.gov/timss/
3. https://nces.ed.gov/surveys/pisa/
4. There is a handful of unique private schools that have been created around a specific idea/philosophy (science/math, languages, a certain pedagogical approach) after the collapse of the Soviet Union. These two schools are great examples that showcase our model.
5. www.theschool.ru/
6. https://letovo.ru/

References

Chankseliani, M., (2015). Escaping homelands with limited employment and tertiary education opportunities: Outbound student mobility from post-Soviet countries. *Population Space Place*, 22(3), 301–316.

Chankseliani, M., (2018). The politics of student mobility: Links between outbound student flows and the democratic development of post-Soviet Eurasia. *International Journal of Educational Development*, 62, 281–288.

Chankseliani, M., & Silova, I. (Eds.). (2018). *Comparing post-socialist transformations. purposes, policies, and practices in education*. Oxford, UK: Oxford Studies in Comparative Education. Symposium Books.

Charon-Cardona, E. (2013). Socialism and education in Cuba and Soviet Uzbekistan. *Globalization, Societies and Education*, 11(2), 296–313.

Engel, L. C., & Megan, M. S. (2017). A cross-national comparison of international strategies: Global citizenship and the advancement of national competitiveness. *Compare: A Journal of Comparative and International Education*, 48(5), 749–767.

Harris, R. (2010). 'Society and the individual: State and private education in Russia in the 19th and 20th centuries'. In D. Johnson (Ed.), *Politics, modernization and educational reform in Russia: From past to present* (pp. 17–58). Oxford: Symposium Books.

Kapuza, A. V., Kersha, J. D., Zakharov, A. B., & Khavenson, T. E. (2017). Academic achievement and social inequality in Russia: Trends and the impact of educational policy. *Educational Studies Moscow*, 4, 10–35. (in Russian).

Kelly, C. (2007). *Children's world: Growing up in Russia, 1890–1991.* New Haven, CT: Yale University Press.

Laruelle, M. (2016). Russia as an anti- liberal European civilization. In B. Helge & K. Pål (Eds.), *The new Russian nationalism: Imperialism, ethnicity and authoritarianism, 2000–15.* Edinburgh: Edinburgh University Press.

Mead, M., & Silova, I. (2013). Literacies of (post)socialist childhood: Alternative readings of socialist upbringings and neoliberal futures. *Globalization, Societies and Education, 11*(2), 194–222.

Offord, D., Ryazanova-Clarke, L., Rjéoutski, V., & Argent, G. (Eds.). (2015). *French and Russian in imperial Russia: Language use among the Russian Elite.* Edinburgh: Edinburgh University Press.

Pevzner, M., Rakhkochkine, A., Shirin, A., & Shaydorova, N. (2019). Internationalization of schools in Russia. *Policy Futures in Education, 17*(6), 715–731.

Silova, I. (2009). 'Varieties of educational transformation: The post-socialist states of Central/Southeastern Europe and the former soviet union. In R. Cowen & A. Kazamias (Eds.), *International handbook of comparative education* (pp. 295–320). Dordrecht: Springer.

Smolentceva, A. (2007). Educational inequalities in the soviet union. In R. Teese, S. Lamb, & M. Duru-Bellat (Eds.), *International studies in educational inequality, theory and policy: Inequality in education systems* (Vol. 2, pp. 143–156). New York: Springer.

Smolentceva, A. (2017). Where Soviet and neoliberal discourses meet: The transformation of the purposes of higher education in Soviet and post-Soviet Russia. *Higher Education, 74*, 1091–1108.

The Economist. (2018, September 13). *A manifesto for renewing liberalism.* Retrieved https://www.economist.com/leaders/2018/09/13/a-manifesto-for-renewing-liberalism

Tsyrlina-Spady, T., & Alan, S. (2017). Russian History Textbooks in the Putin Era: Heroic Leaders Demand Loyal Citizens. In Z. Joseph, T. Tsyrlina-Spady, & L. Michael (Eds.), *Globalization and historiography of national leaders': Symbolic representations in school textbooks.* Springer: Netherlands.

Tsyrlina-Spady, T., & Lovorn, M. (2015). Patriotism, history teaching, and history textbooks in Russia: What was old is new again. In J. Zajda (Ed.), *Globalization, ideology and politics of education reforms.* Globalization, Comparative Education and Policy Research 14, Switzerland: Springer International Publishing.

Yemini, M. (2014). Internationalization of secondary education— Lessons from Israeli Palestinian-Arab schools in Tel Aviv-Jaffa. *Urban Education, 49*(5), 471–498.

Yemini, M., & Fulop, A. (2015). The international, global and intercultural dimensions in schools: An analysis of four internationalised Israeli schools. *Globalisation, Societies and Education, 13*(4), 528–552.

6 Multiple Internationalisations

The Idiosyncratic Enactment of the International Baccalaureate in State Schools in Costa Rica, Peru and Buenos Aires

Jason Beech and Jennifer Guevara

Introduction

The influence of the International Baccalaureate (IB) has grown significantly. There are now a total of 6,311 programmes, running in 4,786 schools, across 153 different countries (as of February 2019, www.ibo. org). The most influential IB programme is the Diploma Programme (IBDP): an assessed programme for students aged 16 to 19 that focuses on students' physical, intellectual, emotional and ethical development through the study of at least two languages, several traditional academic subjects, a course on the theory of knowledge, and community service.[1] In Latin America, until recently, the IBDP could mainly be found in private schools that catered for the most affluent sectors of society. However, since the mid 2000s, the IBDP has been introduced into state schools as well in countries such as Ecuador, Peru, Costa Rica and in the City of Buenos Aires in Argentina (Bunnell, 2008; Resnik, 2016).

This chapter analyses the introduction of the IBDP in state schools across Peru, Costa Rica and the city of Buenos Aires.[2] Our analysis is based on a research project that examined the introduction of the IBDP across public schools in these educational systems (Beech, Guevara, & del Monte, 2018). Data was collected through interviews with high-ranked officials at the ministries of education and in the International Baccalaureate Organization (IBO), school principals, and teachers (61 in total); focus groups with students (1 per school, 9 in total, with 6 to 8 participating young people); document analysis (18 relevant documents); and observations of 27 classes and other activities in three schools in each educational system.

The chapter contributes in two ways to the discussion on the internationalisation of schools. First, through the analysis of the IBDP in three different school systems, it contributes to knowledge about one of the most influential agencies promoting the internationalisation of schooling at a global level. Second, the empirical analyses of the idiosyncratic enactment of the IBDP in each system illuminates the complex ways in which the IBDP, as a global model of pedagogic governance, is recontextualised through local political and pedagogic cultures and aspirations. This suggests the need to think of processes of 'internationalisations'—in the plural—since the IBDP, despite being a global model, is mediated by national and local political and pedagogical cultures.

To examine processes of recontextualisation of the IBDP as a global model, we focus on the trajectories of policies (Ball, 1993) that promote the IBDP in these countries. In particular, we analyse the interaction between the global model and local cultures in two key processes within the trajectories of policies. We examine (i) the rationales for introducing the IBDP in these three contexts and (ii) the infrastructures that were designed to support schools and manage the programme locally and nationally.

There are at least two ways in which the international dimension of the IBDP could make the programme desirable for school systems. First, the IBDP promotes an 'international mindedness' among its students, seeking to educate people with an openness towards global diversity. Second, the IBDP has become an international standard of quality through a curriculum centered on the development of skills, a series of governing practices that provide support to teachers and, most notably, through standardised exams.

We argue that in each of the three educational systems, the international dimensions of the IBDP (ethics and standards) have been appropriated differently, depending on the type of actors that were involved in promoting the IBDP, the ways in which the IBDP was combined with other educational policies, the idiosyncratic characteristics of each educational systems and the kind of issues that the IBDP was set to address in each context. Exploring this differentiation is key to developing nuanced understandings of the diverse elements that can contribute to motivations for the internationalisation of schooling. Furthermore, if the IBDP is to be increasingly introduced across public schools, lessons on how to create the necessary infrastructure to support it, and mechanisms of governance, must be learnt.

Based on our research, we suggest that the IBDP has a very particular way of governing pedagogic practices through what we have called 'horizontal networks of governance', in which teachers are trained by other teachers, external assessment of students is also undertaken by IB teachers and a range of mechanisms for promoting the exchange of know-how and experiences among practitioners have been fostered. The idea of an expert and a hierarchically superior trainer that is distant from classroom practice itself is foreign to the IB culture. Furthermore, the IB has traditionally worked directly with schools, rather than with state bureaucracies. The horizontality of the IB network of governance is an important characteristic of the IBDP because it is very different from the modes of governance that are predominant in Latin America. Thus, in Costa Rica, Peru and Buenos Aires, where public administration in education is mostly bureaucratic and hierarchic, the synthesis of the governing logic of the IBDP and the mechanisms of the state has been a challenge. We argue that in each of our three cases the State has used different mechanisms to overcome these challenges and connect the IBDP network with state bureaucracies.

In order to explore the arguments presented previously, the chapter is divided into five main sections. In the first section, we offer a theoretical framework and a brief analysis of the IBDP and its horizontal network of governance. The next three sections analyse the rationales for introducing the IBDP in each of these school systems and the infrastructure that has been created in each of these systems to govern the IBDP in public schools. In the conclusion, we offer some ideas on the challenges that these cases illuminate for the study of processes of internationalisation of schooling.

Problematisation and Infrastructurisation

Our theoretical point of departure to analyse the initiatives that introduced the IBDP in public schools in Costa Rica, Peru and Buenos Aires is Ball's conception of the trajectories of policies (Ball, 1993). From this perspective, policies are dynamic objects that move between different contexts. As policies move, they transform the contexts to which they move, but at the same time, and as part of the same process, policies are transformed by this context. Policies are interpreted and reinterpreted. Policies are ontologically unstable objects that have different meanings in different contexts, at the same time. So, for example, a policy that distributes computers to students is a political opportunity for a government, a business possibility for the company that supplies the technology, a logistic challenge for the head of a school and a pedagogic complication for a teacher (Beech & Artopoulos, 2016).

Based on these notions, we analyse in this chapter two fundamental aspects of the trajectories of these projects: the processes of problematisation and infrastructurisation. These two concepts, which will be explained in the following paragraphs, will be used to provide a theoretical framework to compare the three cases.

Problematisation is the process through which a given issue—in this case the introduction of the IBDP in public schools—becomes a matter that requires public intervention (Ureta, 2014). In this case, the question we address is how and why at specific times and under particular circumstances the introduction of the IBDP in public schools became a matter of policy concern and enactment (Ureta, 2014) in each of these three cases.

Following what Engel and Ortloff (2009) found in other contexts, we contend that strategies of internationalisation are mediated by national agendas. Thus, although there are certain common conditions that contributed to the emergence of the IBDP as a matter of governmental concern in the three cases, there are also specificities about why the IBDP was reenacted as a solution to be deployed in public schools in each context.

In the three educational systems, the IBDP had been present for several decades as an option for private schools that catered to students from high socio-economic backgrounds. This situation gave the IBDP a certain aura of representing quality education only accessible to privileged groups. In countries with significant socio-economic disparities, such as the ones in question, the possibility of offering the IBDP to students being educated in public schools was mostly justified as a matter of equity, understood as giving students from less privileged backgrounds the opportunity of following an educational programme that was only available to the most affluent sectors of society. Thus, in the three cases, participants who were interviewed tended to emphasise the appeal of the IBDP in terms of the educational quality of the programme, combined with a redistributive logic. The long-standing presence of the IBDP in private schools in these educational systems also contributed to the possibility of having individuals that had worked in IBDP schools to work alongside public schools to develop it. Significant in our findings was that the international dimension of the IB, in terms of its promotion of international mindedness, while valued, was not prioritised as a reason for implementing it. Despite this similarity across the three cases, how these elements were constructed during the process of problematisation was quite different in each educational system. Once the option of introducing the IBDP in public schools was reenacted as an issue that required public intervention, states and other participating actors had to create an infrastructure to support schools, teachers and students that would follow the IB. Ureta (2014) defines the process of infrastructurisation as the sociomaterial practices through which new and existing sociotechnical devices are organised and reorganised in connection with the entities identified in the process of problematisation.

Developing and overseeing the teaching and learning required by the IBDP involves a specific kind of know-how that we have called 'IB know-how'. The IBDP has developed a network of people (e.g. teacher trainers and evaluators) and materials (text books, web pages, exams) through which this IB know-how flows. As we develop further later, this is mostly a horizontal network that connects teachers, schools and the International Baccalaureate Organization. One of the main challenges for these projects that introduced the IBDP in public schools was to combine or at least negotiate the coexistence of the hierarchic and bureaucratic networks of public administration in Costa Rica, Peru and Buenos Aires with the more horizontal network of the IB.

To understand and compare the way in which each educational system addressed this challenge, we introduce some concepts of actor-network theory (ANT): the notion of distributed action (or the actor-network), the concepts of symmetry and assemblage.

One of the main principles of actor-network theory as an approach to the social sciences is the idea of distributed action. From the perspective of ANT, action is always distributed and dislocated. There is no such thing as isolated individuals that act alone. An actor is what is made to act by many others (B. Latour, 2005, 2011). It is a node of a network of multiple sets of agencies linked in a network of heterogeneous relations (Law, 1992). In ANT, these networks that generate actions such as teaching and learning are called assemblages. The principle of symmetry in ANT refers to the way that nonhuman objects are conceptualised in this approach as actors. thinking of hybrid networks or assemblages in which human and nonhuman entities interact to produce effects.

If we accept that action is distributed, it becomes evident that assemblages that produce action are not only composed of human elements. Humans need other humans to act, but also objects. As Latour says, 'without the nonhuman, the humans would not last for a minute' (Bruno Latour, 2004, p. 91). Power is not deployed in the abstract; it requires nonhuman objects, such as text-books, curricula, slideshow presentations, black boards, computers, digital learning environments, etc. In order to teach, a teacher interacts with students, maybe with colleagues, but also with the expert that wrote a text, those who defined the official curriculum, etc. These connections are mediated by material objects. Thus, the social is a hybrid of heterogeneous elements. From the perspective of ANT, the actor and the assemblage in which it is embedded have to be considered as one.

The ANT perspective is relevant for this study because it contributes to understanding how the projects that introduced the IBDP in public schools face the challenge of making some kind of synthesis between the socio-technical assemblages of the IB and the assemblages through which the state governs public education. Even though the analysis of these three cases suggests that the IBDP is a flexible programme that can adapt to different contexts, the IBDP does define an ideal assemblage composed of human and nonhuman entities that generate specific types of teaching and learning practices as an effect in IBDP schools. In the remaining paragraphs of this section we describe the IBDP assemblage, showing its elements and its horizontality. Then, in the next sections, we analyse how this specific assemblage interacted with the vertical assemblages that constitute the systems of governance in public school systems in Costa Rica, Peru and the city of Buenos Aires.

For a school to offer the IBDP, it must be authorised by the IBO. During the process of authorisation schools receive advice from an IBDP educator (usually a teacher or head teacher of an IBDP school with significant experience) to prepare the school for the authorisation process that is done by a group of different IBDP educators. All IBDP schools must have an IBDP coordinator who runs the programme in the school and is the link between the school and the IBO. Schools must also reach certain standards in terms of their internet connection; they must supply a science lab with specifically listed equipment and have a library for students with certain materials that the IBDP demands. Schools must pay an annual fee to be IBDP schools, and there is also a fee for each participating student. Access to teacher training requires an extra fee.

Becoming an IBDP school implies following the IBDP curriculum that is made up of three subjects that constitute the IBDP core (Theory of Knowledge; an extended essay; and Creativity, Activity and Service) and different courses that schools can choose to offer within six subjects groups (Studies in Language and Literature; Language Acquisition; Individuals and Societies; Sciences; Mathematics; Arts). Schools also have to abide by the IBDP learner profile that is based on a broad range of human capacities and responsibilities that go beyond academic success. The IBDP aims to 'develop learners who are inquirers, knowledgeable, thinkers, communicators, principled, open-minded, caring, risk-takers, balanced, reflective' (https://www.ibo.org/benefits/learner-profile/). Students can choose whether to enter the full Diploma Programme or opt into one or many individual IBDP courses. It is up to the school to decide whether students can opt to do individual IBDP subjects or whether they are obliged to sit for the full DP. The IBDP offers training for teachers that is carried out by expert IBDP teachers. It also offers materials such as textbooks for different subjects, and students must have access to a specific kind of calculator. The IBDP also gives teachers access to a platform called 'My IB' in which they can find materials such as exam models and connect with other teachers in other parts of the world to exchange ideas and resources and find solutions to teaching challenges. The IBDP also has an information system in which schools enrol students, upload exams, receive students' marks, provide feedback on the overall performance of each student, etc.

One of the key elements of the IBDP assemblage is the IBDP exam. Students are assessed through direct evidence of achievement against the stated goals of the IBDP courses. There are two examination sessions each year, in May and November. The IBDP uses both external and internal assessment. External assessment is carried out by examinations that form the basis of the assessment for most courses. They include essays, structured problems, short-response questions, data-response questions, text-response questions and case-study questions. Teacher assessment (internal) is also used for most courses. This includes oral work in languages, fieldwork in geography, laboratory work in the sciences, investigations in mathematics and artistic performances. Students prepare for these exams over the course of two years. In the classes we observed, it was evident that the exam in each subject was a strong driver of teaching and learning practices. Thus, the exam is a fundamental actor in the

IBDP assemblage, connecting a certain type of knowledge and skills that students must develop with teaching and learning strategies, with a final grade, the feedback that teachers receive and, in many cases, the opportunities that students will have to access higher education.

Thus, the IBO has developed a complex socio-technical assemblage that supports schools and teachers to follow the DP. The network connects schools and teachers in many parts of the world in such a way that IB know-how can be created and shared. One of the salient characteristics of this network of heterogeneous elements is its horizontality. Teachers are trained by other teachers, schools get advice and are then evaluated by colleagues, and external assessment of student exams is undertaken by teachers. Furthermore, teachers receive feedback from their counterparts and can exchange ideas, resources and experiences with other teachers. The IBO has created a career structure for teachers that is not as flat as in traditional educational systems. Teachers can apply to be part of the IBDP Educators Network (IBEN) and become evaluators or teacher trainers, or perform other roles and gain prestige and earn extra income. Members of the IBEN cannot spend more than two years without actively being an IBDP practitioner in an IBDP school. In this way, the IBDP sustains the principle that the IBDP assemblage is a horizontal network mostly formed by currently active IBDP practitioners.

As we will show when analyzing each case, the kind of assemblage that organises governance mechanisms in these public educational systems has a very different bureaucratic and hierarchic logic to the IB one. In the following sections, we show how each system has found different ways to synthesise and/or negotiate the coexistence of these two different types of assemblages.

Costa Rica

Until recently, the Diploma Programme in Costa Rica was an option available only to those attending some of the most expensive private schools in the country. After an initial project in the Liceo de Costa Rica—a landmark public school whose graduates include some of the most important political figures in the country—a group of philanthropic individuals linked to a local private IBDP school started a project seeking to promote the IBDP across other public schools in the country. The first school to become an IBDP school as part of this initiative was Colegio Palmares in the province of Alajuela.

By 2007 both the Liceo and Palmares were authorised by the IB to offer the DP. In 2008, the Association of IB schools in Costa Rica was founded with the aim of supporting these two schools, as well as implementing the IBDP in 20 additional public schools. The initiative grew rapidly, and by 2016, 15 Costa Rican public schools were offering the IBDP—compared to only 12 private institutions. The goal of having

20 public IBDP schools can also be found in the National Development Plan of Costa Rica—demonstrating a significant political commitment to this endeavour.

In the case of Costa Rica, the quality dimension of the IBDP is what has motivated the champions of the initiative to support its introduction into public schools. There was a strong ethical purpose—to ensure the kind of education offered by IBDP schools is made available to those Costa Ricans who do not have the economic means necessary to make that choice for themselves. In this case, equity is understood as giving students in public schools the same opportunities that more affluent youth have in private schools. Nevertheless, this specific articulation of the principle of equity is also controversial. Critics have pointed out that significant investments have been made in just a small number of IBDP schools and not in others, especially those in the most disadvantaged contexts.

The two key organisations in the governance and support framework of the IBDP initiative in Costa Rica are the Ministry of Public Education (MEP) and the Association of IB schools in Costa Rica (ASOBITICO). One of the characteristics of the process of infrastructurisation in Costa Rica is that the links and distribution of responsibilities between these two entities has been dynamic. At the beginning of the process, ASOBIT-ICO acted as a mediator that connected participating schools and teachers with the horizontal network of the IB. This assemblage had very few nodes of contact with the hierarchic and bureaucratic assemblage of the MEP, resulting in the coexistence of two parallel assemblages. Until 2018 it actually funded the IBDP in public schools by paying school and students' fees to the IBO. Facilitating this, the MEP allowed ASOBITICO to work with the first phase of schools, making bureaucratic exceptions so the IBDP could coexist with the national baccalaureate in these schools. But as the initiative grew, the decision was made to agree to a single IBDP curriculum for all public schools in Costa Rica. Subjects of the IDBP were aligned with subjects of the national curriculum in such a way that students who obtained the IB Diploma only needed to pass Social Sciences and Civic Education in the national tests in order to obtain the national baccalaureate degree simultaneously. This decision contributed to a major synthesis across both assemblages.

As the project continued to develop in small manageable steps, the state got more involved and is gradually taking over as the main organisation leading the process. Even though ASOBITICO continues to be the main provider of 'IB know-how' and the principal mediator with the IB network, the two assemblages have become much more integrated, with the state creating paid posts whose responsibility it is to run the project. In addition, the state has taken on most of the financial commitments.

Thus, one of the particularities of the Costa Rican experience is the key involvement of civil society both in processes of problematisation and infrastructurisation. ASOBITICO was the main promoter of the initiative and the main mediator connecting participating schools and teachers with the horizontal assemblage of the IB. As the project evolved, this ad hoc assemblage became more integrated into the existing assemblages of state bureaucracy, contributing to the stability of the project.

Peru

The Diploma Programme in public schools in Peru is part of a broader project called *Colegios de Alto Rendimiento* (High Achieving Schools), known as COAR. The COAR initiative was created by the Peruvian Ministry of Education to educate academically outstanding students in the public school system. COARs are highly selective boarding schools in which students spend six days a week receiving a holistic education aimed at shaping students' personal, academic, artistic and physical potential as part of their preparation to become future Peruvian leaders with an international mind-set. All expenses for attending these schools are covered by the state.

There are currently 25 COARs, one in each region of Peru, enrolling around 6,700 students in total. In 2014, the COAR network started the authorisation process to offer the IBDP in 13 of its schools, and in 2017 the first cohort of students sat for the IBDP exams. The other 12 COAR schools were going through the process of authorisation at the time of data collection (in 2017).

The context in which the COAR project developed was one of sustained economic growth over the last two decades in Peru. Peru's economy has been growing steadily since 2000. The GDP has increased from 52 billion USD in 2000 to 192 billion USD in 2016, with an average growth of 6% between 2010 and 2016 (World Bank, 2017). This led to many families moving out of poverty, gaining access to various material and symbolic goods, and developing increased educational aspirations for their children. In turn this led to substantial growth in private school enrolments across the country (Balarin, 2016, p. 8). Meanwhile, economic growth has also resulted in a significant increase in government expenditure on education.

The history of the IBDP in Peru can be traced back to 1987, when the first private IBDP school was authorised. Since then, the programme has grown steadily as a form of provision in the private sector. In 2010, the Colegio Mayor in Lima—the first school designed to serve exclusively high achieving students—became the first public school to offer the DP. The initiative to create this school came from President Alan García. The goal was to create an innovative institution that mirrored higher education in terms of its organisation, could respond to the needs of the most talented students in the public system and could prepare the future leaders of the country. Officials in charge of the initiative were attracted to the IBDP because it is recognised by prestigious universities, it has an international reputation and its learner profile was aligned philosophically with their views. The Colegio Mayor enrolled its first cohort in 2010 and started offering the IBDP in 2011. It rapidly gained a strong reputation across Peru as an elite school. After a new Minister of Education was appointed in 2013, a decision was made to expand the COAR initiative to create 24 more schools for high-achieving students, one in each region of Peru, based on the model of the Colegio Mayor.

The main motivation for the COAR project, as expressed in official documents and in the view of officials who were interviewed for our study, is the transformation of Peruvian society through educating the future leaders of the country. This was supported by the school authorities, teachers and even the students interviewed. A key component of the COAR schools is that they only admit Peruvian students who have attended public schools for the last three years of their compulsory secondary education. Merit, as opposed to socio-economic advantage, was argued to be the determining principle behind the initiative, thus promoting social mobility. Critical to the COAR project is also its commitment to reducing regional inequalities across Peru by creating one school in every region and taking a high-quality educational model to the most distant and rural areas of the country. Furthermore, the COAR initiative is understood to offer an education that takes into account the different abilities and aspirations of young Peruvians—in this case talented, high-achieving students in the public sector. Within this, the IBDP was valued as an existing educational model that was internationally recognised and had high prestige. Some of the champions of the COAR project had previously worked in IBDP schools themselves, contributing to the conditions of possibility for the inclusion of the IBDP as a key component of the COAR pedagogic design.

The COAR project has not been without its opposition. Some are concerned about the elitist character of the initiative: it aims to improve public education only for outstanding students by creating a privileged education pathway for a specific group. Thus, it is argued that COAR is investing too many resources on a limited group of students. The state spends 10 times more on each COAR student than on a basic regular education (EBR) student.

Unlike the situation in Costa Rica, it was the Peruvian state that started the initiative and immediately designed a very centralised assemblage of governance that embedded part of the IBDP assemblage within its own governance networks. Since the COAR schools are new, and very different from those providing basic regular education (EBR), the state has created an independent, distinct network of governance in which the IBDP has been a central element. For example, most of the curriculum of COAR schools is constituted by the IBDP. Furthermore, the learner profile promoted by the COAR model mirrors that of the IBDP.

The governance and support frameworks of the initiative are an indicator that the COAR project is central to the national education policies of Peru. COAR schools are overseen by the DEBEDSAR (Directorate of Basic Education for Students with High Performance and Achievement), a division within the Directorate of Special Basic Education that was specifically created to run the COAR project. This is a big division (47 employees) that regulates, supports and evaluates COARs.

The COAR is a highly regulated and vertical project in which the DEBEDSAR defines many detailed aspects of school life. The Ministry of Education in Peru developed a determined and coherent strategy of buying-in IB know-how through hiring professionals with first-hand experience of the IBDP to act as mediators between the broader, global IB assemblage and the COAR project. Given the verticality of the organisational structure in Peru, IB know-how flows mainly from the central state out to schools. Apart from the IB know-how in the form of teacher training, overall support to teachers and the leadership teams of COARs, DEBEDSAR provides for all the material needs of COARs and their students (from food, medical assistance and uniforms to backpacks, computers and calculators).

Thus, different to the Costa Rican case, in Peru the state is the main actor in the project of introducing the IBDP in public schools as part of the wider COAR initiative. In the process of problematisation, even though the educational quality of the IBDP and the search for equity were central elements, they were articulated quite distinctively from the Costa Rican case, as they were combined with the idea of educating future leaders that were needed for the development of Peru. Through the process of infrastructurisation, the state developed a new and separate governance assemblage that included the IBDP as a central element. The state brought in IB know-how through the hiring of practitioners with IB experience who acted as mediators connecting the IBDP horizontal network to the governance mechanisms of the COAR project. In this way, the horizontality of the IB assemblage is, to a certain extent, translated into a much more vertical and hierarchical governance network.

City of Buenos Aires

The project of implementing the IB Diploma Programme in public schools in Buenos Aires is an initiative of the Ministry of Education of the City of Buenos Aires, launched in 2013. However, the IBDP has a long tradition in Argentina, mostly in private schools, but also in two state schools (one in the City itself and one in the Province of Buenos Aires).

The new project saw the implementation of the IBDP across 11 public schools, though these were not evenly distributed across the City. Of the 11 schools, 6 can be found in 3 of the wealthiest districts in the north of the City, and there are no IBDP schools in the southern districts of the City, which are also the most disadvantaged.

The implementation of the IBDP in Buenos Aires has taken place in the context of a general crisis about secondary education in Argentina (Terigi, 2008). Concerns over the quality of secondary schools grew over the last decades due to high student dropout rates and disappointing student outcomes throughout the country. Only 5 out of 10 students who enrolled in secondary education graduated in a timely manner. (Montesinos, 2015).

It was the Minister of Education of the City who made the decision to implement the IBDP in public schools on his return from an IB Conference in the United States, believing it might address some of these education problems. Introducing the IBDP in public schools in the City of Buenos Aires was founded on the principle of equity. As in Costa Rica and Peru, promoters of the project that were interviewed interpreted equity as giving students in public schools opportunities to access a high-quality education that had previously only been available to affluent families. The Secretary of Innovation and Planning who was originally in charge of the initiative also mentioned that they were motivated to show that students from less advantaged backgrounds could perform as well as students in the most privileged socio-economic situations. Here, the IBDP was held up as a reputable education model representing high standards. However, the initiative in Buenos Aires lacked a clear focus. Beyond overcoming the secondary education crisis, there did not seem to be a clear goal that directed the initiative forward, as far as we could ascertain from our interviews and document analysis. While equity appeared to be the driver, this was not in turn translated into more specific aims to organise and mobilise the initiative.

This weak articulation of vision lead to an unstable process of infrastructurisation. One visible characteristic of the initiative in Buenos Aires was its weak institutionalisation as an initiative. There is no regulatory framework overseeing it other than the terms of reference signed between the IBO and the City. The Ministry of Education has not developed a stable network of governance for the project. Neither did it integrate IB know-how within its formal structure, nor have a process for accessing and distributing this kind of knowledge. Unlike the case of Costa Rica and Peru, the promoters of the initiative and officials in charge of the design of support systems in Buenos Aires did not have previous experience of the IB.

Thus, when officials were faced with conflicts between the hierarchic and bureaucratic governance system of education within the City and the IBDP horizontal networks, officials tended to solve these by making exceptions to the logic of public administration. A more entrepreneurial style, often reliant on the enthusiasm of individuals to overcome obstacles, resulted in an unstable support infrastructure. For example, the project was initially placed within the responsibility of the Secretariat of Innovation and Planning, who reported directly to the Minister of

Education. Originally, the Secretary of Innovation and Planning created a division who oversaw what they called 'special projects'. These were mostly innovation projects that experimented with external educational models to promote changes at the school level. Within this division, two people worked full time on the IB project. In an interview with the (now former) Secretary, she told us how she interpreted the IB as a project that required 'high maintenance' to be sustainable, and she told us how the Minister, herself and the team were on top of the project, meeting with principals, teachers and students and providing support.

In the tradition of the Ministry of Education in the City, the Secretariat of Planning is not directly in charge of schools. Thus, when a new administration reorganised the Secretariat of Planning in 2016, closing the 'special projects' division, the IB project came under the supervision of the Director of State Managed Schools, which oversees more than 1,000 schools. In this context, a project that involves only 11 schools was not given as much attention and resources as it had received before. Furthermore, the Director of State Managed Schools retired in the first months of 2017, and while we were visiting schools, coordinators and principals appeared to not know who was now overseeing the project within the Ministry.

The weakening of the support infrastructure led to the IB know-how becoming scarcer and scarcer. For instance, the agreement between the IBDP and the Government of Buenos Aires included only one training workshop to certify teachers. No more formal training was offered after the authorisation of schools. Some of the teachers that were trained retired the next year, while others were promoted to other roles or changed schools and abandoned the project. Since no more official training was offered, teachers and coordinators had to be creative in finding IB know-how on their own.

Perhaps as a response to this lack of institutionalised support structures, a fruitful partnership was established in the City between private and public IB schools by the Association of IB Schools in the River Plate (ACBIRP), which includes private schools that are part of the IB network in Argentina and Uruguay. Each public IB school was assigned an experienced private IB school partner. The support of private schools was very important in transferring some IB knowledge to public schools, but it was limited, given its informality and the fact that it was based on the good will of private schools.

One of the clearest examples of the lack of connections between the state governance network and the IB assemblage is the way in which IB curricular options were defined. Schools were given the freedom to select the IB subjects they preferred; a process that led to 11 unique IB curricular arrangements. School principals and recently appointed IB coordinators had no experience with the IB and very little support from officials, who themselves had no IB experience. In such a context, very few of the

IB subjects were integrated with existing local subjects, not more than one or two per school. Thus, students who followed the IBDP had to do the existing national curricular programme in addition. As a result, students who chose the IBDP had to follow almost two full programmes in order to follow national regulations. Considering that students in typical Argentine schools take 12 to 14 subjects, this implied a huge amount of work. For instance, students in technical schools sometimes have classes from 7 AM to 6 PM.

This weak and imprecise process of infrastructurisation in terms of curricular synthesis between the two existing networks generated further challenges in access to IB know-how and its distribution. Since each school developed a unique IBDP curricular design, the number of IB subjects that are being taught in Buenos Aires is much larger than in Costa Rica and Peru. This is very inefficient in terms of teacher training, access to materials that are subject-specific, the possibility of teachers moving from one IB school to another, the development of a local network of teachers that can potentially exchange experiences and IB know-how, and state supervision and support. For example, one of the schools we visited was very proud of being the only school in the world to offer an IB subject called 'Design of Technology' in Spanish. Even though the pride of the school authorities is understandable, from the perspective of planning, it is evident that having such a rare subject in the school curriculum is a challenge for sustainability and efficiency.

Thus, the IB project in the City of Buenos Aires is far from being stable and institutionalised at the state level. Mechanisms of support for schools are weak, and they have been weakening further with time, especially due to changes in authorities. The challenge of providing IB know-how to schools and teachers by developing connections with the IBDP network has not been met. Schools and teachers had very little support and access to the kind of IB know-how they need to prepare students for the challenging IB exams. Students are overloaded with two parallel and demanding programmes. Furthermore, the number of schools that participate is small in relation to the size of the educational system of the City, and within each school there are very few students in each IBDP cohort (nine students average per school). Thus, at the macro level, we would argue that the sustainability of the initiative in Buenos Aires' public schools is at risk.

Final Thoughts

Throughout this chapter we have sought to illustrate the complexity of contemporary processes of internationalisation of schooling through the example of the IBDP expansion across parts of Latin America. First, we contend that it is necessary to understand the diversity of motivations that education authorities or other significant agencies might have in pursuing international educational programmes such as the International

Baccalaureate. Even though economic competitiveness and promoting cosmopolitan sensibilities are valued, in the three educational systems that we analysed, it was mainly the IB as an international standard of quality education that was considered its most important characteristic. Furthermore, similar to the argument made elsewhere, that internationalisation contributes to increased opportunities for distinction for already privileged groups (Maxwell, 2018), our cases show that internationalisation can promote further access to social mobility for some less advantaged groups. The counter argument, though, has been to question whether it is the fairest and most effective mechanism for promoting equality—to spend significantly more resources on a very limited group of talented and motivated students when all three countries have large socio-economic and educational inequalities, and generally the education institutions have been under-resourced.

Second, we have explored the mechanisms through which the International Baccalaureate—as one of the main contemporary drivers of the internationalisation of schooling—constitutes a more horizontal assemblage of teachers, curricula, materials and general 'IB know-how'. Understanding the variety of ways such horizontal networking can become integrated (or not) with bureaucratic and hierarchic logics is critical to reflecting on how best to roll out the IB and other internationalisation initiatives elsewhere. Our analysis indicated that the way this integration is made possible depends on a number of national or local pedagogic and political cultures.

What is clear is that more research is needed on the internationalisation of schooling. At least in Latin America, as states start to get involved in promoting international models such as IBDP, more empirical evidence and nuanced interpretations are needed in terms of understanding the governance and pedagogic challenges implied in the promotion of international models of schooling. Furthermore, it is important to analyse how these state initiatives are affecting the ways in which international models such as the IB interact with issues of social class and with the role of education in reproducing or reducing inequalities. These issues will become more and more relevant as the momentum of internationalisation of schools seems to be growing steadily in the region.

Notes

1. Information available in the IBO website: www.ibo.org/programmes/diploma-programme/ [accessed on July 5, 2018].
2. The study was financed by the International Baccalaureate Organization.

References

Balarin, M. (2016). La privatización por defecto y el surgimiento de las escuelas privadas de bajo costo en el Perú.¿ *Cuáles son sus consecuencias? Revista de la Asociación de Sociología de la Educación (RASE)*, 9(2), 181–196.

Ball, S. J. (1993). What is policy? Texts, trajectories and toolboxes. *The Australian Journal of Education Studies*, 13(2), 10–17.

Beech, J., & Artopoulos, A. (2016). Interpreting the circulation of educational discourse across space: Searching for new vocabularies. *Globalisation, Societies and Education*, 14(2), 251–271.

Beech, J., Guevara, J., & del Monte, P. (2018). *Diploma programme implementation in public schools in Latin America: The cases of Costa Rica, Argentina (Buenos Aires) and Peru*. Bethesda: International Baccalaureate Organization.

Bunnell, T. (2008). The global growth of the international baccalaureate diploma programme over the first 40 years: A critical assessment. *Comparative Education*, 44(4), 409–424.

Engel, L. C., & Ortloff, D. H. (2009). From the local to the supranational: Curriculum reform and the production of the ideal citizen in two federal systems, Germany and Spain. *Journal of Curriculum Studies*, 41(2), 179–198.

International Baccalaureate Organisation (n.d.). *IB learner profile*. Retrieved from https://www.ibo.org/benefits/learner-profile/

Latour, B. (2004). *Politics of nature*. Boston, MA: Harvard University Press.

Latour, B. (2005). *Reassembling the social: An introduction to actor—Network theory*. New York: Oxford University Press.

Latour, B. (2011). Networks, societies, spheres: Reflections of an actor-network theorist. *International Journal of Communication*, 5, 796–810.

Law, J. (1992). Notes on the theory of the actor-network: Ordering, strategy, and heterogeneity. *Systems practice*, 5(4), 379–393.

Maxwell, C. (2018). Changing spaces—The re-shaping of (elite) education through internationalisation. In C. Maxwell, U. Deppe, H. H. Krüger, & W. Helsper (Eds.), *Elite education and internationalisation: From the early years into higher education* (pp. 347–367). Basingstoke: Palgrave Macmillan.

Montesinos, M. P. (2015). Políticas de revinculación y terminalidad escolar: Reflexiones en torno a los abordajes contemporáneos orientados a universalizar la educación secundaria. In *Serie Educación en Debate* (Vol. 19). Buenos Aires: DiNIECE.

Resnik, J. (2016). The development of the International Baccalaureate in Spanish speaking countries: a global comparative approach. *Globalisation, Societies and Education*, 14(2), 298–325.

Terigi, F. (2008). Los cambios en el formato de la escuela secundaria argentina: Por qué son necesarios, por qué son tan difíciles. *Propuesta Educativa*, 17(29), 63–66.

Ureta, S. (2014). Policy assemblages: Proposing an alternative conceptual framework to study public action. *Policy studies*, 35(3), 303–318.

World Bank. (2017). *GDP growth (annual %)*. World Bank national accounts data, and OECD national accounts data files. Retrieved 19 September 2018, from https://data.worldbank.org/indicator/NY.GDP.MKTP.KD.ZG?locations=PE.

7 On Being Local and International

Indonesian Teachers' Experiences in an International Kindergarten

Vina Adriany

Introduction

The purpose of this chapter is to explore experiences of local Indonesian teachers working in international kindergartens in Indonesia. Internationalisation of schooling is frequently argued to be a leading strategy for providing students with the skills, competencies, and attitudes necessary for the globalised world. Engel and Siczek (2018a; 2018b) argue that internationalisation provides students with intercultural values such as empathy and understanding towards different cultures, offering a space for students to learn about what it means to be a global citizen. Although many systems worldwide espouse the values of internationalisation, the form that internationalisation takes varies (Maxwell, 2018; Yemini, 2014). In this chapter, I focus on international kindergartens in Indonesia as a place where internationalisation is negotiated amongst global and local actors (Adriany, 2018; Heyward, 2002).

Internationalisation in early childhood education[1] (ECE) settings is rarely discussed or researched (for an exception see Mierendorff, Ernst, & Maderin, 2018 and Press & Woodrow, 2018). As there has been no specific theoretical innovation to date about how to conceptualise internationalisation in ECE settings, I will borrow from the literature on internationalisation in schools to frame my analysis. Internationalisation of education has been shown to have positive dimensions, but studies also call for some caution. Yemini (2015) explains how the term 'international school' often carries multiple meanings, many of which are associated more with neoliberal values that frame education simply as a form of economic investment. Parents choose an international school for their children because they believe that it will allow their children to be economically competitive (Adriany, 2018; Weenink, 2008). Earlier research (Miyahara & Miyahara, 1994) also linked international schools with broader, national-level modernisation initiatives. By embracing international values, a system was considered more modern and developed.

Other critiques of international schools have focused on the fact that most of the international schools were established in Global countries (Martin & Griffiths, 2012; Mwebi & Brigham, 2009). Since the 1950s, a growing group of expatriates began to settle in countries around the world, and thus needed or desired international schools. This was preferred by many, who did not want to send their children 'home' to be educated, but have them stay close, while also receiving an education similar to that of 'home' (Heyward, 2002). But a growing provision of international schools arguably, as discussed by Heyward (2002) and Tanu (2014), puts pressure on local residents to become 'international', and often this means being 'Western' (Crossley & Tikly, 2004). Other research also has shown how local students in international schools often feel like 'the other', trapped between two distinctive cultural experiences (Fail, Thompson, & Walker, 2004). Specifically, Tanu's (2014) research has illuminated the extent to which being an international school student in a country like Indonesia has reinforced not only their identity as international but also perpetuates their elite status within the country. Therefore, international education institutions (e.g. schools and kindergartens) can become institutional mechanisms that promote, sustain, and even deepen economic and social inequalities within a country (Adriany, 2018; Maxwell, 2018).

Much of the preceding research has focused on students' experiences in international schools; yet, it is important to also understand international school teachers' perspectives and experiences to fully appreciate the complexities of international schooling spaces. Only a few studies have explored the local teachers' experiences in international school contexts in the Global South, and they frequently focus on expatriate teacher experiences. For example, Tarc and Tarc (2015) explore experiences of teachers from Global North settings, such as the UK, teaching in Global South countries. Bailey (2015), similarly, focused on expatriate teachers' experiences in Malaysia. However, research on local teachers' experiences in an international school, particularly local teachers from a Global South context, remains very scarce.

The purpose of this chapter is to unpack local teachers' perspectives and experiences in the international school sector in Indonesia. Specifically, this chapter focuses on kindergarten teachers because despite the growing numbers of international kindergartens in Indonesia, they are still an entirely under-researched area in the field. This chapter will draw on postcolonial theories to bring a critical lens to the experiences of teachers as they negotiate their identities and power relations within an internationalised context. By focusing on local Indonesian teachers' experiences, this chapter aims to illuminate the micro-politics of internationalisation in lower education levels (Tanu, 2017).

Theoretical Framework

Internationalisation of Education

Earlier research on internationalisation focused on how it attempted to incorporate intercultural and global values into education settings (Yemini, 2015). Internationalisation of education is seen as a strategic endeavour to improve the quality of education in a country. That is, a country and/or an institution engaged in an internationalisation process is thought to benefit from it because of the opportunity to experience intercultural and global experiences (Heyward, 2002).

Yemini (2015, p. 21) draws on traditional definitions from the international higher education sector to define internationalisation of education as 'the process of encouraging the integration of multicultural, multilingual, and global dimensions within the education system, with the aim of instilling in learners a sense of global citizenship'. Here, the link between internationalisation and global citizenship education is clear. Global citizenship education as articulated by Engel and Siczek (2018a, p. 3) is an approach in education that aims to develop 'students' critical thinking and analytic skills about global problems and issues; attitudes of empathy, solidarity and respect for difference and diversity; and the willingness to take action on global problems'. As a goal of internationalisation, global citizenship education aims to equip students as well as teachers with skills needed in today's highly globalised world. Not only that, but global education is also purported to prepare students to develop intercultural literacy (Heyward, 2002).

Despite the noble objectives of internationalisation of education through global citizenship education, previous studies have indicated how the notion of global citizenship education, in reality, can be quite problematic. For example, global values promoted in the schools are often detached from the countries' social context where the schools are situated (Tanu, 2017). Moreover, the teaching of global citizenship education still uses the soft approach where the issue of social justice and power relations between social groups are often usually overlooked (Andreotti, 2014). Heyward (2002) unpacks the notion of 'global values' by questioning whether there is such a thing as global values as very often the values reflect more of a Western and middle-class orientation. Maxwell (2018) also highlights how internationalisation aids the construction of eliteness both on the transnational and national level. In short, internationalisation of education is often perceived to perpetuate neoliberal and neo-colonial values (Heyward, 2002; Tanu, 2014; Weenink, 2008; Yemini & Fulop, 2015).

Using Postcolonial Theories on Internationalisation of Early Childhood Education

This chapter is informed by postcolonial theories (Gupta, 2006, 2008; Viruru, 2001, 2005). Postcolonial theories are selected because they are particularly useful in understanding the process of internationalisation of ECE as a site where there exists an ongoing negotiation between local and global values. The postcolonial lens is used here because previous research on internationalisation of education often focuses on the binary between international versus national values, where internationalism is often perceived as preferred (Tanu, 2017). Hence, previous studies tend to overlook the class, racial, gendered, and colonial elements in the internationalisation of education.

Postcolonial theories can be understood as an approach that is used to explain and understand the living experiences of people who have colonialised experiences (Bhabha, 1994; Spivak, 2000). Postcolonial theories argue that the process of colonisation does not stop when the colonisation ends. Rather, it transforms social relations in more subtle ways, impacting the way people think and behave (Landry & Maclean, 1996; Viruru, 2001).

In the field of ECE, postcolonial theories are particularly useful because, as is the case in many of the Global South countries, the legacy of colonisation is still very pervasive (Gupta, 2006; Viruru, 2005). Many practices of ECE in the countries are predicated on theories and research derived from Western epistemology. The child-centred approach, for example, has been widely adopted in the South. Critics have pointed out the extent to which the approach uses the standards of child development in the North often positioned against child development in the South (Adriany, 2016; Burman, 2008; Walkerdine, 1998). In a report prepared by the World Bank, for example, it was reported that Indonesian children in the village are often seen to be developmentally delayed (Hasan, Hyson, & Chang, 2013). It could be argued that this is because they used a testing instrument that is culturally insensitive towards children indigenous to Indonesia (Adriany & Saefullah, 2015). The implications of these assessments and interventions are that children in the South are often seen as developmentally delayed and different from children in the North (Penn, 2002, 2011).

In addition to these, the legacy of colonisation is also evident since international forces play dominant roles in developing ECE principles and provision in the South (Adriany, 2018; Gupta, 2018; Lee, 2018). In Indonesia, for instance, the penetration of international agencies, such as the World Bank, into the development of ECE has been pervasive (Adriany & Saefullah, 2015).

Importantly, postcolonial theories do not only recognise the ongoing effect of colonisation, but they also acknowledge a form of resistance made by the colonised. As Spivak (2000) and Mohanty (2006) assert, sometimes the only language the colonised need to use is the language of the coloniser. To do that, the colonised will create a 'third hybrid space', the grey space that allows the values of the colonised and the coloniser to be negotiated (Bhabha, 1994). Research conducted by Jahng (2013) in Korean kindergartens demonstrate the extent to which kindergartens adopt both Korean and Western values in their practices. Gupta (2006) also shows how kindergartens in India adjust the notion of Vygotsky's approach and integrate it with their Indian values. Additionally, Adriany (2018) also illustrated how international kindergartens in Indonesia become a hybrid space by expanding the notion of child-centredness by adapting it to the local values.

A few others have used postcolonial theories when studying internationalisation of education. For example, Tanu (2014, 2016, 2017), as well as Tarc and Tarc (2015), have adopted postcolonial theories in their research on internationalisation. By using postcolonial approaches, they are able to understand the intersectionality of the teachers' racial, national, and gender background, as well as unpack forms of teacher privilege they can draw on. I follow in their path, using postcolonial theories in order to deconstruct an apparently 'innocent' practice in the process of internationalisation of kindergartens in various parts of Indonesia. It permits me to assess developments more critically. However, I also draw on postcolonial theories to work with the notion of the hybrid space—focusing in on how global and local cultures are negotiated and integrated in various ways. This enables us to move beyond binary notions of global and local, the West and the East, the North and the South.

The Rise of International Kindergartens in Indonesia

Indonesia is a large country of more than 250 million people (World Population Review, 2018). For the past ten years, the country has enjoyed rapid economic development. As a result, the middle class is increasing; yet, at the same time the disparity and inequality between lower and middle classes are also becoming more visible (Yusuf, Sumber, & Rum, 2014).

The internationalisation of ECE in Indonesia has been informed by three different models (Adriany, 2018). The first model has emerged through cooperation with international donor agencies such as the World Bank (White, 2011). The World Bank, through its loan programme to the Indonesian government, linked this to the development of specific ECE programmes in many villages across Indonesia (Hasan, Hyson, & Chang, 2013). The second form of internationalisation has been promoted by the adoption of 'international-recognised' models and ECE curricula into local kindergartens (Newberry, 2010). Finally, the internationalisation of ECE is being led by the increasing presence of international franchise-based ECE (Dýrfjörð, 2012). This chapter focuses on this third model— a relatively recent development, but also one that is gaining pace and should be more critically engaged with.

Since 1998, Indonesia has undergone major social and economic reforms as a result of the country's democratisation. This has included changes in the education system, more specifically a shift away from centralisation to more decentralised modes of governance (Amirrachman, 2012). Specifically, numbers of international schools, including international kindergartens, increased significantly from 2003 (Tanu, 2017). This has led to the emergence of private kindergartens, including international franchise–based kindergartens (Newberry, 2010).

Kindergartens in Indonesia are divided into formal and non-formal kindergartens (Formen, 2017). They normally serve children ages four to six years old (Ministry of Education and Culture Republic of Indonesia, 2014). Formal kindergartens are led by teachers who have graduated from university, while non-formal kindergartens are normally run by volunteers, and the teachers are not required to have any formal background or ECE-specific qualifications (Adriany & Saefullah, 2015). Kindergartens are not part of the compulsory education in Indonesia, so they are not state-funded, though since 2013, there has been an operational assistance fund provided by the state (Ministry of Education and Culture Republic of Indonesia, 2018). There is often a vast discrepancy between non-formal and formal kindergartens in terms of resources.

Both international and local kindergartens are very much influenced by theories from the Global North, as demonstrated in the utilisation of child-centred approaches within the ECE curriculum in Indonesia. However, in the international kindergartens, these practices are even more pervasive since international kindergartens must adopt prescribed curriculum from international kindergartens programs in the North, such as High Scope, Montessori, and Beyond Circle and Centre Time (BCCT) (Adriany, 2018). Hence, without any doubt, international kindergartens can be seen as a space that prolongs the legacy of colonialisation.

Methodology

This chapter adopts a case study approach to allow the researcher to compare and contrast the different experiences of teachers working in different international kindergartens (Swanborn, 2010; Yin, 2008). Three teachers become the informants—Lia, Grace, and Jenny. Lia is a senior teacher who is also acting as a school principal in an International kindergarten in a city in West Java province in Indonesia. She has been teaching in the kindergarten for more than ten years. Grace is a new teacher in an international kindergarten in another city in the province. She has taught at the kindergarten for one year. Before joining the school, she taught in an international kindergarten in Malaysia. This overseas experience in combination with being Indonesian, as she described it, provides her with a sense of being both local and international. The last participant, Jenny, is also a senior teacher in a kindergarten in another city in the province. Jenny has been teaching in various international kindergartens for more than ten years.

Individual interviews were carried out with each participant. Rather than using a rigid, highly structured interview, I adopted an informal, less-structured interview, which as Swain (2006) elucidates is more like engaging in a conversation. The teachers were asked about their experiences of becoming local teachers in international kindergartens. All of the interviews were transcribed, and the transcripts were returned to the participants so they could check whether the conversation had been accurately recorded. The participants were also given a chance to see whether they would like to omit any information. After the participants expressed their agreement, I then proceeded to analyse them. The analysis was informed by constructivist grounded theory (Charmaz, 2006). Each line was given a code, different codes with similar meaning were gathered, and a theme was assigned. The analysis yielded three significant themes as seen in the finding section.

Findings and Discussion

Being the Other: The Negotiation of Political Belonging

Despite sharing the same educational qualifications as expat teachers, Indonesian teachers in international schools are frequently seen and treated as less competent than expat teachers. The expat teachers in the three kindergartens in this study were from America, the UK, Malaysia, and the Philippines. Structurally, Indonesian teachers experienced a number of discriminatory practices, such as receiving a lower salary, and despite having more years of experience and a higher education degree, they are always put in the classroom as an assistant teacher. As Jenny explained the practice in her kindergarten:

> It is the policy of our kindergarten to have the expatriate teachers as the lead teachers. We, the local teachers would only act as an assistant teacher . . . (laugh) . . . despite the fact that I have more teaching experience than them . . . but what can I say? It is one way to attract parents to enrol their children to our school because we have the lead teachers who are expat.

Jenny further explained:

> Of course it (the role as an assistant teacher) affects everything, including my salary. Even though I am an assistant teacher, I am still doing many things that are supposed to be done by the lead teacher. I am in charge of the lesson plan, even with the assessment but still, my salary is far below the lead teacher (laugh) . . .

Jenny's experiences illuminate the type of discrimination she regularly encounters due to her Indonesian status and the privilege that expat teachers possess due to their international status. Even though common definitions of an expatriate means a person who lives in a foreign country, similar to an immigrant, the status attached to both words is often very different. The distinction between the use of the concepts of immigrants and expatriates symbolises 'the complex configurations of racialisation, gender, class and nationality, often involving problematic reproductions of the colonial past' (Kunz, 2016, p. 89).

The local teachers not only have a lower salary, but they are also given different benefits. In Lia's school, for example, the expat teachers are provided with health insurance, a first class return flight ticket to go back to their countries of origin once a year, a housing allowance, and so forth, while the local teachers do not receive these advantages. Even among the expat teachers, there exists a hierarchy, with those coming from Western countries like the UK and the US receiving more recognition (monetarily and in terms of their skills) than those from non-Western countries, according to Lia. As Tanu (2017) argues, an international school often becomes a place where being Western is hegemonised. Here, the apparent different experiences between the local and expat teachers might demonstrate the extent to which international kindergartens become a space where 'social making group in the transnational scene' is created (Tarc & Tarc, 2015, p. 39). International kindergarten in this sense becomes a vehicle that sustains global inequality between people from the North and the South.

The experiences of the local teachers are, to put it in Lia's words, 'confusing, but what can we do?' A similar but not identical feeling is also experienced by the expat teachers. Research conducted with Canadian expat teachers working in Global South countries also illuminates a sense of conflict (Tarc & Tarc, 2015). The expat teachers feel trapped between their elite status and the lived realities of the local people they encounter in their daily life.

The experience of the local teachers also affects the relationship with the parents, where parents too often prefer to interact with the expat teachers. According to Grace, parents favour expat teachers to whom they have paid the expensive tuition fees, in part due to the expat teachers being employed at these international kindergartens. In her attempt to understand parents' behaviour, Grace states,

> I understand if parents prefer expat teachers. They pay more because they want their children to be exposed to international cultures. So, if their children are only taught by the local teachers, there is not worth sending them here (to international kindergartens). Having expat teachers is like the first step to have international cultur[al exposure] for their children.

Lia also explains further the reasons why parents desire the presence of expat teachers: 'Expat teachers speak better English, and of course, when they put their children here [in the international kindergartens], they want their children to speak good English'. The parents' attitudes towards local and expat teachers might illuminate how international kindergartens are seen as key to their children's future success. Underlying this idea is a neoliberal view of education as an investment in higher long-term economic returns (Adriany, 2018). International kindergartens and, consequently, access to international teachers are preferred because they are assumed to be able to provide their children with the language skills that would allow them to be successful in the global world (Engel & Siczek, 2018a). Thus, the local teachers in these international settings find themselves in an in-between space—arguably a 'hybrid third space' (Bhabha, 1994)—not fully 'belonging'. They do not feel like full members of this international community—operating more at the periphery (Lave & Wenger, 1991), and yet they are no longer part of the local community of teachers either, as detailed in the next section.

Being Exclusive

Even though local teachers are constructed as 'the Other' in relation to expat teachers, the local teachers at the same time also see Indonesian teachers who teach in Indonesian kindergartens as somehow less competent than themselves. This becomes one of the reasons that prevent the Indonesian teachers in the international kindergartens from leaving the schools. They feel somehow that their competencies are overqualified if they have to teach in local schools. As Grace says, 'they [the teachers who teach in the local schools] do not really understand about child-centredness. Their teaching is very much teacher-centred. I think what they do is wrong . . . really, really wrong'.

The findings suggest how the thinking of the local teachers in this research echoes the reflection of the expat teachers. Research suggests that expat teachers often see local teachers as 'old-fashioned and indoctrinate[ing]' (Bailey, 2015, p. 10). As Foucault (1984) indicates, a person might be rendered powerless in one situation, while at the same time adopting a more dominant position in another situation. By seeing the Indonesian teachers who teach in the local kindergarten as less competent, the local teachers in this research were themselves complicit in promoting social structures that further sustained inequality not only between the expat and local teachers but also between local teachers employed in different kinds of kindergartens—where the global/international is seen as having more value than the local.

While local teachers in international kindergartens in this study received lower salaries than their expat counterparts; their salaries were

usually arguably higher when compared to most kindergarten teachers
in Indonesia. For example, local teacher participants' salary per month
ranged from Rp. 3,000,000 (USD 207) to Rp. 12,000,000 (USD 829)[2]
depending on their qualifications, position, and years of experience;
while teachers in Indonesian kindergartens received around Rp. 150,000
(USD 10.4) to Rp. 5,000,000 (USD 345.4). Furthermore, teachers who
taught in non-formal ECE centres received an even lower salary. Some
of them as low as Rp. 50,000 (USD 3.5) per month. The teachers in
this research, however, seemed unaware of this significant discrepancy in
terms of wages. Instead they highlighted their marginalization by other
local teachers. Lia, explained:

> I used to feel marginalised by my colleagues (who teach in Indone-
> sian kindergartens). When I was young, I was even bullied by them
> whenever I attended the regional meeting. They would give me so
> many assignments, but luckily I always managed to do it. I want to
> prove to them that I am not as exclusive as they think.

Working in an international kindergarten arguably detached many local
teachers from the social reality of ECE provision in Indonesia and the
conditions so many teaching colleagues and differently resourced children were working/being educated in. Even though international schools
are argued to promote global citizenship values, sometimes it is ironic to
see, as Tanu (2017) asserts, that taking such a global outlook often means
overlooking local problems and taking for granted economic privilege.

The notion of being exclusive seems to be derived from their identity
as teachers in the international kindergarten. As Grace admits, 'maybe it
is because we teach in the International kindergarten and speak English,
that they think we are different from them'.

Lia's account indicates that in a Global South country like Indone-
sia, speaking English becomes a signifier of one's eliteness. As Tarc and
Tarc (2015) argue, English is a form of symbolic advantage in the Global
South.

Lia's and Grace's stories seem to suggest the navigation of their identity and belonging from being local to international. Inhabiting the local
versus global context becomes part of the everyday of teachers' experiences in these spaces. Here, they encounter being 'the Other' within the
international kindergartens, yet at the same time, they are perceived as
being 'exclusive' in relation to local teachers in Indonesian kindergartens.
Through this process another line of fracture is opened up within Indonesian society, just as those children whose families can afford a place
in an international kindergarten are being set apart from their peers in
a process of distinction that begins through the first stage of education/
childcare provision in the schooling process. Yet simultaneously, the process of internationalising education is making available to some local

teachers opportunities for social mobility and the potential to be at the forefront of negotiating relations of belonging.

Friendship: A Space for Resistance and Negotiation

Friendship plays an essential role in international kindergartens. Friendship becomes a strategy developed by the local and expat teachers to negotiate their belonging within these spaces (Achinstein & Meyer, 1997). In Lia's school, for example, the local teachers are informally assigned to assist the expat teachers whenever the latter need to see the doctor—to assist with translation. While one could position such a 'service' as embedding a racialised form of friendship where the local teachers should become the expat teachers' 'helpers' (Tanu, 2017; Tarc & Tarc, 2015), the participants describe it as opening up the possibility for establishing friendship and understanding. At first, Lia herself admitted that she felt this arrangement was an additional burden on her. However, after some time, she started to understand how difficult it must be for a foreigner to be in another country without knowing the language. She said, 'I could only imagine it must be difficult to leave your own country and move to another'. She also revealed that the expat teachers often start to show an interest in learning Indonesian.

Through friendship, a desire to facilitate knowledge transfer between both groups also begins. As Jenny explained:

> We get to know each other better. I have to admit, there is so much I can learn from them, especially on how to manage the class, but at the same time, I think they can learn from me, especially on how to understand Indonesian parents and children more.

Jenny's statement arguably demonstrates how mutually learning from one another through forming friendships can become an act of decolonisation. Here power relations start to become re-negotiated. At the same time, friendship becomes a tool for local teachers to re-construct their national identity—emerging in Jenny's comment is a sense of pride in being able to make sense of and explain the practices of Indonesian parents and children to an outsider. As Rizvi (2010) argues, one of the effects of internationalisation is in fact to strengthen one's national identity in an attempt to make sense of the world and to resist so-called 'international' or 'global values'.

Conclusion

This chapter explores a small sample of Indonesian teachers' experiences teaching in international kindergartens in Indonesia. By framing internationalisation through a postcolonial lens and emphasising teachers' voices, this chapter is able to identify the micro-politics that take place in international kindergartens, which I have argued reinforce postcolonial relations of power between North and South and global and local. As an under-researched area, in a space that is increasingly being internationalised and marketized—and, critically, using a postcolonial frame—I suggest that like other trends within the internationalisation of education, ECE is following suit. Overall, international kindergartens can be seen potentially as places that construct transnational and national elites and that serve as a vehicle that sustains global inequalities between the South and the North. Not only in legitimising Western credentials through higher salaries for expat teachers, but also through the creation of economic and positional differentiations between local teachers working in international settings and those working in state-run/local forms of provision.

Yet, my research also highlights ways in which the internationalisation of ECE could potentially serve as a vehicle for promoting global values, inter-cultural modes of understanding, and construction of new practices of education and belonging that take in local and more Western values. For internationalisation of education to be successful, it has to be implemented with high sensitivity to local practices.

My findings also emphasise the need to promote a form of global citizenship education that is not detached from local context and issues. This can be done by drawing on a reflexive approach to global citizenship, as developed by Rizvi and Lingard (2009). Engel (2014) defines reflexive approaches to global education as an understanding that 'the global is not an abstract concept existing separate from students' everyday lives, but rather that local communities around the world are now more interdependent than ever before' (p. 242). In other words, an individual's positionality and reflexivity should create a linkage between an individual and local, as well as global, spaces. By developing this reflexivity further, students and teachers in education institutions could be equipped with an understanding that would not separate them from the society they are living in. The cases I draw on in this chapter emphasise the separation and fracturing that occurs within these internationalised settings, but also how this could be challenged.

Findings illuminated in this chapter also powerfully reveal how friendship can become a tool to dismantle the legacy of neo-colonialisation within international kindergartens. Perhaps on a larger scale, this could mean that international schools provide spaces where learning occurs, through the facilitation of mutual respect and understanding between local and expat teachers. First, teachers and students in international schools should acknowledge their privilege in being in such an environment, and then be encouraged to forge productive networks with individuals from local settings to mutually exchange ideas, learn from each other's experiences, and have the opportunity to form lasting relationships. Perhaps in doing so, more ethical and culturally sensitive practices of internationalisation of education can be achieved.

Notes

1. In this chapter, I am using the term *kindergarten* to refer to schooling within a larger framework and set of discourses around early childhood education (ECE).
2. By the time this chapter is written, the currency between US Dollars against Indonesian Rupiah is USD 1 equals to Rp. 14476.5.

References

Achinstein, B., & Meyer, T. (1997). *The uneasy marriage between friendship and critique: Dilemmas of fostering critical friendship in a novice teacher learning community.* Paper presented at the Annual Meeting of the American Educational Research Association (Chicago, IL, March 24–28, 1997).

Adriany, V. (2016). Gender in pre-school and child-centred ideologies. In J. Warin, I. Wernersson, & S. Brownhill (Eds.), *Men, masculinities and teaching in early childhood education* (pp. 70–82). London: Routledge.

Adriany, V. (2018). The internationalisation of early childhood education: Case study from selected kindergartens in Bandung, Indonesia. *Policy Futures in Education, 16*(1), 92–107. doi:10.1177/1478210317745399

Adriany, V., & Saefullah, K. (2015). Deconstructing human capital discourse in early childhood education in Indonesia. In T. Lightfoot-Rueda, R. L. Peach, & N. Leask (Eds.), *Global perspectives on human capital in early childhood education: Reconceptualizing theory, policy, and practice* (pp. 159–179). New York: Palgrave Macmillan.

Amirrachman, R. A. (2012). *Peace education in the Moluccas, Indonesia: Between global models and local interests.* (PhD Dissertation), University of Amsterdam.

Andreotti, V. O. (2014). Soft versus critical global citizenship education, *Development education in policy and practice* (pp. 21–31). New York: Springer.

Bailey, L. (2015). Reskilled and 'Running Ahead': Teachers in an international school talk about their work. *Journal of research in international education, 14*(1), 3–15. doi:10.1177/1475240915572949

Bhabha, H. K. (1994). *The location of culture.* London: Routledge.

Burman, E. (2008). *Deconstructing developmental psychology.* East Sussex: Routledge.

Charmaz, K. (2006). *Constructing grounded theory: A practical guide through qualitative analysis.* London, California, New Delhi, Singapore: SAGE Publication Ltd.

Crossley, M., & Tikly, L. (2004). Postcolonial perspectives and comparative and international research in education: A critical introduction. *Comparative Education, 40*(2), 147–156. doi:10.1080/0305006042000231329

Dýrfjörð, K. (2012). *Infected with neo-liberalism: The new landscape of early childhood settings in Iceland.* Paper presented at the Creating Communities: Local, National and Global Selected papers from the fourteenth Conference of the Children's Identity and Citizenship in Europe Academic Network, London.

Engel, L. C. (2014). Global citizenship and national (re)formations: Analysis of citizenship education reform in Spain. *Education, Citizenship and Social Justice*, 9(3), 239–254. doi:10.1177/1746197914545927

Engel, L. C., & Siczek, M. M. (2018a). A cross-national comparison of international strategies: Global citizenship and the advancement of national competitiveness. *Compare: A Journal of Comparative and International Education*, 48(5), 749–767.

Engel, L. C., & Siczek, M. M. (2018b). Framing global education in the United States: Policy perspectives'. In L. D. Hill & F. J. Levine (Eds.), *Global perspectives on education research*. (pp. 24–47). New York: Routledge.

Formen, A. (2017). In human-capital we trust, on developmentalism we act: The case of Indonesian early childhood education policy. In M. Li, J. Fox, & S. Grieshaber (Eds.), *Contemporary issues and challenge in early childhood education in the Asia-Pacific Region* (pp. 125–142). Singapore: Springer Singapore.

Foucault, M. (1984). The order of discourse. In M. Shapiro (Ed.), *The language of politics*. Oxford: Blackwell.

Gupta, A. (2006). *Early childhood education, postcolonial theory, and teaching practices in India: Balancing Vygotsky and the Veda*. New York: Palgrave Macmillan.

Gupta, A. (2008). Tracing global—Local transitions within early childhood curriculum and practice in India. *Research in Comparative and International Education*, 3(3), 266–280.

Gupta, A. (2018). How neoliberal globalization is shaping early childhood education policies in India, China, Singapore, Sri Lanka and the Maldives. *Policy Futures in Education*, 16(1), 11–28.

Hasan, A., Hyson, M., & Chang, M. C. (Eds.). (2013). *Early childhood education and development in poor villages of Indonesia: Strong foundations, later success*. Washington, DC: International Bank for Reconstruction and Development/The World Bank.

Heyward, M. (2002). From international to intercultural: Redefining the international school for a globalized world. *Journal of Research in International Education*, 1(1), 9–32.

Jahng, K. E. (2013). Reconceptualizing kindergarten education in South Korea: A postcolonial approach. *Asia Pacific Journal of Education*, 33(1), 81–96. doi :10.1080/02188791.2012.751898

Kunz, S. (2016). Privileged Mobilities: Locating the Expatriate in Migration Scholarship. *Geography Compass*, 10(3), 89–101. doi:10.1111/gec3.12253

Landry, D., & Maclean, G. (1996). *The Spivak reader: Selected works of Gayatri Chakravorty Spivak*. New York: Routledge.

Lave, J., & Wenger, E. (1991). *Situated learning: Legitimate peripheral participation*. Cambridge: Cambridge University Press.

Lee, I. F. (2018). (Re) Landscaping early childhood education in East Asia: A neoliberal economic and political imaginary. *Policy Futures in Education*, 16(1), 53–65.

Martin, F., & Griffiths, H. (2012). Power and representation: A postcolonial reading of global partnerships and teacher development through North—South study visits. *British Educational Research Journal*, 38(6), 907–927.

Maxwell, C. (2018). Changing spaces—The re-shaping of (elite) education through internationalisation. In C. Maxwell, U. Deppe, H. H. Krüger, & W.

Helsper (Eds.), *Elite education and internationalisation: From the early years into higher education* (Vol. 347–367). Basingstoke: Palgrave Macmillan.

Mierendorff, J., Ernst, T., & Maderin, M. (2018). Embedded Internationalisation and Privilege in German Early Years Provision. In C. Maxwell, U. Deppe, H. H Krüger, & Helsper, W. (Eds.), *Elite education and internationalisation: From the early years into higher education* (pp. 121–138). Basingstoke: Palgrave Macmillan.

Ministry of Education and Culture Republic of Indonesia. (2014). *2013 Curriculum of Early Childhood Education* (Vol. 146). Jakarta. Technical Guidance on Special Funding Allocation Non Physical Operational Cost for ECE Centres, (2018).

Miyahara, K., & Miyahara, H. (1994). 'Internationalisation' and early childhood education in Japan: Responsive education for young children. *Cambridge Journal of Education*, 24(2), 175–181.

Mohanty, C. T. (2006). Under Western eyes: Feminist scholarship and colonial discourse. In B. Ashcroft, G. Griffiths, & H. Tiffin (Eds.), *The post-colonial studies reader* (pp. 242–245). Oxon, New York: Routledge.

Mwebi, B. M., & Brigham, S. M. (2009). Preparing North American preservice teachers for global perspectives: An international teaching practicum experience in Africa. *Alberta Journal of Educational Research*, 55(3).

Newberry, J. (2010). The global child and non-governmental governance of the family in post-Suharto Indonesia. *Economy and Society*, 39(3), 403–426. doi: 10.1080/03085147.2010.486217

Penn, H. (2002). The world bank's view of early childhood. *Childhood*, 9(1), 118–132.

Penn, H. (2011). Travelling policies and global buzzwords: How international non-governmental organization and charities spread the word about early childhood in the global south. *Childhood*, 18(1), 94–113.

Press, F., & Woodrow, C. (2018). Marketisation, elite education and internationalisation in Australian early childhood education and care. In C. Maxwell, U. Deppe, H. H. Krüger, & W. Helsper, (Eds), *Elite education and internationalisation: From the early years into higher education* (pp. 139–160). Basingstoke: Palgrave Macmillan.

Rizvi, F. (2010). International students and doctoral studies in transnational spaces. In P. Thompson & M. Walker (Eds), *The Routledge doctoral supervisor's companion: Supporting effective research in education and the social sciences* (pp. 158–170). London: Routledge.

Rizvi, F., & Lingard, B. (2009). *Globalizing education policy*. London: Routledge.

Spivak, G. C. (2000). Translation as Culture. *Parallax*, 6(1), 13–24. doi:10.10 80/135346400249252

Swain, J. (2006). An ethnographic approach to researching children in junior school. *International Journal of Social Research Methodology*, 9(3), 199–213. doi:10.1080/13645570600761346

Swanborn, P. (2010). *Case study research: What, why and how?* London, California, India, Singapore: SAGE Publications Asia-Pacific Ltd.

Tanu, D. (2014). Becoming 'international': The cultural reproduction of the local elite at an international school in Indonesia. *South East Asia Research*, 22(4), 579–596.

Tanu, D. (2016). Going to school in 'Disneyland': Imagining an international school community in Indonesia. *Asian and Pacific Migration Journal*, 25(4), 429–450.

Tanu, D. (2017). *Growing up in transit: The politics of belonging at an International School*. New York: Berghan Books.

Tarc, P., & Mishra Tarc, A. (2015). Elite international schools in the Global South: Transnational space, class relationalities and the 'middling' international schoolteacher. *British Journal of Sociology of Education, 36*(1), 34–52. doi:10.1080/01425692.2014.971945

Viruru, R. (2001). Colonized through Language: The case of early childhood education. *Contemporary Issues in Early Childhood, 2*(1), 31–47. doi:10.2304/ciec.2001.2.1.7

Viruru, R. (2005). The impact of postcolonial theory on early childhood education. *Journal of Education, 35*(1), 7–30.

Walkerdine, V. (1998). Developmental psychology and the child-centered pedagogy: The insertion of Piaget into early education. In J. Henriques, W. Hollway, C. Urwin, C. Venn, & V. Walkerdine (Eds.), *Changing the subject: Psychology, social regulation, and subjectivity* (pp. 153–202). London: Routledge.

Weenink, D. (2008). Cosmopolitanism as a form of capital: Parents preparing their children for a globalizing world. *Sociology, 42*(6), 1089–1106.

White, L. A. (2011). The internationalization of early childhood education and care issues: Framing gender justice and child well-being. *Governance, 24*(2), 285–309. doi:10.1111/j.1468–0491.2011.01520.x

World Population Review. (2018). *Indonesia Population 2018*. Retrieved from http://worldpopulationreview.com/countries/indonesia-population/

Yemini, M. (2014). Internationalisation discourse: What remains to be said? *Perspectives: Policy and Practice in Higher Education, 18*(2), 66–71. doi:10.1080/13603108.2014.888019

Yemini, M. (2015). Internationalisation discourse hits the tipping point. *Perspectives: Policy and Practice in Higher Education, 19*(1), 19–22. doi:10.1080/13603108.2014.966280

Yemini, M., & Fulop, A. (2015). The international, global and intercultural dimensions in schools: An analysis of four internationalised Israeli schools. *Globalisation, Societies and Education, 13*(4), 528–552.

Yin, R. K. (2008). *Case study research: Design and methods (Applied Social Research Methods)*. London, New Delhi, Singapore: SAGE Publications Inc.

Yusuf, A. A., Sumber, A., & Rum, I. A. (2014). Twenty years of expenditure inequality in Indonesia, 1993–2013. *Bulletin of Indonesian Economic Studies, 50*(2), 243–254.

8 Inclusive Internationalisation in an International School in Amsterdam—Illusion or Reality?

Boris Prickarts

Introduction

Denise is a school which constitutes a part of the Dutch Esprit School Group in Amsterdam, a consortium of fourteen state-funded primary and secondary schools. In 2011, Esprit adopted a policy called *Esprit International*, which aimed to internationalise all of its schools. Denise was established in 2013 as an integral part of this policy. However, it has a unique position within the internationalising Esprit School Group since it focuses on recruiting a more heterogeneous population rather than the typical middle-class international students and thus claims to promote a unique type of inclusive internationalisation. In this way, Denise accommodates the growing demand for internationalised, English-based education from many middle class and mobile families while at the same time being committed to equality of opportunity for all students to access good schools. In this way, I argue, Denise resists creating greater cleavages within local education spaces, often resulting from increasing availability of international forms of education (Bates, 2011; Maxwell, 2018).

Since 2016, there has been an accelerated growth of internationally mobile families in the Amsterdam region, causing a surge in demand for international schooling. Apart from the Esprit School Group itself, the Amsterdam municipality has also taken an active interest in internationalising education by promoting various cross-sectorial initiatives and measures. The United Kingdom's impending withdrawal from the European Union (Brexit) acted as a catalyst for the municipality to step up its activities since more companies and banks were expected to leave their UK bases and potentially relocate to Amsterdam.

International schools are emerging as a main site for mobile professionals' cultivation of middle-class privilege (Yemini & Maxwell, 2018) as well as a safe choice for local elites (Yemini & Fulop, 2015). Traditionally, these schools would cater for the children of privileged, globally mobile families, but recently this market has been reorganised to address the needs of local middle classes and, to some extent, the less privileged migrants who cannot or do not want to assimilate within national education systems (Weenink, 2008). The rising numbers of international schools is also being fiercely promoted by the International Baccalaureate Organisation (IBO) and, as in the case of the Netherlands, by the national and regional governments as well.

This chapter focuses specifically on Denise because it gained public attention as it set out to take a rather different, arguably 'more locally sensitive' and inclusive approach to internationalisation of education. Right from the start, Denise agreed to use both English and Dutch as the languages of instruction, and to recruit a diverse student body that should include local Dutch students, as well as less resourced refugee/migrant students alongside more privileged children from international or globally mobile families. As a Dutch senator observed: 'The social and cultural benefits of this [Denise] international classroom are evident. . . . Is the government prepared to allow this [Denise] experiment?' (EK, 2015).

This chapter starts with a brief overview of engagements with internationalisation in Dutch education policy-making, followed by a section on the theoretical orientation shaping my research. Some of the ideas in this text have been published before (Prickarts, 2010, 2016), but new research is included here, allowing me to consider further the impact of Denise in the Amsterdam internationalised schooling space. A specific focus is taken to understand the role of the 'Esprit School Group policy agents' in determining the format of inclusive internationalisation that is promoted, and to articulate more specifically what an 'inclusive' form of internationalisation can look like. I also illuminate the important role of government in facilitating more inclusive modes of internationalisation, as they seek to balance the desire for internationalisation alongside a focus on equality in general and integration of immigrant and refugee communities in local education systems.

Internationalising Dutch Education, 1979–2018

Internationalisation within the Dutch education system is longstanding. As early as 1979, the Dutch Minister of Education, Van Kemenade, was looking for ways to attract foreign multinational companies to the Netherlands by providing appropriate schooling for the children of their employees. With the understanding that international education is key for such companies' employees, he hosted the first European Ministerial Conference on the International Baccalaureate (IB) in The Hague. In 1982 this event inspired three Dutch secondary school leaders to set up the first three international secondary departments in their schools, called Dutch International Secondary Schools (DISS), in Eindhoven, Hilversum and Oegstgeest. The Dutch international primary schools followed suit in 1984, and thus an association of Dutch international primary schools (DIPS) was established. At the same time, the extra funding required to set up and run the Dutch International Schools (DIS) was made available by the government.

However, in order to manage the financial expenditure of the policy commitment to internationalise education in the Netherlands, at this stage such schools were only allowed to recruit expatriate students. In the course of the 1980s, 'in the slipstream' of the development of the DIS, it became clear that many Dutch, often professional, middle-class parents whose children did not meet the mobility/nationality criteria, were nonetheless interested in receiving such an 'international education'. Thus, in 1989, the government sponsored a, predominantly Dutch-English, bilingual education programme (TTO, or TweeTalig Onderwijs). TTO rapidly spread into many mainstream Dutch schools from the mid-1990s, making it one of the most well-developed in Europe (Prickarts, 2010, p. 229). At the Dutch secondary school level, there has been an increase in the provision of internationalised programmes, from five schools offering a special internationalised programme in 1993 (Weenink, 2008, p. 1090), to around 130 schools in 2019 (Nuffic, 2019).

The Dutch government has been trying for over thirty years to keep the balance between preparing students for the perceived needs of the (global) knowledge economy;, accommodating the growing demand for internationalised, English-based education; and guarding a commitment to equality of opportunity for all students to access good, local schools, which sometimes can be threatened when international schools compete over students and resources with mainstream state schools. Finding a way to balance these aspirations came under increasing pressure since, according to a World Bank study, the percentage of low-performing, less advantaged fourteen-year-old students in regular Dutch schools rose from 14% in 2000 to 48% in 2015 (Herrera-Sosa, Hoftijzer, Gortazar, & Ruiz, 2018, p. 19). Both the Dutch Education Council and the Dutch Education Inspectorate recently confirmed this trend. The Dutch Education Council observed growing school segregation which 'limits the potential of Dutch education to contribute to Dutch social cohesion' (Onderwijsraad, 2018, p. 2), and the Dutch Education Inspectorate reported that segregation produces a 'bubble of the more and less privileged' (Onderwijsinspectie, 2018, p. 5). This mirrors the growing segregation found elsewhere in the world, and it can be attributed in part to the growing inequality in access to global competencies (Goren, Yemini, & Maxwell, 2018).

It took a very long time for the Dutch government to develop a coherent strategic vision regarding internationalisation of education. Only in 2016 did the Dutch Education Council, an advisory body to the Dutch government, offer the 'building blocks' for such a vision, based on the concept of 'internationalisation at home' (Knight, 2004; Onderwijsraad, 2016). It advised the government to *recommend* to all schools to work in different ways to contribute to developing international competencies in a local context (Onderwijsraad, 2016, p. 29–30). One year later, in 2017, the government set up a special taskforce to help manage the demand and supply of international education in order to keep the Netherlands attractive for transnational companies (TNCs) and to safeguard good quality international education for the children of their workers (Ministerie van Onderwijs, 2017).

Theoretical Framework and Research Design

This research makes use of critical social theory (Bhaskar, 1978), a lens of inquiry which posits an ontological assumption that *relations* (e.g. between state and individual, or school and parent) generate phenomena (e.g. inequalities) and that they should be the core focus of a researcher. A related assumption made in critical social theory is that agents and their social positions are located in a 'field'. The field theoretical paradigm posits reality as a *social construct* 'in the eye of the beholder', i.e. a *perception* organised by a set of cultural dispositions called *habitus* (Bourdieu, 1977, p. 81) and a perception 'in terms of making sense of a prestructured causal world' (Levi-Martin, 2003, p. 24). International education can be seen as such a field (Bunnell, 2014, p. 37–38; Weenink, 2008, p. 1102, 2012, p. 39; Brown & Lauder, 2011, p. 48), in which agents manoeuvre within the limits of structures and their generative mechanisms, co-creating and sustaining their 'day-to-day interactions, practices and meaning making' (Al-Youssef, 2009, p. 132–33). This research builds on a suggested notion of 'embedded agency' and 'structuration' (Cambridge, 2013, p. 195), coming from institutional theory (DiMaggio & Powell, 1983; Giddens, 1991). This perspective argues that the institutional context influences expectations and actions of social agents. Thus, social agents may in principle be paradoxically embedded within the institutional context or perpetuate existing patterns and structures whilst their intention is actually to try to change them.

It may have been that structuration pressures on Denise have subjected it to some degree of isomorphism (Shields, 2015). Isomorphism is understood as a 'constraining process that forces one unit to resemble other units that face the same set of environmental conditions' (Hawley, 1968, cited by DiMaggio, & Powell, 1983, p. 149). So far, research supports a tendency towards isomorphism, when the organisational arrangements, publicity materials and other features of schools in competition with each other frequently appear to show convergence (Cambridge, 2013, p. 195).

In order to operationalise structuration theory, I studied the process and rationales of the internationalisation of education at Denise by focusing on three elements: (1) its organisational structure, (2) its expectations for schooling and (3) its policy agents' actions (i.e. of the students, teachers, parents, school director and board manager) regarding policy, curriculum and pedagogy. My data originated from eight semi structured interviews (carried out in November and December 2018 with the board manager, the Denise director, two Denise teachers, two Denise students and two Denise parents), two lesson observations at Denise (using a standardised observation template) and the analysis of Denise/ Esprit documents (e.g. the 2018 Esprit strategic management report, the Denise budgets 2014–2018, the minutes of Esprit management meetings, the Denise School Guide 2018–2019 and the Denise website).

Denise as an Organisational Structure

From its establishment, Denise has found itself under pressure from within and outside of the Netherlands. According to the Esprit board manager, it is a constant challenge to innovate education but also 'to keep things within the parameters of the [Dutch] law'. For example, Denise is using English as the language of instruction for more than the legal maximum amount of educational learning time due to its desire to allow the students to reach an advanced level in spoken and written English. However, and untypically for an international school, its student body includes Dutch local and underprivileged refugee/migrant students who cannot afford to pay tuition fees, as well as students from internationally mobile privileged families. These students often possess a lower level of English and lack the external resources for private tutoring and extra lessons. In such a situation, Denise is the only place in the Netherlands where less privileged children might gain high English language proficiency and avoid tracking based on previous achievements. Moreover, this school is unique in its structure, since it integrates primary school and secondary education together, thus avoiding competition to enter different tracks for secondary schooling, which so often fosters inequality. Some parents viewed this focus as an attractive feature of Denise, as illustrated by a Dutch father who said that he chose for his sons to go to Denise because he felt it offered an important alternative to the mainstream Amsterdam education system:

> My kids have joined the school recently and our primary motivation is that they, as Denise students, will not be subjected to the current system for Amsterdam secondary school selection. As Denise primary and—later on—Denise secondary school students, they will stay at Denise [the whole way through] and they don't need to draw lots for an Amsterdam secondary school.

Clearly, an important feature of Denise is that it is perceived by all interviewees to help less privileged and migrant students to 'do so much better' in dealing with a heavily standardised, stratified and segregated Dutch education system. Here, a fourteen-year-old student explained that for her Denise is:

> . . . extra help, an extra opportunity. . . . I have been at different schools, here in the Netherlands and abroad. [Denise helps me] to make a good start in life. Life is long enough and school is but a small part. So it is important to make good use of that short period of time.

During my previous research in 2016, parents and students expected the school to provide them with an open-minded disposition as well as a set of 'global competencies'. These were regarded as critical if they were to make their way in international social and work arenas. During this most recent phase of the research on this school, the Denise parents considered the school not only as opening up 'the international', but also as an alternative to the Dutch national education system. The following parent explained why such an alternative *within* the Dutch education system was so welcome:

> Here in the Netherlands, education can be really stratified and performative. The moment you're earmarked as a 'vocational' student for example, it's difficult to get rid of that label, which is seen as a negative label.

Inclusive Internationalisation at Denise

While some parents and students addressed the organisational structure of Denise as unique and appealing, it seems that the school's management stressed the global dimensions instilled through the school's curriculum and settings as outstanding. For example, the Esprit board manager and the Denise director see Denise as a school where an awareness of global interdependencies is taught; as a place where a more active stance towards the world's problems is encouraged, and where skills to deal with difference and diversity and taught. There is a mutual awareness among participants in Denise that they are involved in a common enterprise, which is embedded in the school's nature. Denise's inclusivity helps, as a teacher explains:

> For example a married off Pakistani girl and a group of Amsterdam girls can explain to each other really well why all of them are happy with the choices they have (at school)! And we have students who don't have enough money for the tram making friends with students who are taken to school in a taxi. Diversity is the norm here.

Denise students and the school leader certainly desire 'to be a different school' and 'to be more international than the average international school'. They want to position their school alongside the Amsterdam International Community School (AICS), but also perform a different function. The AICS is one of the other Esprit schools described as a 'golden opportunity' and—with Denise—as a 'winning team'. The Esprit board manager said that Denise offers 'an alternative to children who are on the waiting list of the AICS' and to those internationally mobile children who 'are considering staying more long term in Amsterdam'. A teacher even indicated that Denise is filling 'a gap between wealthy expat schools and less affluent local schools', providing less affluent migrant students with the opportunity to do the IB Diploma Programme (DP). When I asked an immigrant mother (who has two children at the AICS, one at Denise) what she hopes from Denise, she responded:

> To help migrant students and other students who are living here long term, to work together and learn in an Amsterdam, Dutch context (. . .) I hope that Denise students realise that they need to remember what their roots are and that they should avoid locking themselves up in a, sometimes elitist, bubble. . . . What happens at some large and popular schools [is that] students arrive as individuals but leave again looking just like each other.

The global dimension of Denise is actually used to provide the necessary glue to facilitate an inclusive environment among such a heterogeneous student population—this on top of other stated goals of international education. For example, the Esprit board manager framed Denise's unique approach to internationalisation of education in managerial terms: 'It is not a matter of copying AICS' IBDP and that's that. Denise staff need to 'own' what they develop together'.

Therefore a continued concerted motion was observed between field structuration and *heterogenisation*, accentuating Denise's specific local context. In other words, the reactions to these different and typical types of structuration pressures were guided by a strong desire or vision of Denise to be different and do things differently. This may indicate a process of *anisomorphism*, of Denise developing its own type of international school instead of becoming 'more of the same' (e.g. the AICS).

Denise's Expectations for What Its Education Will Lead To

As in other cases, Denise's stakeholders (e.g. parents, teachers and managers) held various and sometimes conflicting expectations as to what exactly the school should achieve. A typical characteristic of a pragmatic take on international education is to restrict international learning to English as the main language of instruction, which is regarded as an asset and leading to a competitive advantage (Weenink,

2008, p. 1097). When I asked a father what he hoped to achieve for his children by them attending Denise, he said, 'To help [them] transition from Denise, with the help of the IPC [International Primary Curriculum] and the IB, to other schools abroad. And to obtain a bilingual education'.

One teacher argued they needed to be trained to be internationally minded teachers, articulating a number of eclectic rationales, 'Amsterdam itself is a multicultural city and in order to live and work here one requires an international mindset. And for world peace and a job in the future. True relationship-making is needed and this starts at school'. Other actors, mainly from the managing team, seemed to therefore suggest a range of ideological reasons as the main drivers of the Denise initiative. These included 'knowing about and dealing with your own and different backgrounds'; 'becoming free from stereotyping'; and 'to educate world citizens' who are prepared to act on 'the world's problems, like war'. Interestingly, the Esprit board manager set these expectations for Denise schooling against those she had for the AICS:

> An extra expectation—like a cherry on top—for the AICS is that it enables students to transition more easily to schools in other parts of the world. Parents pay for that. Their careers force them to buy temporary, joined-up schooling in different places in the world where their work takes them. For Denise it is different. It helps to educate world citizens.

This expectation is supported by the findings of this research, including the internal Denise/Esprit documents. They confirm that 'For the next five years, the aim of internationalising our education is to increase the equality of opportunity and social coherence in Amsterdam, the Netherlands and the world' (Esprit School Group Archives, 2018b). In addition, 'international cooperation within the Esprit School Group, with the AICS as a central focus, needs to increase and feasibility studies need to be carried out to explore the possibilities of the introduction of more international programmes at more Esprit schools' (Esprit School Group Archives, 2018c).

Internationalisation of education is something that needs to be articulated and implemented. It comes with espoused objectives and with people putting them in practice, as Archer (2007, p. 9-10) argues:

> the pursuit of human projects in the social domain frequently encounters structural properties and activates them as powers. In such cases there are two sets of causal powers involved in any attempt to develop a successful social practice: those of subjects themselves and those of relevant structural or cultural properties . . . agents have the capacity to suspend the exercise of constraints (and enablements) through their circumventory (or renunciatory) actions.

The Denise case illustrates this point, challenging again the idea of a trend towards isomorphism.

Denise's Policy Agents' Actions Regarding Policy, Curriculum and Pedagogy

At Denise, particular factors led to a context where it could emerge as a more inclusive international school focused on local forms of citizenship and integration in a local education market system. These factors include the schooling needs of less resourced refugee/migrant students, institutional rapprochement with the other Esprit schools because the Denise format was not possible within Dutch education policy at the time, children on the waiting lists of other international schools and the increase of 'internationals' settling more long term in Amsterdam.

Particularly parents and teachers were observed to be active international education policy agents. The parents clearly supported the idea of an inclusive, local form of internationalisation. They expressed their objections to a typical international school being focused on English-based, 'international education' for the preparation of predominantly middle-class children for globally located destinations (in terms of higher education and work). A globally mobile mother reacted in the following way to her children being in a school that is not a typical international school, which she saw as 'very pushy, homework-heavy and factory-like. Education should give students the opportunity to do things their own way, regardless of the marks you get or any level of performance. Here in the Netherlands, education can be really streamed and performative'. The teachers have been observed adopting a more transformative rather than an instrumentalist dimension to their pedagogy, didactics and curriculum. Their teaching, learning and programmes were seen to be geared more towards students' transformative (open-ended, risky to the Self) than instrumentalist (converging towards set goals) experiences (Tarc, 2013). This pedagogy is not typical of Dutch mainstream schools (Meijer, 2013, p. 38) nor of typical international schools (Cambridge, 2013).

In a lesson about the 'reality of Mathematics', for example, with a group of sixteen- and seventeen-year-olds, the teacher left a lot of room for deviation from the planned lesson structure and her own preconceived ideas. She asked her students to produce a video presentation which would evidence a creative take on the issue of abstract, theoretical versus practical, real-life Maths. The video presentations invited both the teacher and the students to reflect on and question different ways of knowing. For example, the following questions were asked:

STUDENT 1: Is it possible to calculate something you don't know?
STUDENT 2: If Maths is real, where can we find evidence and justification in real life for it?
STUDENT 3: Does mathematical proof provide us with completely certain knowledge?

Students were challenged to disagree with, and question the reliability of different perspectives, without dismissing them. A teacher-initiated but student-driven dialogue developed during the lesson. Various perspectives were considered and critiqued, without ending up with 'the right one'. Students were enabled to act as student teachers and intervene when they thought the lesson needed the teacher's explanation. Twice during the lesson students successfully asked the teacher to change course. In those instances, she stopped the video and the note-taking from the whiteboard and discussed the students' questions.

In another lesson, seven- and eight-year-olds were asked to write up and act out a conversation with *Sinterklaas*. He is a typical Dutch Santa Claus—with Spanish/Turkish roots—who celebrates his birthday on 5 December by giving presents to children. A student unexpectedly took over the *Sinterklaas* part from the teacher when he was acting out a conversation with another student. The teacher, instead of trying to stick to his planned lesson objectives of that moment, encouraged this intervention and taught the whole class a lesson about acting:

TEACHER: This is real acting! You are intruding my conversation, but you are pretending to be someone you are not! You are a real actor!

The teacher made conscious use of situations which allowed students to reflect on their own behaviour, instead of telling them how to behave exactly. When he asked a student what he would like to have as a present, a long pause followed. The following quote shows how the teacher uses his skills to create a 'post-experiential moment'. He deliberately adopted a focus on developing dispositions, instead of creating a 'pre-experiential moment' with a focus on competencies:

TEACHER: It seems you would like to think about it. And that's fine. Perhaps—judging from your silent pose—you would like a statue?

His students were encouraged to find out how play acting a conversation with *Sinterklaas* really works, instead of just doing well. He was interested in the process more than in the product, the actual roleplay. The teacher exemplified cooperation between himself and the students and connected with them. He was also an active listener and asked a lot of questions himself, instead of only telling the students what was required. Here again, we can see how traditions and worldviews of students were taken into account, and teachers succeeded in managing potentially complex situations, while proactively fostering inclusive pedagogy.

Conclusions

I argue that schooling at Denise, despite the adoption of the IBDP (Esprit School Group Archives, 2018a) and the fact that it is managed by the same organisation, has been engaging in a unique form of inclusive internationalisation. This form of internationalisation might be interesting to explore in other settings, as it is aimed not only at reaching out to the world, but also for reaching into local communities, through engaging local, sometimes immigrant communities from less privileged backgrounds, and including them in this more globally oriented education. I suggest that so far, Denise has been able to continue to resist general isomorphism processes and has not become a school claiming to offer an English-based 'international education' for predominantly middle-class international students as is found in so many places elsewhere in the world (Cambridge, 2013). The reactions of the Esprit staff, parents and students to the different and typical types of structuration pressures were guided by a strong desire or vision of the Esprit School Group to be different and to do things differently.

Despite my research finding (Prickarts, 2016) that particularly Esprit parents and students expected more of the same type of international-mindedness and global job market opportunities from the Esprit schools, the Denise policy agents have resisted becoming a 'bargaining zone' and converging to a more uniform model for international schooling: the Esprit board manager, Denise director, teachers and parents continued to perceive the internationalisation of education as a desirable, ideologically driven supplement to national education programmes. The particular shape of internationalisation adopted by Denise was largely supported by them as it met their needs. Particularly parents and teachers have been able to take the space to support a holistic, international dimension to education that is aimed at equal opportunities and social cohesion, as opposed to an individual, personalised approach framed towards a 'projected' market (standardisation, performance) requirement (Engel & Siczek, 2017). True 'open-mindedness' is the opposite of political correctness and means that one learns how to come to know one's own and the Other's interpretative capacity (Tarc, 2013, p. 114).

References

Al-Youssef, J. (2009). *The internationalisation of higher education institutions: A case study of a British university* (EdD thesis), University of Bath.

Archer, M. S. (2007). *Making our way through the world: Human reflexivity and social mobility.* Cambridge, UK: Cambridge University Press.Bates, R. (2011). *Schooling internationally: Globalisation, internationalisation and the future for international schools.* Abingdon, Oxon: Routledge.

Bhaskar, R. (1978). On the possibility of social scientific knowledge and the limits of naturalism. *Journal for the Theory of Social Behaviour, 8*(1), 1–28.

Bourdieu, P. (1977). *Outline of a theory of practice.* Cambridge, UK: The Press Syndicate of the University of Cambridge.

Brown, C., & Lauder, H. (2011). The political economy of international schools and social class formation. In R. Bates (Ed.), *Schooling internationally:*

Globalisation, internationalisation and the future for international schools (pp. 39–58). Oxford, UK: Routledge.

Bunnell, T. (2014). *The changing landscape of international schooling: Implications for theory and practice.* Abingdon, Oxon: Routledge.

Cambridge, J. (2013). Dilemmas of international education: A Bernsteinian analysis. In R. Pearce (Ed.), *International education and schools. Moving beyond the first 40 years* (pp. 183–204). London: Bloomsbury.

Dimaggio, P. J., & Powell, W. W. (1983). The iron cage revisited: Institutional isomorphism and collective rationality in organizational fields. *American Sociological Review, 48*(2), 147–160.

EK 2015–2016, (2015, September 22). *Verslag van de vergadering van 22 September 2015 (2015/2016 nr. 1).* Retrieved from www.eerstekamer.nl/verslagdeel/20150922/onderwijs_in_de_engelse_duitse_of

Engel, L. C., & Siczek, M. M. (2017). A cross-national comparison of international strategies: Global citizenship and the advancement of national competitiveness. *Compare: A Journal of Comparative and International Education, 48*(5), 749–767.

———. (2018a). *Denise diploma programmes.* Retrieved from https://denise.espritscholen.nl/home/english/diploma-programmes/

———. (2018b). *Esprit strategic management report.*

———. (2018c). *Minutes of Esprit management meetings.* (accessed 6 November 2018).

Giddens, A. (1991). Structuration theory: Past, Present and Future. In C. Bryant & D. Jary (Eds.), *Giddens' theory of structuration: A Critical Appreciation* (pp. 201–222). London: Routledge.

Goren, H., Yemini, M., & Maxwell, C. (2018). Israeli teachers make sense of global citizenship education in a divided society-religion, marginalisation and economic globalisation. *Comparative Education, 55*(1), 1–21.

Hawley, A. (1968). Human ecology. In D. L. Sills (Ed.), *International encyclopaedia of the social sciences.* New York: Macmillan.

Herrera-Sosa, K., Hoftijzer, M., Gortazar, L., & Ruiz, M. (2018). *Education in the EU: Diverging learning opportunities?* Washington, DC: World Bank. Retrieved from https://openknowledge.worldbank.org/handle/10986/30007

Knight, J. (2004). Internationalization remodeled: Definition, approaches and rationales. *Journal of Studies in International education, 8*(1), 5–31.

Levi-Martin, J. (2003). 'What is Field Theory?' *American Journal of Sociology, 109*(1), 1–49.

Maxwell, C. (2018). Changing spaces—The re-shaping of (elite) education through internationalisation. In C. Maxwell, U. Deppe, H. H. Krueger, & W. Helsper (Eds.), *Elite education and internationalisation: From the early years into higher education* (pp. 347–367). Basingstoke: Palgrave Macmillan.

Meijer, W. A. J. (2013). *Onderwijs, weer weten waarom.* Amsterdam: SWP.

Ministerie van Onderwijs. (2017). *Voorbereid op de toekomst. Actieplan van de Taskforce Internationaal Onderwijs (The Hague).* Retrieved from www.rijksoverheid.nl/documenten/rapporten/2017/06/13/voorbereid-op-de-toekomst

Nuffic (2019). *Is er een tto school bij mij in de buurt? (Nuffic, Den Haag).* Retrieved from www.ikkiestto.nl/is-er-een-tto-school-bij-mij-in-de-buurt/

Onderwijsinspectie (2018). *Hoofdlijnen van de Staat van het Onderwijs 2018 (The Hague: Onderwijsinspectie).* Retrieved from www.onderwijsinspectie.

nl/documenten/rapporten/2018/04/11/hoofdlijnen-stelseloverzicht-de-staat-van-het-onderwijs-2018

Onderwijsraad (2016). *Internationaliseren met ambitie, uitgebracht aan de Staatssec-retaris van Onderwijs, Cultuuur en Wetenschap* (The Hague: Onderwijsraad). Retrieved from www.onderwijsraad.nl/publicaties/2016/internationaliseren-met-ambitie/volledig/item7414

Onderwijsraad (2018). *Doorgeschoten differentiatie in het onderwijsstelsel.* Retrieved from www.onderwijsraad.nl/upload/documents/publicaties/volledig/Publiekssamenvatting-sven.pdf

Prickarts, B. J. A. (2010). Equality or equity, player or guardian: The Dutch gov-ernment and its role in providing access opportunities for government spon-sored international secondary education, 1979–2009. *Journal of Research in International Education, 9*(3), 227–244.

Prickarts, B. J. A. (2016), *Shifting borders: A case study of internationalisation of education within a Dutch School Group in Amsterdam* (Unpublished EdD thesis), University of Bath.

Shields, R. (2015). Measurement and isomorphism in international education. In M. Hayden, J. Levy, & J. J. Thompson (Eds.), *The SAGE handbook of research in international education* (Chapter 32, 2nd Ed.). London: Sage Publications.

Tarc, P. (2013). *International education in global times: Engaging the pedagogic.* New York: Peter Lang.

Weenink, D. (2008). Cosmopolitanism as a form of capital: Parents preparing their children for a globalizing world. *Sociology, 42*(6), 1089–1106.

Yemini, M., & Maxwell, C. (2018). Discourses of global citizenship education: The influences of the global middle classes. In *The Palgrave handbook of global citizenship and education* (pp. 1–14). London: Palgrave Macmillan.

9 Pedagogy for Internationalisation

An Australian Secondary School Case Study

Sherene Hattingh

Introduction

Pedagogy for internationalisation is a pivotal concept for education institutions, especially in the current climate. To date, research into pedagogy for internationalisation has been examined within higher education (Leask, 2013), but it has not been a focus in studies of secondary schooling. In this chapter I seek to examine pedagogical approaches for internationalisation by looking closely at the case of one school in Australia which, through enrolling an increasing number of international students from abroad, is having to meet their needs and consider how to adapt their pedagogy to suit. This will enable me to theorise a little more broadly about pedagogy for internationalisation within secondary schooling.

One might argue that internationalisation is no longer an option for schools to engage with, but has become a requirement, similarly to higher education. It involves more than simply enrolling international students; it means also learning to appreciate and work with the similarities and differences found in an increasingly linked world (Leask, 2011). Knight defines internationalisation as 'the process of integrating an international, intercultural and/or global dimension into the purpose, functions (teaching, research and service) and delivery of (higher) education' (Knight, 2006, p. 13). According to Knight (2004), there are two key ways in which internationalisation occurs—where students are encouraged to go abroad or the development of initiatives that seek to internationalise at 'home'. These forms of engagement can happen simultaneously as well as online (Pitts & Brooks, 2017). The focus in this chapter is on internationalisation that occurs at home through the curriculum, and the various teaching and learning approaches developed to meet the needs of a changing cohort of students, all with a focus at school level.

More than 3.7 million students are enrolled across Australian schools. The Australian Curriculum intends to provide a national standard where the same content is accessible to all students and where achievement can be measured consistently with national standards. The Australian

Curriculum has seven general capabilities it aims to develop in students, which are seen as 'vital for life and work in the 21st century', and some of them are directly related to the global dimensions of education (Australian Curriculum Assessment and Reporting Authority (ACARA), 2010). Goren and Yemini (2017) note that many countries have similarly adapted their curricula to develop curricula and related pedagogical approaches that seek to prepare their students to become global citizens as part of their internationalisation agenda. A global citizen is defined by Pitts & Brooks (2017) as someone who is able to understand and be open to '"diverse modes of being"; learns to appreciate and accept cultural enigmas; and has the ability to look beyond cultural divides and assumptions' (p. 264). Goren and Yemini (2017) present global citizenship as more than just emerging out of facilitated trade, extensive immigration, increased mobility and changes in state relationships, including the development of supra-natural organisations. Global citizenship also includes how people perceive themselves, their civic duty, and reflecting on the changes they go through as a result of these global processes. This means that many teachers and education policy-makers promote global citizenship education as a key outcome of mandatory schooling today.

Alongside this development, mobility for schooling continues to rise. Many students are choosing to study abroad, taking secondary schooling qualifications in English-speaking countries (Curtis & Ledgerwood, 2018; Pope, Sánchez, Lehnert, & Schmid, 2014). The prospect of receiving an English-medium education while developing English proficiency, as well as learning to live in a different culture, and the possibility of being able to stay in the new country long-term means mobility for secondary schooling is increasing (Yang, Zhang, & Sheldon, 2018). It is believed to be critical in furthering students' opportunities for accessing elite forms of higher education and future employment opportunities in their home countries as well as abroad (Henard, Diamond, & Roseveare, 2012; Nilsson & Ripmeester, 2016). For students entering English-medium education, who come from oftentimes quite different cultures and environments (Hogan & Hathcote, 2014), the different kind of pedagogy they encounter can lead to challenges for their integration and academic success.

Australian Schools Actively Recruiting International Students

Recruiting international students is a growing trend in Australian schools and elsewhere (Meng, Zhu, & Cao, 2018). Focus is often placed on the financial gain that institutions experience when enrolling international students. The Australian Government actively markets Australia as 'a leading global education powerhouse with some of the world's best facilities and educators, providing local and international students with a range of quality study options' (Engel & Siczek, 2017; 'Study in Australia', 2018). Australia is the third most popular study destination for international students, behind only the United States of America and the United Kingdom. Australia is also listed as having five out of the thirty best student cities world-wide. International education is Australia's third largest export valued at $19 billion (Study in Australia, 2018). As part of the focus in growing the international student numbers across the schooling sector, a specific national strategy has been developed—the *National Strategy for International Education 2025* (published in 2016).

International student enrolment across Australian schools has steadily been rising for the last four years from 19,440 in 2015 to 25,866 in 2018 (Department of Education and Training, 2018). Australian secondary schools are choosing to enrol overseas students, with the financial benefits of high tuition fees seemingly driving this move. The other potential benefits—such as opportunities for promoting cultural awareness, international networking and collaboration, particularly for the future, as well as local economic benefits for the community (Luo & Jamieson-Drake, 2013)—often appear to be overlooked by institutions and staff (Hattingh, Kettle, & Brownlee, 2017).

Key Features of Internationalisation for a School

Across the literature I identified key institutional features that affect how internationalisation is conceived, practised and embedded in a school: the organisation and management of the school; the school culture; how cultural knowledge is offered to the students; and the teaching and learning approach. Critically, my review emphasises how significantly the first three key institutional features impact the pedagogy at a school. Engaging in internationalisation pursuits requires preparation, planning and responsibility across a school, so as to ensure that there is a welcoming and supportive community for the international student (Engel & Siczek, 2017). All school stakeholders—staff, students and parents—need to be involved in this process. A school that internationalises needs policies and practices that are implemented and followed across the institution by the administration team, teachers, students and parents (Hattingh, 2016).

The Organisation and Management of the School

The administration team—which usually includes a principal, school council and other administrative staff—of a school ensures that the school meets the legal requirements for internationalisation (Education Services for Overseas Students [ESOS] Act, 2000). Another part of the organisation and management of the school is the compiling, dissemination and implementation of school policies directly connected with internationalisation, ensuring that all stakeholders are aware and guided by these policies (Kyriakides, Creemers, Antoniou, Demetriou, & Charalambous, 2015). Research has found that school policy has a direct effect on teachers' actions, which indirectly affects teaching and learning (Kyriakides et al., 2015). This planning, organisation and management within a school forms part of the school culture directly impacting well-being for all, as well as contributing to internationalisation.

The School Culture

The organisation and management of the school determines and significantly directs the school culture in regards to whether diversity is valued and integrated into efforts to promote equality for all enrolled students (Hattingh, 2016). This means that the international students should be treated fairly by: being able to enrol in all offered subjects, being part of the planning and organisation within the class and assessments, being able to revise and prepare their learning in their first language, having their home culture acknowledged, being protected from discrimination and being able to actively and fully participate in school life (Clegg, 1996). School culture determines the sense of belonging which impacts membership for both students and their families, as well as their academic achievement (Harris, 2018). Including the student's family via open communication is essential to cultivating positive support and connections (Hoy & Miskel, 2008), which, in turn, affects the international students' wellbeing. A school administration that promotes and develops a school culture where all work together and take responsibility for the international students is a school culture that promotes internationalisation (Hattingh, 2016).

The Services Provided for Cultural Knowledge/Cross Cultural Competency

Another role of school management that impacts teaching and learning for internationalisation, according to research (Hattingh et al., 2017; Popadiuk, 2010), is that of providing resources and equipping staff with cultural knowledge and cross cultural competency. This means that specific and specialised help and support needs to be available for teachers and students when required. By providing these services, a school is investing in the care and general wellbeing of all, including the international students. Schools that internationalise need to regularly audit their management of services and planning as part of their investment into the future. Included in this process is the provision of pastoral care through translators, counselling and guidance assistance (Jin & Wang, 2018), establishing and maintaining staff engagement by allocating time and collaborative opportunities for staff (Brigaman, 2002; Gibbons,

2006) and professional development for internationalisation (Karathanos, 2010). Australian secondary schools already have diversity within the student and teacher population; however, internationalisation also presents different social, educational and linguistic student profiles that are unfamiliar to teachers. Internationalisation challenges established patterns and expectations of interactions for teachers, particularly pertaining to teaching and learning (Hattingh et al., 2017).

Pedagogy for Internationalisation

Teachers are at the forefront of internationalisation efforts when interacting with international student cohorts in their classes. In reviewing the limited literature with regards to teaching and learning for internationalisation, four pivotal elements emerge as central for teachers to proactively facilitate internationalisation. I draw on these to construct the concept of 'pedagogy for internationalisation'—a critical tool for analysing internationalisation efforts in schools and for developing approaches to improve these efforts. The four elements are: the teacher's attitude towards the international students; the teacher's cross cultural competency and cultural knowledge; the choice of teaching approach and perception of learning styles; and classroom communication patterns. These listed elements are intertwined and affect each other, ultimately shaping the teaching and learning experience for all. Given this is the central focus of this chapter, I will outline in a little more detail these various elements that shape pedagogical approaches in classrooms containing international students in secondary schools. After this review, I will examine how a school I studied engages with pedagogy for internationalisation.

The teacher's attitude towards the international student can be varied and depends on their own educational experiences, English as a Second Language (ESL) training, experience in teaching ESL students, gender and personality, as well as any previous contact they have had with different cultures (Youngs & Youngs, 2001). Teachers may perceive international students as either challenging or enriching within their classroom. This belief will impact the manner in which the teacher then models and demonstrates equity, learning and inclusion within their classroom through their planning, organising and implementation of their teaching (Hachfeld Hahn, Schroeder, Anders, Stanat, & Kunter, 2011). Reeves (2006) found that teachers did not want to modify coursework for English learners in their mainstream classes but preferred to give them more time to complete the tasks. Her research also found that the teachers felt unequipped to work with ESL learners in their mainstream classes. These perceptions of feeling inadequate will impact the teacher's attitude towards the international students and towards the pedagogy they implement.

Cultural knowledge and/or cross cultural competency is critical to making teachers feel confident about engaging with local and international students. Cultural knowledge is displayed when someone understands and acknowledges diversity and difference and knows about a range of cultural values and norms (Lareau, 2015). Cross cultural competency is demonstrated when an individual is able to successfully interact and communicate with people from different cultures, as well as be sensitive and display emotional competence across cultures by being able to understand and interpret a different way of life and competently explain it to others who live in another culture (Fantini, 2000). This means that teachers need more than just the understanding and knowledge of a student's culture, they need to interact and become involved with the culturally and linguistically diverse student and their wide-ranging educational needs. Linked directly to this is the need for the teachers to engage in professional development in these areas. Love and Arkoudis (2004) found that mainstream teachers were not aware of the resources they had access to or the support they needed for internationalisation. Researchers have found that Western teachers hold particular cultural expectations of their students which are often perceived negatively and impact on the teaching and learning within a classroom (Faltis & Wolfe, 1999; Gunderson, 2000; Li, 2004). For example, teachers expect students to hold eye contact when spoken to, to actively participate in groups and to ask questions to clarify. However, when students do not do this, teachers perceive them as inattentive, lazy and/or disrespectful. Teachers' expectations of students link with the choice and use of teaching approach and perception of learning styles implemented within the classroom.

Effective pedagogy is practised by teachers who have an understanding and knowledge of their students as learners. Including international students within classes requires teachers to have an understanding and awareness of second-language pedagogy. According to research, second language learners need explicit instruction regarding the rules and grammar of English for academic writing and literacy (Lightbrown & Spada, 2006); this is particularly the case in the Australian context where English is both the medium and target of learning (Gibbons, 2003). A key element in second-language pedagogy is knowing the learner and their background, specifically their previous pedagogical experience and language proficiency (Karathanos, 2010). Pedagogy also requires the teacher to create a safe, secure and supported classroom to address individual student needs. Teachers who know their students hold reasonable expectations and plan well for their learners (Hattingh et al., 2017).

Classroom communication is pivotal in pedagogy for internationalisation. Part of classroom communication is academic communication, which differs from spoken English. Teachers who are unfamiliar with the difference between academic English and conversational English are often impatient and/or surprised with the international students.

This difference also affects the international students when they do not achieve as well as they hoped or expected because of this differentiation in the type of language they are required to demonstrate (Heydon, 2003; Reeves, 2006). International students enrolled in Australian secondary schools have met the entry English proficiency requirements but often experience difficulty in their English communicative competence, for example, critical evaluation, comprehension and writing, and presenting substantial written and spoken texts (Hattingh et al., 2017). Talk is a significant element of any classroom and is a crucial aspect to learning and language development, which assists in the process of meaning making, negotiation, clarification and rewording (Davies & Pearse, 2000; Gibbons, 2002). According to Lewis and Fusco (2017), teacher talk matters and, as stated previously, is especially important in pedagogy for internationalisation. Teachers talk in order to direct, question, explain and prompt their students. Researchers have found that teachers need to reflect on their teacher talk in regards to their vocabulary, syntax, talking speed, subject expectations, etc. (Lewis & Fusco, 2017) when working with culturally and linguistically diverse students.

Teachers are paramount in the process of internationalising a school. Pedagogy is the business of schools, and teachers are responsible for implementing the curricula within the classroom and assessing it as part of their role. Effective teachers, I argue, create authentic relationships with their pupils, preserve suitable learning expectations for their students, implement a variety of teaching approaches, participate in classroom curriculum development, regularly evaluate and reflect on their classes to improve teaching and learning, and network with other teachers focusing on discussing their pedagogy (Grant & Gillette, 2006; West, 1998). The way in which a teacher conducts themselves in their classroom reveals their practised pedagogy. These six effective teaching principles are the heart of pedagogy for internationalisation as the focus is on getting to know the student and their learning needs.

The Case Study Context

The case study school is a non-government educational facility referred to as an independent school. This case study school operates as a Foundation to Year 12 centre of learning. International students have been enrolled at this school since 1992. International students enrolled at this school have come from various countries, including South Korea, China and Japan. More broadly, students and staff at this case study school represent a diverse range of ethnic backgrounds from Australia, China, Cook Islands, Croatia, Ethiopia, Japan, South Korea, Mauritania, New Zealand, Niue, Papua New Guinea, Samoa, Serbia, Solomon Islands, South Africa, Tonga and the United States of America. This range of cultural diversity exists within Australia and already contributes to internationalisation within Australian schools. For this investigation I focused on the secondary campus of this school that had 29 staff and 320 students enrolled, including 16 international students, in 2013. At that time, I was the ESL teacher at the school, and so this study was initiated as a response to the requests I had for help from the secondary teachers regarding teaching international students.

Data was gathered through questionnaires, focus groups, individual interviews and document analysis. The data gathered was used to answer two questions:

1. *What features of internationalisation have been implemented in the case study school that shape pedagogy?*
2. *What impact does enrolling international students have on the school, particularly on the teaching and learning?*

Features of Internationalisation Already Implemented at the Case Study School

In response to question one, 'What features of internationalisation have been implemented in the case study school that shape pedagogy?', four administrative processes emerged that significantly impacted this process. These four administrative processes were communication, school climate, the provision and support of teacher professional development and staff collaboration opportunities. Policies for internationalisation at the case study school were developed and had been implemented since 1995. Although these policies were in place, only a few individuals on the administration team were aware of them.

Communication as an administrative process is a key area for internationalisation, which at this case study school appeared limited. Two teachers indicated a mistrust in the enrolment process for internationalisation, stating, 'I think some of the ones we had before they really didn't qualify to get in and somehow they managed to get in a back door . . .' This comment raises a perception of underhanded manipulation somewhere in the process, highlighting communication gaps and potential enrolment issues. One administrator acknowledged that the enrolment policy and internationalised programme were not discussed or communicated with the teachers which she felt linked to the teachers' negative attitude towards internationalisation. She also stated that there was a lack of information gathered regarding students' backgrounds and that this was often not shared readily with teachers. Overall, the teachers were not familiar with the enrolment process or of what assessments were used in this process. Interestingly, the enrolment of students was processed by the administration; however, a key player stated, 'if I am not here no-one knows . . . The reason why I say this is that we could have incidents where there could be issues, but nobody else here knows all the information for international students'. Relying on one person limits the extent to which the process is understood and legitimate in the eyes of the other staff at the school. This lack of dissemination of information appears to have negatively impacted the teachers and their attitude, planning and teaching in working with the international students, which are all factors affecting the development and sustainment of a pedagogy for internationalisation (Hachfeld et al., 2011; Youngs & Youngs, 2001).

School culture—especially a caring one—was another administration process identified through the data as affecting the potential success of integrating internationalisation. Staff and students expressed that they perceived the case study school as a caring environment: 'I think . . . the kids feel really liked, loved, cared for in the school. I think that is pretty strong'. An international student said, 'You get to know everyone in here. I like the small school, it is better'. As part of assisting students to become integrated into the school, a buddy system was operated. This system had proved to be helpful in allowing a smooth transition into the school as expressed by Admin 1:

> Our students are great like that. They help whether it's local students from outside or international they help them fit in. I think students coming into our school transition nicely because they are not coming into a school where they feel threatened.

Comments such as this show positive features contributing to the school culture, which appears to provide opportunities for students to engage, participate and contribute to the environment in which they study, which also aligns with the values underpinning being a global citizen (Pitts & Brooks, 2017).

However, school culture is more than an atmosphere of friendship and inclusiveness for students. Hoy and Miskel (2008) emphasise that this needs to also include the student's family. Open communication with parents cultivates a sense of belonging and impacts international students' wellbeing (Hoy & Miskel, 2008). The perception by teachers at the case study school was that it was too difficult and not their responsibility to communicate directly with parents who did not speak English. One teacher said, 'We can't do it ourselves . . . we get others to write letters to the parents to tell them; but we have awful trouble with the agents trying to get it through to the parents'. Another teacher added to this saying, 'A lot of the students in the senior school are old enough. They take it upon themselves to be their own guardian and they sign everything themselves'. There were other teachers who did support direct communication with family. The data shows that an evening event was planned especially for the international students and their families so that they could meet the teachers; however, this was limited to those family members who could attend the event in Australia. Beyond this event there was no evidence nor were there any on-going plans to implement direct communication with international students' families. Yet research emphasises how important this is (Finley, 2018; Harris, 2018; Hoy & Miskel, 2008).

As part of an internationalised school culture, teachers need to demonstrate cross cultural competency. They display this through cultural knowledge, open-mindedness, communication skills, empathy and the understanding and knowledge of what is required to be successful in diverse and multiple environments. One teacher said, 'Identifying with things that we value in our culture, you know, in order to fit in they have to cross that cultural gap'. This statement places all the responsibility on the international student. Interestingly another teacher said, 'I think the other thing is we really have to understand what it's like being there. Being away from home without mom and dad and maybe we would be a bit more sympathetic and not just dismiss them'. The fact that the teachers at the case study school were concerned about academic support, language proficiency as well as their own limited cultural knowledge insinuates that these teachers are not confident about cross cultural competency (Hattingh et al., 2017; Popadiuk, 2010) or engaging with notions of global citizenship.

During my investigation at the case study school, the school leadership established a specific committee with a written purpose and direction. This committee was to 'provide service for the international students, strengthen the transition between the Primary and Secondary campuses in this area, change staff perception on the international students by providing information for them, investigate ways to improve internationalisation at [name of school]'. In essence this committee was tasked to review and improve procedures and policies related to internationalisation, to address teaching and learning for internationalisation, and also to help with the communication between the administration team and the teachers. This was a clear response to the needs the administrative team were identifying as part of the internationalisation process. Granting permission for my research to progress at this site was also part of the administrative team intentionally focusing on developing and improving internationalisation.

Professional development was another administrative area identified in the data which forms part of the process for equipping staff to collaborate, discuss, communicate and plan for internationalisation (Hollingworth, Olsen, Asikin-Garmager, & Winn, 2018). Overall the data from the teachers expressed limited and inadequate knowledge and skill for internationalisation, particularly for professional competence and capacity in knowing how to provide pedagogy for internationalisation. One teacher summed it as,

I feel like they're [international students] here, but we don't seem to have much of a process to actually help them succeed. We talk about it a bit, but what do we actually do, now I'm talking from a teacher, and it's different possibly for that room over there [indicates the ESL room]. What do we do? We definitely seem to just abandon them almost. That's what it seems like.

The greatest area of need identified by the teachers was in knowing how to teach international students. The data identifies that there is a lack of teacher knowledge on constructing and running an effective classroom with second-language learners. This is a key concern that is also identified in other research (Gibbons, 2003; Karathanos, 2010). Most teachers were eager to participate in further professional development to assist them with knowledge of curriculum and culture as well as other topics related to internationalisation.

The administrative team was responsible for fostering a culture of collaboration, professional exchange and communication for internationalisation. Interestingly across the data, especially from the teachers, there was the recurring question of whether there was a process where information for internationalisation was shared and, if there was, they were unaware of it. One teacher stated:

> Do we have a mechanism where we keep a tab on all of this? . . . Surely there needs to be a mechanism . . . where we know what's happening. Where we get in touch with each other, whether it's pastoral support . . . academics . . . ESL, whatever it is, some sort of liaison so we actually know what is happening with these kids.

All the teachers agreed that staff collaboration would reduce gaps and assist in providing vital information they needed for their pedagogy. Teachers also indicated a willingness to participate in regular meetings and discussions with other teachers as part of internationalisation in order to enhance their teaching and learning. Clearly there are insufficient opportunities provided at this case study school currently to discuss, communicate or plan for internationalisation. The data showed that the teachers felt they needed direction and guidance so that they could be intentional about their pedagogy for internationalisation. To advise the school on how best to meet this need, I had to assess what was already being implemented within classrooms around teaching and learning (research question 2).

Pedagogy for Internationalisation

Across the data I looked for evidence of understandings connected to pedagogy in working with culturally and linguistically diverse students. Teachers were asked, *Have you instigated any changes to your mainstream classes/work to cater specifically for the international students?*

If yes, what are the changes and why did you make them? Sixty-five percent of the teachers stated that they had made changes to their practice with regards to teacher-talk and communication within their classrooms, teaching and learning strategies used in their classrooms, their classroom management, and school curriculum and assessment modifications.

The teachers were clear in their understanding that their work included a significant amount of expository talk. Three teachers had intentionally slowed their speech as a changed practice within their classroom, for example, 'I try to talk slower because I talk very fast . . . and I find myself deliberately taking things slower and talking slower . . . but I really try and make an effort to slow down'. Although this teacher noted her efforts to change, the other 15 teachers noted their rapid tendency in talk but no mention was made in the data of addressing this aspect of their pedagogy. Four teachers highlighted that they were aware of and addressed discipline-specific vocabulary within their classes. The literature notes that modifications to classroom talk are essential for internationalisation (Lewis & Fusco, 2017). This was clearly an issue noted by the international students: 'I can't really understand what he's saying . . .', 'I can't really understand his class . . .', 'It's a big problem'. One international student described a teacher as 'just mumbling', while another international student said, 'They just talk and it's pretty hard to listen to it . . . and it's hard to make the written notes'. The international students agreed with each other in their focus groups and presented the amount and nature of teacher-talk as a problematic classroom practice they experienced. Teachers need to be aware of their learners and address their language needs within their classroom, which other research shows as well (Gibbons, 2002).

The teachers indicated that they had made some changes to their pedagogy. These changes included stressing important information by 'signalling too what's most important' and the use of specific words, for example, 'tips, very, good, etc'. This aligns with effective second language pedagogy and the explicit teaching of listening strategies which are important for learners (Gibbons, 2002). Another pedagogical strategy used by the teachers was that of repeating concepts. Teachers stated that they revisited content for their students, thus reinforcing concepts in various forms and ways. They reworded, clarified statements, repeated lessons or parts of lessons and used multiple options to enhance understanding or in order to review a concept or idea again aligning with second language pedagogy (Gibbons, 2002). Modelling and scaffolding were other teaching and learning strategies identified as a change the teachers had implemented for internationalisation. Four teachers discussed how they scaffolded their students' learning, for example, 'I also do a lot of editing/ conferencing at home for assignments with email', 'and I do put a lot of effort in to help them a lot', 'model right for them and all of that kind of things'.

In addition, translated texts are provided in the school library for students in their first language as another form of scaffolding. Further, working one-on-one with students or in small groups was implemented in classes as well. A teacher stated, 'I have taken to when I have the time . . . I go to those students and just start helping them. Where are you up to, what are you doing? And I will help them as much as I can'. These teaching and learning strategies were confirmed by all of the international students, for example, '. . . he explains like to the end, right until we understand; and, . . . because he is always like willing to help students even at lunch time or after school'. Together with group work four teachers also implemented peer teaching as an additional learning and teaching strategy. This was particularly used in English classes where these teachers allowed international students to assist each other, drawing from their own cognitive and linguistic resources. For example,

> I had some Year 12 girls come and say what about this, this and this and I explained it and they were still looking at me blankly and I said you could ask [names a resident student] or somebody who I've seen them talk to before and who seems to be able to explain things to them. And that helps both sides.

The fact of having to explain something to another person is argued in the literature as consolidating understanding, which contributes to academic competence (Gibbons, 2006; Saville-Troike, 1984), thus assisting both students. All of these strategies demonstrate a pedagogical approach actively engaging students and supporting second-language pedagogy.

The teachers' view of their learners impacts on the teaching and learning within the school. The teachers in this study found the international students generally reserved, reluctant to participate in class and quiet, which aligns with the literature (Gibbons, 2003). Teachers stated that they did not know who the international students were or much about them. 'Knowing' students includes knowledge of their previous educational experience and background. Furthermore, teachers did not directly ask the students about their previous learning experiences or what they already knew. This aligns with previous research which found that international students arrived at a school and felt like they are treated as 'blank slates' (Grant & Gillette, 2006; Karathanos, 2010; West, 1998).

Finally, teachers felt ill-equipped to assess or tackle the gap between the international students' mastery of academic English versus conversational English. 'You know you can sit down and have a conversation with them, but when it comes to subject specific language . . .' The teachers were largely unaware about the ways they could help their students or even diagnose language problems or ascertain language proficiency levels vital for addressing learner needs.

Conclusion

Clearly across the case study school the research found evidence of pedagogy for internationalisation—such as the use of some specific teaching approaches suited to second language learners, as well as the intentional focus on classroom communication. More focus needs to be on the teachers getting to know their students and their educational needs. The case study teachers appear open to more and intentional professional development which this investigation recommends in the area of working with linguistically and culturally diverse students. Even though the case study school has a small number of international students, implementing pedagogy for internationalisation benefits the whole student body. Institutions with larger international student enrolments will need to embrace pedagogy for internationalisation in various ways and develop initiatives where relationships can be built, curriculum developed, and where there is regular evaluation and reflection of the teaching and learning that happens within the classroom.

References

Australian Curriculum Assessment and Reporting Authority (ACARA). (2010). *General capabilities*. Retrieved from www.australiancurriculum.edu.au/f-10-curriculum/general-capabilities/

Brigaman, K. J. (2002). *The culturally diverse classroom: A guide for ESL and mainstream teachers*. Paper presented at the TESOL Convention (2003). Retrieved from https://eric.ed.gov/?id=ED474938

Clegg, J. E. (1996). *Mainstreaming ESL case studies in integrating ESL students into the mainstream curriculum*. Clevedon: Multilingual Matters Ltd.

Curtis, T., & Ledgerwood, J. (2018). Students' motivations, perceived benefits and constraints towards study abroad and other international education opportunities. *Journal of International Education in Business, 11*(1), 63–78. doi:10.1108/JIEB-01–2017–0002

Davies, P., & Pearse, E. (2000). Development in English teaching. In *Success in English Teaching* (pp. 185–204). Oxford: Oxford University Press.

Department of Education and Training. (2018). *International student enrolments in Australia 1994-2018*. Retrieved from https://internationaleducation.gov.au/research/International-Student-Data/Pages/InternationalStudentData2018.aspx

Education Services for Overseas Students (ESOS) Act. (2000). *ESOS legislation*. Retrieved from www.legislation.gov.au/Series/C2004A00757

Engel, L. C., & Siczek, M. M. (2017). A cross-national comparison of international strategies: Global citizenship and the advancement of national competitiveness. *Compare: A Journal of Comparative and International Education, 48*(5), 749–767.

Faltis, C., & Wolfe, P. M. E. (1999). *So much to say: Adolescents, bilingualism, and ESL in the secondary school*. New York: Teachers College.

Fantini, A. E. (2000). *A central concern: Developing intercultural competence.* Retrieved from www.sit.edu/SITOccasionalPapers/sitops01.pdf

Finley, A. M. (2018). Fostering success: Belongingness pedagogy for English language learners. *BC TEAL Journal*, 3(1), 37–48.

Gibbons, P. (2002). *Scaffolding language, scaffolding learning: Teaching second language learners in the mainstream classroom.* Portsmouth: Heinemann.

Gibbons, P. (2003). Mediating language learning: Teacher interactions with ESL students in a content-based classroom. *TESOL Quarterly*, 37(2), 247–273.

Gibbons, P. (2006). *Bridging discourses in the ESL classroom: Students, teachers and researchers.* London: Continuum.

Goren, H., & Yemini, M. (2017). The global citizenship education gap: Teacher perceptions of the relationship between global citizenship education and students' socio-economic status. *Teaching and Teacher Education*, 67(2017), 9–22.

Grant, C. A., & Gillette, M. D. (2006). *Learning to teach everyone's children: Equity, empowerment, and education that is multicultural.* Toronto: Thomson Nelson.

Gunderson, L. (2000). Voices of the teenage diasporas. *Journal of Adolescent & Adult Literacy*, 43(8), 692–706.

Hachfeld, A., Hahn, A., Schroeder, S., Anders, Y., Stanat, P., & Kunter, M. (2011). Assessing teachers' multicultural and egalitarian beliefs: The teacher cultural beliefs scale. *Teaching and Teacher Education: An International Journal of Research and Studies*, 27(6), 986–996. doi:10.1016/j.tate.2011.04.006

Harris, J. (2018). Speaking the culture: Understanding the micro-level production of school culture through leaders' talk. *Discourse: Studies in the Cultural Politics of Education*, 39(3), 323–334. doi:10.1080/01596306.2016.1256271

Hattingh, S. (2016). A review of literature: What is an ideal internationalised school? *Educational Review*, 68(3), 306–321. doi:10.1080/00131911.2015.1087970

Hattingh, S., Kettle, M., & Brownlee, J. (2017). Internationalising a school: Teachers' perspectives on pedagogy, curriculum and inclusion. *TESOL in Context*, 26(1), 45–62. doi:10.21153/tesol2017vol26no1art704704

Henard, F., Diamond, L., & Roseveare, D. (2012). *Approaches to internationalisation and their implications for strategic management and institutional practice: A guide for higher education institutions.* Retrieved from OECD: www.oecd.org/education/imhe/Approaches%20to%20internationalisation%20-%20final%20-%20web.pdf

Heydon, R. (2003). A touch of . . . class! Literature circles as a differentiated instructional strategy for including ESL students in mainstream classrooms. *The Canadian Modern Language Review*, 59(3), 463.

Hogan, K., & Hathcote, A. (2014). Issues in curriculum and instruction for culturally and linguistically diverse students. *Multicultural Learning and Teaching*, 9(1), 93–102. doi:10.1515/mlt-2013-0024

Hollingworth, L., Olsen, D., Asikin-Garmager, A., & Winn, K. M. (2018). Initiating conversations and opening doors: How principals establish a positive building culture to sustain school improvement efforts. *Educational Management Administration & Leadership*, 46(6), 1014–1034. doi:10.1177/1741143217720461

Hoy, W. K., & Miskel, C. G. (2008). *Educational administration: Theory, research and practice* (8th ed.). Boston: McGraw-Hill.

Jin, L., & Wang, C. D. C. (2018). International students' attachment and psychological well-being: The mediation role of mental toughness. *Counselling Psychology Quarterly, 31*(1), 59–78. doi:10.1080/09515070.2016.1211510

Karathanos, K. A. (2010). Teaching English language learner students in US mainstream schools: Intersections of language, pedagogy, and power. *International Journal of Inclusive Education, 14*(1), 49–65.

Knight, J. (2004). Internationalization remodeled: Definition, approaches, and rationales. *Journal of Studies in International Education, 8*(1), 5–31. doi:10.1177/1028315303260832

Knight, J. (2006). *Internationalization of higher education: New directions, new challenges: 2005 IAU global survey report.* Paris: UNESCO.

Kyriakides, L., Creemers, B. P. M., Antoniou, P., Demetriou, D., & Charalambous, C. Y. (2015). The impact of school policy and stakeholders' actions on student learning: A longitudinal study. *Learning and Instruction, 36*, 113–124. doi:10.1016/j.learninstruc.2015.01.004

Lareau, A. (2015). Cultural knowledge and social inequality. *American Sociological Review, 80*(1), 1–27. doi:10.1177/0003122414565814

Leask, B. (2011). Assessment, learning, teaching and internationalisation—Engaging for the future. *ALT Journal, 11*(Summer), 5–20.

Leask, B. (2013). Internationalizing the curriculum in the disciplines—Imagining new possibilities. *Journal of Studies in International Education, 17*(2), 103–118.

Lewis, T., & Fusco, J. C. (2017). Lingua anglia: Bridging language and learners. *English Journal, 106*(5), 83–85.

Li, Y. (2004). Learning to live and study in Canada: Stories of four EFL learners from China. *TESL Canada Journal, 22*(2), 25–43.

Lightbrown, P., & Spada, N. (2006). *How languages are learned* (3rd ed.). Oxford: Oxford University Press.

Love, K., & Arkoudis, S. (2004). Sinking or swimming? Chinese international students and high stakes school exams. *Australian Review of Applied Linguistics, 58–72.*

Luo, J., & Jamieson-Drake, D. (2013). Examining the educational benefits of interacting with international students. *Journal of International Students, 3*(2), 85–101.

Meng, Q., Zhu, C., & Cao, C. (2018). Chinese international students' social connectedness, social and academic adaptation: The mediating role of global competence. *Higher Education, 75*(1), 131–147. doi:10.1007/s10734–017–0129-x

National strategy for international education 2025. (2016). Retrieved from https://nsie.education.gov.au/sites/nsie/files/docs/national_strategy_for_international_education_2025.pdf.

Nilsson, P. A., & Ripmeester, N. (2016). International student expectations: Career opportunities and employability. *Journal of International Students, 6*(2), 614–631.

Pitts, M. J., & Brooks, C. F. (2017). Critical pedagogy, internationalisation, and a third space: Cultural tensions revealed in students' discourse. *Journal of Multilingual and Multicultural Development, 38*(3), 251–267.

Popadiuk, N. (2010). Asian international student transition to high school in Canada. *The Qualitative Report, 15*(6), 1523–1548.

Pope, J. A., Sánchez, C. M., Lehnert, K., & Schmid, A. S. (2014). Why do Gen Y students study Abroad? Individual growth and the intent to study Abroad. *Journal of Teaching in International Business, 25*(2), 97–118. doi:10.1080/08 975930.2014.896232

Reeves, J. (2006). Secondary teacher attitudes toward including English-language learners in mainstream classrooms. *The Journal of Educational Research, 99*(3), 131–142.

Saville-Troike, M. (1984). What really matters in second language learning for academic purposes? *TESOL Quarterly, 18*(2), 199–219.

Study in Australia. (2018). Retrieved from www.studyinaustralia.gov.au/english/ why-australia

West, M. (1998). Quality in schools: Developing a model for school improvement. In A. Hargreaves, A. Lieberman, M. Fullan, & D. Hopkins (Eds.), *International handbook of educational change* (Vol. part 2, pp. 768–789). Dordrecht: Kluwer Academic Publishers.

Yang, Y., Zhang, Y., & Sheldon, K. M. (2018). Self-determined motivation for studying abroad predicts lower culture shock and greater well-being among international students: The mediating role of basic psychological needs satisfaction. *International Journal of Intercultural Relations, 63*(2018), 95–104.

Youngs, G. S., & Youngs, G. A. J. (2001). Predictors of mainstream teachers' attitudes toward ESL students. *TESOL Quarterly, 35*(1), 97–120.

10 Learning From Internationalisation Scholarship in Higher Education

Commonalities, Divergences and Possible Research Directions for Internationalisation in Schools

Tatiana Fumasoli

The purpose of this chapter is to consider how the more longstanding, extensive and coherent scholarship around internationalisation and higher education could offer theoretical tools for the nascent field of internationalisation in compulsory schooling. Being a scholar specialising in the former field, who has done research on the structure and function of higher education, this has been a useful exercise, as I seek to contextualise the concepts and processes of internationalisation and add some thoughts to this emerging field of studies.

Definitions and Major Characteristics of Internationalisation

First, I turn to the various definitions of the term suggested in the literature on internationalisation in higher education (de Wit, 2002, Knight, 2004; Vincent-Lancrin, 2009). I introduce several ways of understanding the process and motivations of internationalisation, initially developed in the context of higher education, and consider their possible applicability to schools. Contemporary pressures to internationalise can be grouped into three categories: Political, economic and social. Politically, internationalisation of higher education has been advocated in order to boost innovation and consolidate or further strengthen countries' and regions' competitive advantage in the 'knowledge economy'. Here, international staff and students are sought in order to enhance local and regional technological and industrial hubs. Several actors have been involved in facilitating this development, from businesses, small and medium enterprises and corporations, to local, regional and national authorities (Knight, 2013a). Economically, internationalisation has increasingly offered universities the possibility to earn a profit as they become more and more autonomous in handling their own growth strategies, while simultaneously seeing public funding either shrinking or at least stagnating. While this type of internationalisation has been significantly visible in

Anglophone countries, the UK and Australia in particular, it is still less pronounced in others, e.g. in continental Europe (Huisman & van der Wende, 2004). Finally, from a social perspective, internationalisation has provided countries that are not (yet) capable of fulfilling the increasing demands for higher education of their populations with the possibility of seeking out such provision elsewhere (van der Wende, 2001).

Internationalisation in higher education is broadly defined as a process 'integrating an international, intercultural or global dimension into the purpose, functions (primarily teaching/learning, research, service) or delivery of higher education' (Knight, 2004, p. 85). This definition became central and widely used in the field, and is also often utilised in research related to compulsory schooling. Knight (2003) specifies that *international* addresses relationships between countries, *intercultural* relates to national contexts (in particular to country, community and institutional cultures) and *global* reflects a general worldwide perspective. While this definition is broad and all encompassing, if we focus on higher education practices more directly, mobility is usually the major articulation of internationalisation. In schools, however, except for a small but growing number of international schools that have been traditionally populated with students from globally mobile families, internationalisation relies less on the physical mobility of students and staff and more to integrating locally an international dimension. To emphasise this critical element, in this chapter I elaborate on the role of mobility in internationalisation of higher education, and then question its relevance for schools.

Student and staff mobility, both incoming and outgoing, has traditionally been the most visible aspect of internationalisation. However, while staff and students' mobility has always existed in academia to some extent, the drivers thereof have changed in the last decades, differentiating several types of internationalisation processes and practices, which have equally grown in scope and scale. Originally, mobility across borders, regions and institutions was motivated by the normative frameworks of scholarship and science, whereby scholars and students would visit and stay in different institutions and countries in order to engage with their peers' academic knowledge and practices. With the consolidation of the nation-state since the 19th century, higher education became instrumental to nation-state development, and thus more influential in the shaping of national identities and socio-economic progress (Bloch, Kreckel, Mitterle, & Stock, 2018). More recently, and particularly after World War II, student and staff mobility has reflected political and geostrategic rationales, at times overlapping with the intent to build capacity and foster development in peripheral and developing countries by more economically advanced countries. This could be related to former colonies and close allies (e.g. former Communist Bloc and several African countries where scholars' and students' mobilities were used by the governments and by the receiving countries like the former Soviet Union to promote political goals). At the beginning of the 21st century, yet other drivers have hastened mobility to new levels. Here, to some extent, the standardisation of the accreditation of degrees has led to mobilities from East to West, South to North. Alongside the recognition and pursuit of degrees from, and employment in, globally acknowledged top universities, higher education institutions have been strengthening their engagement with practices of global citizenship to foster their graduates' contributions as members of democratic societies and as part of an instrumental logic aimed to prepare globally competent graduates for the labour markets. Although in some countries students' mobility for secondary education is increasingly pursued, such as in East Asia, where families strategically and temporally immigrate to receive 'English' education (Waters, 2006), internationalisation is actually practised through its embedding in pedagogical approaches related to cosmopolitanism and global citizenship (Yemini, 2014) or its pursuit of the International Baccalaureate (IB) qualifications. By drawing on one of the overarching characteristics of internationalisation in higher education—mobility—I have illustrated how different the context of compulsory schooling is, and therefore why we cannot simply borrow concepts and developments from the higher education sector in our analyses of forms and outcomes of internationalisation in the former.

Explaining Internationalisation as a Response to Globalisation

While internationalisation can be understood as constituting a range of practices and being driven by a variety of factors, globalisation as a process is central to our conceptualisations of the term itself (Altbach & Knight, 2007; de Wit, 2002; Kehm & Teichler, 2007; Knight, 2004; Marginson, 2006; Middlehurst, 2002). Interestingly not much effort has been made to unbundle globalisation and its analytical link to internationalisation. Several contributions in this book, however, seek to directly address this. For example, Auld and Morris (Chapter 1) reflect on the growing role of intergovernmental organisations and the OECD, in particular, as a globalising actor bringing to the assessment cycle, contents (e.g. global competencies) which are likely to generate a greater engagement with internationalisation across curricula. In addition, in Bunnell's (Chapter 3) and Beech and Guevara's (Chapter 6) contributions, there is a focus on the globalising role of the International Baccalaureate in the internationalisation of schooling, and the ways in which it differentially impacts local and national contexts, a thread also picked up in the chapter by Engel and Gibson (Chapter 4).

To facilitate this more theoretical linkage between globalisation and internationalisation, scholarship in political science and sociology is useful. For some scholars it is a matter of growing economic relationships across nation states (Scharpf, 1997) and of power and interdependence in the contemporary polity (Keohane & Nye, 1977). For other writers, globalisation leads to the diffusion of ideals (or 'global scripts' (Meyer, Ramirez, Frank, & Schofer, 2007; Thornton, Ocasio, & Lounsbury, 2012)), such as the ideal university or the business school standard, that travels across the globe and is then translated locally (Czarniawska & Wolff, 1998). Unterhalter and Carpentier (2010) distinguish between globalisation conceived as a technology-driven process that reduces physical distance and induces collaborations across the globe, and globalisation as a market-driven phenomenon penetrating all spheres of society. For the purposes of this chapter, I define globalisation as the increasing relationships, interconnectedness and interdependence between national, local and supra-national organisational actors. Consequently, internationalisation can be understood as the process of the establishment of relationships across all relevant aspects of the higher education enterprise beyond nation-states (see also Knight, 2004). This definition is helpful in the context of internationalisation in schools, too, as it uncovers processes of diffusion and translation of practices of internationalisation, as well as points to the relationships between actors and such practices at the local, national and international levels.

When it comes to defining globalisation, or 'the widening, deepening and speeding up of worldwide interconnectedness' (Held & McGrew, 2000, p. 2), two aspects are particularly relevant for internationalisation in higher education. The first is the changing role of the nation-state, which is losing to some extent its capacity to regulate the higher education sector. In many ways, internationalisation is an outcome of the increasing institutional autonomy of higher education institutions, which have been able to access new opportunities, whether across borders, at the international level (e.g. the EU funding schemes) or at the local level (cities, regional and local authorities). Equally, universities are able to engage with broader society, such as industry and business or the third sector (Fumasoli, 2015). This development does not affect secondary schooling in the same way, as compulsory schooling remains more tightly under the competence of the state. This said, the increasing power of supra-national organisations (like the OECD in particular) is potentially shaping how nation-states and policy-makers at the federal level develop and seek to regulate schooling (see Engel & Gibson in Chapter 4, Engel & Siczek, 2018 and Lewis, 2017). A well-known example of these pressures in higher education is the Bologna Process, which has harmonised the standards and quality of higher education qualifications in 48 countries.

The second aspect of globalisation that is particularly relevant is that of the students and their families. Faced with the opening up of further opportunities and innovative forms of higher education, which appear to be within reach for large numbers, students have begun to show more agency and opportunistic behaviour in relation to their higher education choices, sometimes showing signs of acting more like consumers. While these processes are abundant in higher education, some of them have also begun to appear in the schooling sector in relation to internationalisation—particularly with increasing privatisation and formation of schools seeking to promote themselves as 'elite' within national, regional or international fields. In such cases we arguably see enactments of internationalisation in higher education occurring in secondary spaces (Maxwell, 2018).

Clearly the emergence of global arenas in which higher education institutions compete creates opportunities for potentially extending relations of inequality (between social groups as well as between and within nations). Students are variously located in countries and regions that are more or less exposed to internationalisation processes, that have better or less access to higher education provision. Within the internationalised higher education space, economic, social and cultural forms of capital play an important role in student choice availability (Courtois, 2018). In this respect public policies are central, as they can enhance or aggravate opportunities for some or even to reach all (Nogueira & Alves, 2016). Linked to opportunities are also the ways in which universities themselves seek to include more diverse communities of students. Programmes such as *Erasmus*, put in place by the European Commission, have positively impacted student mobility and the academic and cultural enrichment this makes available, even though some research highlights that the stratification of subjects and destinations still occurs, largely driven by students' socio-economic status (Courtois, 2018; for similar dynamics in North America, see Engel, 2017).

By specifically highlighting the links between globalisation and internationalisation and emphasising several elements that are crucial to the definition and characterisation of internationalisation in higher education, I have developed four ideal types of internationalisation that can be found in higher education (Olsen, 2007). I would propose that these four types could be applied to the compulsory schooling space to better understand and differentiate various practices of internationalisation found in schools.

Articulating Internationalisation in Higher Education: Four Ideal Types

Internationalisation of higher education takes place at multiple levels and in different locations, linking together several sets of actors through distinctive practices and according to multifaceted ideals and discourses on internationalisation. The inherent dynamics of internationalisation can be grouped in four ideal types (see Table 10.1), which I have developed drawing from the typology of universities presented by Olsen (2007).

Table 10.1 Four Ideal Types of Internationalisation in Higher Education

Internationalisation	*Academic*	*Political*	*Democratic*	*Economic*
Institution	Self-governed community of scholars	Instrument for national political agendas	Representative democracy	Service enterprise
Rationale	Building expertise by scientific quality	Implementing national political objectives	Representing diversity	Supplying a service in a market
Actors	Scholars and scientists	State authorities	Interest groups (incl. students)	Institutional leadership
Dynamics	Science and scholarship	Bureaucratic, state delegated	Political and bargaining	Competitive advantage
Scope	Global	Selected groups of countries	Unrelated selected countries	Lucrative markets
Outcome	Elitist	Geopolitical	Differentiated	Profitable

Source: Adapted and further developed from Olsen, 2007.

These ideal types can be observed empirically as occurring in combination, leading to tensions and paradoxes.

The first ideal type is *academic internationalisation*. Its rationale is the pursuit of excellence in the university's core mission of teaching and research. It is globally understood by everyone since it refers to the highest standards of academic quality, which it aims to maintain and diffuse worldwide. Only high-status universities can lead this process, be it in attracting talented students and staff, opening exclusive offshore campuses or arranging partnerships with outstanding institutions in other countries. By definition, academic internationalisation cannot serve large numbers of students and cannot be present in every country.

Political internationalisation reflects the interests and related policies of the respective governments when it comes to international relations. Against this backdrop, universities address their internationalisation efforts to specific regions and countries that are either historically related (e.g. former colonies) or are being targeted to enhance political, economic and technological exchanges. The notion of soft power can be drawn on to conceptualise this type of internationalisation, where universities might have state-induced incentives in order to establish such relationships and enhance capacity and institutional building in targeted countries. Different from democratic internationalisation (discussed next), this type of internationalisation is more likely to target distinctive fields of knowledge (political science or engineering, for instance) and elite students from relevant countries, as there is an understanding that these students will be trained to become the future elites in their countries of origin (Singapore is an example of this; see Ye & Nylander, 2015). In this case, too, scope and scale are limited since they are targeted and depend on the resources available provided by national geopolitical agendas.

Democratic internationalisation, meanwhile, aims to make higher education as accessible as possible, since it sees higher education as a fundamental human right. It is structured around widening participation initiatives and large partnerships with local providers in peripheral and developing countries. Furthermore, it is organised around ideals of global citizenship and mutual and intercultural understanding, whereby students from different countries come together to learn about each other's languages, values and beliefs. A foundational ideal is that education forms good citizens that will be able to integrate themselves and participate in contemporary societies by means of the civic expertise acquired at university. The students who are most targeted by this type of internationalisation often come from resource-poor backgrounds, developing regions and countries. When resources are available, the scope and scale of such projects can be quite significant.

Economic internationalisation is organised around a commercial enterprise where the provision of international higher education reflects market analysis, student demands and the identification of a particular niche. As such, this type of internationalisation might either be quite innovative—types of partnerships and provisions, modes of delivery, countries targeted, fields of knowledge offered—or isomorphic, that is, providers compete for students in the same markets in similar ways (Engel & Siczek, 2017). This depends on the risk assessment and on the entrepreneurial character of the actors involved (i.e. institutional leadership). This type of internationalisation can have three main consequences. The first is related to the standards of quality, whereby narrow logics of profit can lead to the creation of diploma mills and so-called visa factories for international students. Second, and related, student fees become a barrier to all those that are unable to pay the considerable fees expected. Finally, the sustainability and long-term contribution to the communities in which they are located is often a lesser priority in such business-like higher education provision. Here, the role of host governments can be quite significant in shaping local relations between universities and local communities.

These ideal types enable us to single out the different dynamics at play in internationalisation of higher education, and how specific elements of higher education provision become the focus of such initiatives. This framework helps us also to reflect on how different actors are involved and could be drawn on in shaping the space within which internationalisation occurs, the parameters governing it and the outcomes. As for schools, each of these types can potentially exist in the various contexts and conditions where schools might engage in internationalisation. For example, Prickarts (Chapter 8), in his study of a Dutch school embedded in a socio-economically marginalised community, and Adriany (Chapter 7), in her study of internationalisation of a kindergarten in Indonesia, both argue for the democratic, all-encompassing nature of internationalisation, while Auld and Morris (Chapter 1) emphasise the exclusive nature of this process and its hegemonic (political) power. In a sense, schools might be considered as more obligated to promote inclusive modes of the process, given most schools are state-funded and required to provide basic and compulsory education as part of their public mission. Nevertheless, historically, internationalisation has been perceived as an elitist and exclusive practice (see Engel and Gibson, Chapter 4), and thus public authorities must at times proactively seek to challenge such outcomes (as governments across Latin America have done in introducing the IB through public provision—see Beech and Guevara, Chapter 6). Internationalisation in Russian schools (Bodovski and Apostolescu, Chapter 5) and in Latin American contexts (Beech and Guevara, Chapter 6) demonstrate diverse enactments of internationalisation—they are concerned with both political and academic forms simultaneously.

Linking Internationalisation in Higher Education and Schooling

Against this backdrop, this section discusses the practices of internationalisation in schooling presented in this book, and connects them to the various types and characteristics of internationalisation presented previously. As all the stages of educational trajectories are inherently interconnected, pupils and their families are equipped with different resources (or capitals) which shape the choices available to them.

An overarching theme in the book is how engaging with practices of internationalisation is directly linked with different sets of ideals around the purpose of internationalisation and the resources available to people and institutions. These are variably located and interrelated in the educational field. The OECD carries Western and industrialised country values that have global influence (see Chapter 1 by Auld and Morris) on educational policies, even though they have to be translated nationally and locally. This can be understood as the perpetuation of Western democratic models that promote competition and individual responsibility. When such imperatives are promoted across the globe, we find it increases the cleavage between wealthier and poorer countries and also creates pockets of privilege in developing nations when resources and institutional capacity are unable to properly adapt and translate such policies to benefit all. The IB is an example of an internationalisation practice that aims to operate globally by offering a distinctive curriculum at the high school level. Bunnell in Chapter 3 and Beech and Guevara in

Chapter 6 explore its patterns of diffusion, pointing to how the IB strives to reach state schools but with uneven results, while resourceful private schools recontextualise IB according to their national and local environments (see also Prosser, 2016). Both chapters on the IB illustrate how the rationales for internationalisation in schools might be modified during the process of their implementation. The OECD example demonstrates how a misalignment between a discursive democratic ethos (global competences for everybody) and the differential diffusion and reception of these ideas varies across space and time. The IB cases point to how a social rationale for internationalisation in schools has partly lost its original ambition to reach wider audiences and, while being translated in local settings, can become elitist.

A second key theme is how the national context in which internationalisation is taking place directly affects its interpretation and outcomes. In many cases, the outcomes are either rather contradictory to the original intentions or become quite muddled because of the competing influences shaping the promoted forms of internationalisation. Bodovski and Apostolescu (Chapter 5) illustrate how the national level is able to engage with and balance opposite ideals of internationalisation, drawing on the case of Russia. The latter continues to show historical ambivalence between Western and Eastern values, an attempt to maintain its geopolitical role, a desire to seek a competitive edge in strategic industrial and economic sectors, all the while attempting to strengthen its national identity—and leading to quite unique articulations of internationalisation—in the most elitist schools in Russia. This complex picture shows that localised educational spaces can be cherished and serve groups of pupils and families with an interest in cosmopolitan forms of education. Comparably, Waters and Brooks (Chapter 2), elaborating on the engagement of internationalisation by state schools in resource-rich areas of England, demonstrate that internationalisation efforts are concentrated in a commitment to participate in expensive service-learning or charity-oriented trips to former colonies of the United Kingdom. Here, an attempt to build a global social consciousness occurs at the same time as promoting a patronising discourse that can be linked to the imperial past of the country.

But internationalisation can yield more positive outcomes, too, as other chapters in the book illustrate. Boris Prickarts' case study of Denise (Chapter 8) demonstrates how a school's providers have launched a specific school which provides an international programme with a dual language component to children from both privileged and less privileged socio-economic backgrounds (with diverse migration/transnational mobility experiences). Interestingly this has been possible thanks to the school policies rooted in specific local arrangements and without significant interventions from public authorities and policies. Equally, cases from schools in Australia (Chapter 9) and the United States (Chapter 4), as well as from kindergartens in Indonesia (Chapter 7), uncover the subtle activities of mediation and negotiation between local actors in engaging, interpreting and adapting the local dimensions of internationalisation within their broader global ideals.

The contributions in this book thus show how global, international, national and local levels interconnect and how actors engage in different, and at times compartmentalised, processes, shaping practices and achieving successful outcomes. They reveal how education spaces are differentially located and thus profit from different resources, illustrating that under certain conditions, all actors can engage successfully in modifying their local educational space to make it more equitable through providing access to different groups of pupils. The four ideal models of internationalisation in higher education are reflected, in combinations, in these contributions: some schools have a mission of academic excellence and recruit according to selective quality criteria; for them internationalisation is part of a continuous enhancement of their exclusive offer to specific groups of academically high-performing pupils. National identities have also come to the forefront, acting as an implicit or explicit filter in the interpretation and enactment of internationalisation practices. For other schools, it is primarily a mission of inclusion of the different groups present in their (local) communities. Finally, private schools compete in their educational provision and interpret internationalisation as a significant tool to position themselves strategically and ensure their long-term sustainability.

Avenues for Further Research on Internationalisation in Education

Research on internationalisation is in many ways still underdeveloped. Scholarly work has focused on the detailed illustration of practices and outcomes, while theory and conceptualisations are borrowed rather uncritically from other disciplines, as in the case of globalisation, or approaches remain descriptive in illustrating the different internationalisation practices.

The importance of actors making sense of and engaging with global models of internationalisation in education cannot be underestimated. Even more so, a fine-grained conceptualisation of the distinctive actors at different levels becomes helpful in uncovering the changing dynamics of education. Pupils, students and their families, schools and universities with their teaching staff and leadership teams, policy makers and public authorities, as well as interest groups and local and national organisations are all part of the educational field and, through their ideas and actions, participate in its continuous reconfiguration.

As a corollary, this theoretical approach implies that compulsory schooling and higher education should be considered proximate and connected sub-fields, whose actors, resources and linkages can be investigated accordingly (Yemini, 2015). Equally, researchers should engage with appropriate methodologies that include in-depth qualitative case studies as well as quantitative and longitudinal analyses that allow for a comprehensive understanding of the changing education field.

European studies offer an important lens to look at internationalisation of schooling and higher education. For decades, the EU and European policies (i.e. by the Council of Europe) have addressed intercultural understanding, European citizenship, civic engagement and democracy and, since the late 1990s, have equally prioritised global competitiveness. In this sense, Europeanisation can be understood as a regional form of internationalisation where supranational and intergovernmental actors have actively engaged in steering policies through practices of internationalisation both at schools and universities (Engel, 2012; Fumasoli, Stensaker, & Vukasovic, 2018). The schools in this context might take a more active role in internationalisation through EU-based governance, funding and regulations.

Standardisation represents another force related to globalisation and, subsequently, to internationalisation. As myriad schools and universities attract students by means of their international profile, quality assurance and accreditation become more than ever the necessary infrastructure to guarantee coherence and fairness in process and output. Higher Education studies have addressed this topic extensively, and the literature on the OECD and international testing (see also Chapter 1 in this book) is large and comprehensive. The national, regional, local and institutional translations of such global standardisation pressures continue to be a central topic in the studies of internationalisation.

Finally, albeit often mentioned, the technological dimension of internationalisation deserves further scrutiny. It can potentially transform the distinctions between schools and higher education institutions, but also it may change the way internationalisation is enacted in both cases. Not only does technology rapidly evolve, but also it allows for innovative teaching and learning, reaching growing numbers of students. Technology also provides connections that build networks of various actors and can be used with different aims and unintended consequences. Thus, the conceptualisations made through the contributions in this book might further develop in light of the upcoming technological advances.

This chapter has sought to review the insights from the field of study of internationalisation in higher education. By using this frame, it has enabled me to propose four ideal types which researchers might find helpful to facilitate a deeper and more critical analysis of internationalisation in the schooling sector. I have also used my understanding of the field of internationalisation of (higher) education to assess the contributions found in this book—an attempt by me, in closing this volume, to offer readers some key conclusions offered and also some avenues for further research needed to extend the field.

References

Altbach, P. G., & Knight, J. (2007). The internationalization of higher education: Motivations and realities. *Journal of Studies in International Education,* 11(3/4), 290–305.

Bloch, R., Kreckel, R., Mitterle, A., & Stock, M. (2018). Stratification through internationality in German higher education. In C. Maxwell, U. Deppe, H. H. Krüger, & W. Helsper (Eds.), Elite education and internationalisation: From the early years into higher education (pp. 257–278). Basingstoke: Palgrave Macmillan

Courtois, A. (2018). 'It doesn't really matter which university you attend or which subject you study while abroad'. The massification of student mobility programmes and its implications for equality in higher education. *European Journal of Higher Education,* 8(1), 99–114.

Czarniawska, B., & Wolff, R. (1998). Constructing new identities in established organization fields. *International Studies of Management & Organization,* 28(3), 32–56.

de Wit, H. (2002). *Internationalization of higher education in the United States of America and Europe.* Westport: Greenwood.

Engel, L. C. (2012). Autonomy in the global era: Euro-regionalism and new policy spaces in education. In R. Brooks, A. Fuller, & J. Waters (Eds.), *New spaces of education: The changing nature of learning in the 21st century* (pp. 81–95). London: Routledge.

Engel, L. C. (2017). *Underrepresented students in US study Abroad: Investigating impacts.* (Research and Policy Brief Series No. 1). New York: Institute of International Education (IIE).

Engel, L. C., & Siczek, M. M. (2017). A cross-national comparison of international strategies: Global citizenship and the advancement of national competitiveness. *Compare,* 48(5), 740–767.

Engel, L. C., & Siczek, M. M. (2018). Framing global education in the United States. Policy Perspectives, in Hill, L. D., Levine, F. J. (Eds.). *Global Perspectives on Education Research* (pp. 26–46). Routledge.

Fumasoli, T. (2015). Multi-level governance in higher education. In Huisman, J., de Boer, H., Dill, D. & Souto-Otero, M. (Eds.). *Handbook of higher education policy and governance* (pp. 76–94). Thousand Oaks: Palgrave Macmillan.

Fumasoli, T., Stensaker, B., & Vukasovic, M. (2018). Tackling the multi-actor and multi-level complexity of European governance of knowledge: Transnational actors in focus. *European Educational Research Journal,* 17(3), 325–334.

Held, D. & Mc Grew, A. (2000). The great globalization debate, an introduction. In D. Held, & A. Mc Grew (Eds.), *The global transformations reader* (pp. 1–50). Cambridge, MA: Polity Press and Blackwell.

Huisman, J., & van der Wende, M. (2004). *On cooperation and competition, national and European policies for the internationalization of higher education.* Bonn: Lemmens.Kehm, B. M., & Teichler, U. (2007). Research on internationalization in higher education. *Journal of Studies in International Education,* 11, 260–273.

Keohane, R. O., & Nye, J. S. (1977). *Power and Interdependence: World Politics in Transition.* Essex, UK: The Book Service.

Knight, J. (2003). Updated internationalization definition. *International Higher Education*, *33*, 2–3.

Knight, J. (2004). Internationalization re-modeled: Definition, approaches, and rationales. *Journal of Studies in International Education, 8*(1), 5–31.

Knight, J. (2013a). Education hubs: International, regional and local dimensions of scale and scope. *Comparative Education, 49*(3), 374–387.

Knight, J. (2013b). The changing landscape of higher education internationalization—For better or worse. *Perspectives: Policy and Practice in Higher Education, 17*(3), 84–90.

Lewis, S. (2017). Governing schooling through 'what works': The OECD's PISA for schools. *Journal of Education Policy, 32*(3), 281–302.

Marginson, S. (2006). Dynamics of national and global competition in higher education. *Higher Education, 52*(1), 1–39. Maxwell, C. (2018). Changing spaces: The re-shaping of (elite) education through internationalization. In C. Maxwell, U. Deppe, H. H. Krueger, & W. Helsper (Eds.), *Elite education and internationalization: From the early years into higher education* (pp. 347–367). Basingstoke: Palgrave Macmillan.

Meyer, J., Ramirez, F., Frank, D., & Schofer, E. (2007). Higher education as an institution. In P. Gumport (Ed.), *Sociology of Higher Education: Contribution and Their Contexts.* (pp. 187–221). Baltimore: Johns Hopkins University Press.

Middlehurst, R. (2002). Variations on a theme: Complexity and choice in a world of borderless education. *Journal of Studies in International Education*, 6, 134–155.

Nogueira, M. A., & Alves, M. T. G. (2016). The education of Brazilian elites in the 21st century: New opportunities or new forms of distinction? In Maxwell, C. & Aggleton, P. (Eds.), *Elite Education: International Perspectives* (pp. 162–172). London: Routledge.

Olsen, J. P. (2007). The institutional dynamics of the European university. In P. Maassen & J. P. Olsen (Eds.), *University dynamics and European integration* (pp. 25–54). Dordrecht: Springer.

Prosser, H. (2016). Servicing Elite interests: Elite education in post-neoliberal Argentina. In C. Maxwell & P. Aggleton (Eds.), *Elite education: International perspectives* (pp. 173–185). London: Routledge.

Scharpf, F. (1997). Introduction: The problem-solving capacity of multi-level governance. *Journal of European Public Policy, 4*(4), 520–538.

Thornton, P., Ocasio, W., & Lounsbury. M. (2012). *The institutional logics perspective: A new approach to culture, structure, and process.* Oxford: Oxford University Press.

Unterhalter, E., & Carpentier, V. (Eds.). (2010). *Global inequalities and higher education and higher education whose interests are we serving?* New York: Palgrave-MacMillan.

Van der Wende, M. (2001). Internationalisation policies: About new trends and contrasting paradigms. *Higher Education Policy, 14*(3), 249–259

Vincent-Lancrin, S. (2009). *Cross-border higher education: Trends and perspectives, Higher Education to 2030* (Vol. 2, pp. 63–88). Paris: OECD.

Ye, R., & Nylander, E. (2015). The transnational track: State sponsorship and Singapore's Oxbridge elite. *British Journal of Sociology of Education, 36*(1), 11–33.

Yemini, M. (2014). Internationalisation of secondary education: Lessons from Israeli Palestinian-Arab school in Tel Aviv-Jaffa. *Urban Education*, *49*(5) 471–498.

Yemini, M. (2015). Internationalisation discourse hits the tipping point. *Perspectives: Policy and Practice in Higher Education*, *19*(1) 19–22.

Notes on Contributors

Vina Adriany is a Lecturer and Researcher in the Department of Early Childhood Education, Universitas Pendidikan Indonesia. Using post-developmental theories, her research focuses on the issues of gender and social justice in early childhood education as well as the internationalisation of kindergarten. She has published a number of peer review articles and book chapters on the topic. She has also been invited as a visiting lecturer in Sutan Qaboos University, Oman; Gothenburg University; and University West, Sweden. She was a guest editor for several journals, and currently, she is an editorial board member of Policy Futures in International Education.

Ruxandra Apostolescu is a Doctoral Candidate in the Department of Education Policy Studies at the Pennsylvania State University. Her research interests include socio-emotional learning, education policy and comparative and international education.

Euan Auld is Assistant Professor at The Education University of Hong Kong. He holds a master's in Educational and Social Research and a PhD in International and Comparative Education from the UCL Institute of Education. His research to date has focused primarily on international large-scale assessments and their influence on education governance, research and policy.

Jason Beech teaches Comparative Education and Sociology of Education in Universidad de San Andrés in Buenos Aires. He is researcher of the National Council for Scientific and Technical Research of Argentina (CONICET), and Director of the PhD in Education at Universidad de San Andrés. He has a PhD in Education from the Institute of Education, University of London. He has taught in several universities in the Americas, Europe and Australia. He is interested in the globalization of knowledge and policies related to education and in exploring the link between cosmopolitanism, citizenship and education.

Katerina Bodovski is Associate Professor of Educational Theory and Policy in the Department of Education Policy Studies at the Pennsylvania

State University. She received her master's in Sociology from the Hebrew University in Jerusalem, Israel, and her PhD in Sociology from the Pennsylvania State University, USA. Her research interests lie in the intersection of sociology of education and childhood, and comparative international education. She is the author of two books, *Across Three Continents: Reflections on Immigration, Education, and Personal Survival* (Peter Lang Publishing, 2015) and *Childhood and Education in the United States and Russia: Sociological and Comparative Perspectives* (Emerald Group Publishing, 2019).

Rachel Brooks is Professor of Higher Education at University College London in the UK and an Executive Editor of the *British Journal of Sociology of Education*. Her research focuses primarily on the sociology of higher education, and she is currently leading a five-year European Research Council–funded project on the ways in which students are conceptualised across six European countries. She has published over 55 journal articles and 12 books. Her recent publications include: *Education and Society* (Red Globe Press, 2018); *Materialities and Mobilities in Education* (Routledge, with Johanna Waters, 2017); and *Student Politics and Protest: International Perspectives* (Routledge/SRHE, 2016).

Tristan Bunnell is a Lecturer in International Education at the University of Bath, UK, since 2014. Prior to that, for 25 years, he taught International Baccalaureate Diploma Programme Economics at the International School of London and Copenhagen International Schools. He has written extensively about trends and developments in international schooling and international curricula. He has undertaken research on 'international mindedness', funded by the International Baccalaureate. He is the author of several books, the latest being *International Schooling and Education in the 'New Era': Emerging Issues* (Emerald Group Publishing, 2019).

Laura C. Engel is Associate Professor of International Education and International Affairs at the George Washington University (US) where she directs the MA International Education Program. Her research focuses on globalisation studies, citizenship and education policy in federal systems. Her work has appeared in over 50 articles, book chapters, and policy briefs, including two briefs commissioned by the International Association for the Evaluation of Educational Achievement (IEA). She is author of two books: *New State Formations in Education Policy* (Sense, 2009) and *Globalizing Cultural Studies* (Peter Lang, 2007).

Tatiana Fumasoli is Associate Professor at UCL Institute of Education (London, UK), where she is also the Director of the Centre for Higher Education Studies. Her research interests lie at the intersection of management studies, organisation theory and sociology of professions and expertise. She has published extensively on strategy, the academic profession and transnational higher education, Tatiana is co-editor of *Higher Education Quarterly* and is a member of the editorial board of several scientific journals in the field.

Heidi Gibson is the Director for the Global Schools First (GSF) Program at Childhood Education International. GSF works with primary schools around the world to support and celebrate their global citizenship education efforts. Heidi had a leading role in the research team looking at impacts of the DCPS Study Abroad program, was a founding member of the K12 Global Forum, and led the development of a learning progression used by the Smithsonian Science Education Center to guide students towards transformative action. She is a former U.S. diplomat and holds a master's degree in International Education from George Washington University.

Jennifer Guevara is Postdoctoral Fellow of the National Scientific and Technical Research Council for Argentina (CONICET). She holds a PhD in Education from Universidad de San Andrés (Argentina). She has taught in Universidad de San Andrés, Universidad Nacional de General San Martín y Facultad Latinoamericana de Ciencias Sociales in Argentina. She is interested in governance of education policies and systems in Latin America.

Sherene (Sherry) Hattingh is the Primary Course Convenor—Education in the Faculty of Business, Education and Science at Avondale College of Higher Education. She has worked, researched and presented in the Primary, Secondary and Tertiary education sectors as a teacher, administrator and researcher. Her publications in peer-reviewed and church journals and books cover the areas of internationalisation, ESL students and pedagogy, assessment and Christian discipleship.

Claire Maxwell is a Sociologist of whose work focuses on how processes of globalisation and stratification are shaping social class identities, education practices and desired futures of young people and families from highly resourced social groups. She works closely with various colleagues located across different parts of the world—USA, Canada, Israel, Germany, Australia, Sweden and China—on writing and research projects. She has published in *British Journal of Sociology of Education, The Sociological Review, Sociology, Gender & Education, L'Année sociologique, Discourse: Studies in the Cultural Politics of Education*, and *International Journal of Qualitative Studies in Education, Pedagogy, Culture and Society*. She has edited international collections such as *Elite Education and Internationalisation. From the Early Years Into Higher Education* (Palgrave Macmillan, 2018), *Elite Education. International Perspectives* (Routledge, 2016), and *Agency, Affect & Privilege* (Palgrave Macmillan, 2013).

Paul Morris is Professor of Comparative Education at the Institute of Education, University College London. From 1976 to 2000 he worked at Hong Kong University where he was Dean of the Education Faculty for six years. From 2000 he was Deputy President of the Hong Kong Institute of Education (since renamed EDUHK) and the President from 2002 to 2007.

Boris Prickarts is Deputy Director of the Amsterdam International Community School (AICS), chair of the association of Dutch International Primary Schools (DIPS) and a member of the Board of Trustees of the Alliance for International Education (AIE). Prior to setting up the AICS in 2003, he was a history teacher and junior administrator for nine years at the International School of The Hague (ISH). Both the AICS and the ISH are Dutch government–sponsored international schools. In the UK (1992) and Australia (2001), he worked for a short period as a visiting history teacher in government schools. From 1992–2002 he was author and editor of various history school books in Dutch and English. He holds a doctorate in international education from the University of Bath, UK.

Johanna Waters is a Reader in Human Geography and Migration Studies at University College London, having previously worked at the universities of Oxford, Birmingham and Liverpool in the UK. Her research focuses on the intersection of migration/mobilities, (international) education and family life. She is co-editor of the journal *Migration and Society*. Her latest book, written with Rachel Brooks, is titled *Materialities and Mobilities in Education* (Routledge, 2017).

Miri Yemini is a Comparative Education scholar at Tel Aviv University. Her research interests include globalisation of and in education, global citizenship education, internationalisation, and intermediaries in education and the global middle class. She succeeded to secure substantial funding for her research from (among others) the EU, UNESCO and MoE. This year she holds honorary visiting positions at UCL, Institute of Education; Freie Universität Berlin; and The Friedrich-Alexander-Universität at Nuremberg. She published her research at *Journal of Education Policy*; *Comparative Education Review*; *Teaching & Teachers Education*; *Globalisation, Societies and Education*; *Discourse: Studies in the Cultural Politics of Education*; *Compare: A Journal of Comparative and International Education*; *Educational Management Administration and Leadership* and others. In recent years Dr. Yemini published four books: *Internationalisation and Global Citizenship* (Palgrave, 2017); *Project Management in Schools* (with I. Oplatka and N. Sagie; Palgrave, 2018); *Entrepreneurship in Education* (with N. Sagie; Magness Press, 2017) and *Cosmopolitanism and Localism in Education* (Magness Press, 2015).

Index

82–83; internationalisation pathways in 73–74; introduction to 70–71; literature on internationalisation of 74; in North Carolina 75–77; research methods used 75; in Washington, DC 79–82
universities 37, 40; internationalisation and 165–167, 168–171, 174–175; Peru 111–112; Soviet 90–91, 98–99

Washington, DC: demographics 79–80; equity-based/inclusive programming 75; internationalisation in 79–82
World Bank 123
World Values Survey 94–96, 100

Yemini, M. 37, 40, 56, 99–100, 119, 121, 149

Zolotoe Sechenie (Russian school) 98–100

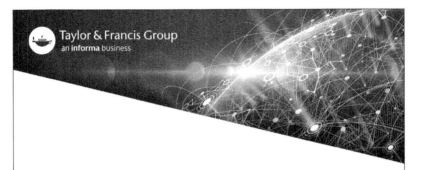